Golfing Reliques

A Captain's Memoir

Gordon A Gilchrist

Ryemuir
Publishing

First published in 2014 by Ryemuir Publishing

ISBN 978-0-9928133-0-7

Acknowledgements
The author wishes to express his thanks to the following for their various means of assistance in enabling production of this book:

For information relating to the text:
Linda Briggs (*Glenrothes*), Roy Bulmer (*Wallasey*), Julie Cooke (*Barrow-in-Furness*),
Archie Fulton *(Ayr)*, Andrew Lochhead *(Prestwick GC)*, Motherwell Heritage Centre,
John Williamson *(Motherwell)*

For the provision of, and permission to include, photographs:
Ayrshire Ladies County Golf Association, Ayrshire Post, Willie Baird *(Peebles Golf Club)*,
Murray Bothwell *(Prestwick St Nicholas GC)*, Sandy Crawford *(Crawford Photography)*,
David Coid *(Prestwick St Nicholas GC)*, Derek McCabe *(DMC Photo Gallery)*

For miscellaneous advice:
Stewart Crichton *(Burnside)*

Typeset in Adobe Garamond, designed and produced by
Gilmour Print www.self-publish-books.co.uk

Gordon A. Gilchrist

(Crawford Photography)

Contents

Prologue

Yet another book on the subject of Golf! Is it likely that anyone other than a few personal acquaintances of the Author will be much interested in the ramblings of someone who has no credentials either as a writer or as a celebrated player? Perhaps not; for this publication is the product of a hitherto lowly member who became Captain of what is generally considered to be the world's twenty-sixth oldest golf club. And, in truth, it is something of a personal indulgence in that he has utilised the prestige accorded by that position to express his opinions, to reminisce on his past experiences and to share something of his golf-related interests. In providing an account of his year in office, not only does he reveal to his fellow members what captaincy entailed for him, but his comments might unwittingly be of some assistance to other golfing captains as they confront the complexities and obligations inherent in the post. Alastair Sim's observation that a bad example can often be more beneficial than a good one is still relevant, but hopefully there are enough items of a positive nature within these pages to provide some ideas or guidance as to how the Captain's role might be enacted.

So, how did this account come to be written? From the outset, and only as a personal record of what for him would be an unprecedented year, it had been the Author's intention to make a note in his pocket diary of the various events that had entailed either his attendance or his attention in the role of golf club captain. However, a few weeks into his term of office, his vice-captain suggested to him that he keep a diary of his experiences, and that proved to be the motivation to record a more detailed account. A short time later, whilst referring to the content of his previous speeches, it occurred to him to retain these along with the diary entries. And from such musings the seed was sown to produce this little volume.

He does not claim that his speeches are in themselves a good example of the public speaker's art, but he has committed them to print as a means of preserving miscellaneous facts unearthed in his researches and of acknowledging the selfless commitment of many people whose names would not otherwise have appeared within the memoir.

In order to preserve the authenticity of what is a very personal account, the Author refrained from seeking corroboration or tacit approval in the course of compiling this work, but he acknowledges elsewhere those who assisted in providing him with information, or who permitted photographs to be used in illustration of the text.

The Author apologises for the repetition of words, phrases and facts, and the occasional irregular use of tense; but that is surely the nature of a diary. Although all of the views and opinions expressed in these writings are his own, he does not claim that they are either original or correct; they are, however, his sincere understanding of the circumstances as known to himself. Furthermore, he has no desire to give offence to anyone when relating some of the incidents which occurred in the course of carrying out his duties as Captain, but to have expunged whatever was contentious or unwelcome would have rendered the account both flawed and incomplete. Nevertheless, anything that is private, or was expressed to him in confidence, has been honoured.

G. A. Gilchrist

Chapter 1

March

The evening of Thursday, 25th March 2010 heralded my election as Captain of Prestwick St. Nicholas Golf Club and the culmination of what for me had been one of life's most significant days. But its commencement was more akin to the prospect of facing the rigours of a professional examination than anything relating to the pursuit of an indulgent pastime. Upon awakening at 7am, my immediate reaction was to commit to paper the various threads of a speech that had been formulating in my mind right up to the moment when I had fallen asleep just after midnight. My usual routine of shaving, showering and breakfasting was suspended whilst I applied myself to the task of drafting out the basis of my oration. Not that I was starting from scratch, because this particular day had been in my thoughts ever since seventeen months earlier Bill Rae had invited me to be Vice-Captain. I had not until now made any notes, but all the various ideas as to what was relevant were very much in my head. And that is how the day progressed; totally focused on putting together a coherent speech that would do justice to the occasion, and very mindful of the importance of making a favourable impression upon the general membership of the Club, to many of whom I was still an unknown quantity.

In my previous experience, inspiration of thought tended to be more prevalent when I was working with pen or pencil rather than at a computer but, as the latter was temporarily out of commission, the question of there being an alternative to everything being hand-written did not arise. That meant, when I would eventually get up to speak, my writing needed to be sufficiently large to allow me to read it easily; and the whole laid out neatly and methodically so that I could readily establish at which point I had reached and, more importantly, pick-up on the key words and phrases that would trigger my thoughts and avoid my delivery being hesitant or disjointed. Thankfully, the inspiration which I craved was forthcoming and, as I set down my words, random ideas and personal notions drifted into my mind and I was able to produce a speech with which I was at least comfortable. As to my being better motivated when using a pen or pencil, that estimation was revised rather speedily as the subsequent weeks and months unfolded.

The format of the Annual General Meeting dictates that the incumbent Captain chairs the formal business relating to annual reports and the like, and it is only later in the proceedings that the election takes place of Office Bearers and Committee for the following season. That is surely the best arrangement as there must be a host of incoming captains throughout the country whose previous experience of chairing meetings of any significance is at best limited, if not almost nil. I certainly would not have relished the prospect of being exposed to spontaneous questioning and comment from the floor based upon my hitherto meagre involvement in golf politics. As matters stood, the 2010 AGM was of considerable importance since it contained a proposal to alter the club's constitution whereby ladies would become eligible for full membership. For many gentlemen members this would be considered as being a fundamental alteration to the ethos of the club, and the Management Committee, having instigated the proposal, was fully expecting that the topic would be the subject of much debate and controversy. The meeting proceeded uneventfully with the adoption of the previous year's minutes, the Captain's Report, the Financial Report and the setting of the Annual Subscription. The next item on the Agenda was Alterations to Constitution, and the atmosphere was heavy with expectation as Captain Bill Rae invited the Secretary, Tom Hepburn, to speak in support of the motion. How relieved I was not to be in the Chair at this juncture! Images of the ghost of an old colonel, recumbent in his bath chair, rotund, beetroot faced with handle bar moustache, and waving a shooting stick in the air, pervaded my thoughts. This was where the AGM was going to come alive! And with what can only be described as a *tour de force*, Tom Hepburn totally diffused the situation with an eloquent and convincing argument as to why our club should embrace this unprecedented change to its constitution. When the vote was taken only four members, out of nearly one hundred present, registered their dissension. If ever the persuasive powers of oratory carried through a motion that might otherwise have split a meeting in two, this was it! And the Agenda moved on to the election of the Honorary President and Office Bearers – and to my induction!

Captain Bill Rae proposed that I be elected as Captain for the forthcoming year, and this was approved by acclamation. Thereupon the time had arrived to deliver my acceptance speech.

Past Captain Bill, Honorary President Bill, Past Captains, Gentlemen:
It was with eager anticipation, whilst on the Waiting List, that I looked forward to the prospect of being admitted into this club and of playing linksland golf. Thanks to being sponsored by Hugh Currie and Miller Douglas that day eventually arrived and, until four years ago, I enjoyed a very low profile among the membership. I never countenanced the thought of being asked to serve on Committee, far less being invited to become an Office Bearer. But, and this might not be the appropriate expression, thanks to Past Captain Jim Pettigrew, and latterly Bill Rae, I find myself standing before you as Captain.

I hope no one will misunderstand me when I say that, for me, this moment does not represent the fulfilment of some personal ambition. This is not something which I ever sought; but it does mark a very willing acceptance on my part to take on the responsibilities of Captain and to face the challenges that are involved.

Over the past year I have researched the role of a golf club captain, and what I have found is that there is no standard job description, there is no specific type of person for the post, and that his profile within the club varies from region to region, indeed from club to club. The recurring advice which appears to emerge for all captains is 'Don't attempt to act like someone else; be yourself. After all, that is why you have been appointed.'

Gentlemen, in my period of office I shall endeavour to be worthy of the position, to uphold the best traditions of the Club, and when called upon to be its representative, to do so in its best interest.

As I have already said, the role of captain varies. Recently quite a few members have said to me 'Well, Gordon, it won't be long now till you're the boss.' In truth, I don't envisage myself as being autocratic. Ours is a democratic club. Management decisions and policy are formulated by our Committee, and day-to-day administration is overseen by our Secretary. If a decision is required urgently, then I shall take on that responsibility. However, as regards the Management Committee, if I feel that something is not in the best interest of the club or its members, I shall try to influence the debate but, in the end, the majority decision will prevail.

Could I perhaps say something on a personal note? I am not by nature a gregarious person. Others of my age will vouch for, and understand, when I say that putting names to faces or recalling the circumstances in which one met previously is not my strongest suit. Please, if I appear awkward or hesitant, be assured that there is no personal slight intended. If you are able to put me at ease, I shall appreciate that very much.

In a perverse kind of way, I rather wish that this was March 2011 and that I was able to report that the good ship St. Nicholas Golf Club was safely back in its own anchorage. In that regard I am rather envious of Bill Rae. He has guided the Club with a steady hand and a deceptively light touch this past year, and the warmth of his personality and enthusiasm for the Club have shone throughout his Captaincy. He has chaired meetings in a most efficient manner and has given unstintingly of his time and abilities. In carrying out his duties as Captain within the confines of the course and clubhouse, or when representing us at other clubs, he has done so with great dignity.

Bill, we, as members, are indebted to you for the wonderful contribution you have made, and continue to make, in the service of our Club and it is with great pleasure that I invite you to accept your Past Captain's tie, and also a tie and Certificate of Life Membership of the Scottish Golf Union.

Gentlemen, in accordance with Rule 8 of the Constitution, I propose that Past Captain Bill Rae be elected an Honorary Vice-President of St. Nicholas Golf Club.

Following this acceptance speech, my first duty as Captain was to introduce the prospective Vice-Captain.

Gentlemen:
The tradition within the Club for the appointment of the Vice-Captain is that he be proposed by the incoming Captain. This appointment is not something to be entered into lightly and, on reflection, may prove to be the most significant decision a Captain has to make during his term in office. The Club is fortunate in that it possesses several members who would fill the post admirably. It may well be considered advantageous if the Captain and Vice-Captain are alike-minded but, for me, that is not a priority. The Club is a diversity of characters, opinions, ages, temperaments, strengths and weaknesses, as is already reflected in Committee. Accordingly, I can think of no reason why the Vice-Captain should be a clone of the Captain.

In terms of age and golfing ability my nominee and I have nothing in common. As to our characters, some may think that there is little similarity. As to our opinions, whilst they often coincide, that is not always the case. However, he is articulate and reasoned in his arguments, he has an obvious love of the game of golf and, to my mind, has already demonstrated his commitment to this Club, not just in word, but in action through his dedicated work on Committee over the past three years.

Gentlemen, I seek your approval to elect Mr. Alan Poole as Vice-Captain for the forthcoming year.

Upon obtaining approval by acclamation of Alan's election, I managed without undue trouble to pilot the meeting through the Election of Committee and Any Other Competent Business. But I was completely unprepared thereafter to be greeted so warmly by members, many with whom I was unfamiliar, who shook my hand and expressed their good wishes to me for my year as Captain. What a wonderful gesture on their part, and what a relief, and joy, to realise that I had been so readily accepted into my new role!

Upon conclusion of the AGM, I met upstairs with all members of the new Committee, together with those who had just retired, and announced the Convenerships that I had allocated to each of them for the forthcoming year, and arranged for a smooth transfer of files among them.

Friday, 26th March: Courtesy visit to Secretary

Waking up to my first morning as Captain was a surreal experience; 'surreal' in the sense that I felt myself to be a different person. My world had changed! An unexpected lightness of spirit consumed me; of pleasurable anticipation similar to that which one experiences at the outset of a long train journey. I was setting out on an adventure which would last for the next twelve months and which I knew would be both challenging and exhilarating. Apprehension did not enter my mind. It was within my own power to establish the manner and direction of my Captaincy. And it never occurred to me otherwise than that my first action as Captain would be to pay a courtesy call to the Secretary's office. The very act of coming out of my house and getting into the car to drive down to the golf club produced a completely new feeling within me. What previously had been automatic and unthinking assumed the status of a ritual. No new Prime Minister was more aware of that first journey to the Houses of Parliament than I was this day. Not for me the privilege of a chauffeur, but the thrill was just the same. Upon entering the clubhouse car park I had the pleasure of driving into the parking space reserved for the Captain. It suited me ideally that no one was about, for I was more than happy to make my arrival as unobtrusive as possible. And so I entered the vestibule and made my way upstairs to the Office. Tom and his assistant, Margaret, welcomed me in their usual friendly manner and I was aware immediately that I could rely upon their support and guidance in relation to what would be required of me in the months ahead. Their enthusiasm and willingness to please was something which I valued greatly, and the prospect of enjoying a happy and informal working relationship with them was very reassuring. This first visit was an opportunity to establish our respective roles, and for me to be made aware as to the means by which we could best operate as a team.

Saturday, 27th March: First round as Captain

Just as I had been happy to arrive at the clubhouse car park the previous day in an unostentatious manner, so also did I want my first venture on to the course to be unheralded. Unlike many clubs, St. Nicholas does not have the tradition of a formal ceremony at which the Captain drives himself into office, and I had no personal desire to draw attention to my first appearance as Captain. For the past ten years George Hunter and I had often partnered each other in competitions and in casual games, and it was my wish that my initial round as Captain should be played in his company and, if possible, without distraction. This first round was very special for me and I particularly wanted George to be the person with whom I could share it. So we arranged to meet just before noon, when we knew the first tee would be relatively quiet, and hopefully would be able to play our game away from the limelight. The favourable weather added to our enjoyment and I was aware that this would probably be one of the few opportunities that George and I would have to play in our usual 'low profile' fashion without my presence attracting the attention of others on the course. Not that I wished to be secretive, nor that I was averse to speaking to or acknowledging other players – in fact, quite the contrary – but it was simply a case that, if possible, this first round should be one that we could enjoy together in circumstances similar to those with which we were hitherto accustomed. What was unexpected, however, was the discovery, upon entering the clubhouse at the conclusion of our round, that both lounges were totally empty and that we had the premises to ourselves!

. . . . 27th: Dinner at the clubhouse

Continuing the theme of starting my year among those golfing partners with whom I most closely associated, I had invited Hugh McKail and George, along with their wives, Kate and Fiona, to join Jeanette and me for dinner in the clubhouse. Unfortunately Andrew Taylor was away on holiday, otherwise he too would have been included. I would not have wanted to spend these first few days in any other manner but, in retrospect, I was perhaps subconsciously boosting my confidence by surrounding myself with friends in whose company I was comfortable. As things turned out, we had a delightful evening, and the staff and fellow members made our company very welcome in their midst. In my capacity as Captain it behove me in the course of the meal to rise from the table and to mingle briefly with the other diners and to exchange pleasantries; not my strongest suit, but something which I considered as being expected of the Captain. Needless to say everyone was generous towards me and helped considerably in allaying my nervousness. The meal itself was very appetising and representative of the consistently high quality of service that Grant Hood and his catering staff provide for members and their guests.

Eden Golf Tournament 1954

If asked to recall when I first took an interest in golf, my earliest recollection is August 1954 during a family holiday in St. Andrews. I was 12 years old and, if memory serves me correctly, my parents and I travelled there by rail from Buchanan Street Station in Glasgow and transferred to the local train at Leuchars. There was no history of anyone in our family having played golf, yet I vividly remember my mother saying that it was something which she would like to have done. This I found very surprising, but on hindsight I now realise that it was in her genes. Brought up by the shores of Loch Fyne in Argyllshire, an area not noted for producing golfers, she was immersed in a community whose passion was shinty; that distinctly Highland game which the uninitiated refer to as being 'hockey without rules'. Her father, who was known locally as 'The Drover', had been Captain of Furnace Excelsiors shinty team in the 1890s and was reputed to have been its outstanding player. So the impulse to whack a ball with a stick was very much an inherent trait on my mother's side of the family.

There was a lovely simplicity about summer holidays in Scotland during the 1950s, when only the 'better-off' families could afford to seek the sun-filled promise of the English Riviera. With few exceptions, most Scottish resorts relied upon their essential assets of attractive beaches, paved esplanades, privately-owned shops, tea rooms, cafes, public gardens, outdoor bathing pools, boating ponds, putting greens and illuminations which, in the latter's case, were often not much more than a single row of fairy lights extending the length of the sea-front. For the vast majority of working class families the fortnight summer holiday was an opportunity to escape the rigours of everyday living and to spend it walking along the promenade, sitting on benches or on the grass or on the sand, eating ice cream cones, browsing through the shops, keeping the children amused, and looking with interest upon the activities of the more adventurous among them as the latter rowed their boats, fished from the harbour walls, splashed about in the water, or golfed on the links. Ours was that kind of passive enjoyment; except that our holiday coincided with St. Andrews hosting its annual Lammas Fair when Market Street and South Street were filled with fairground attractions and to which, of an evening, we also went along to capture the atmosphere and to enjoy some of the fun.

It must have been on the first Wednesday of our holiday that perchance we walked out to the links and discovered that a golf competition was in progress. We ascertained from a spectator that it was the annual Eden Tournament and we followed some of the players for a few holes. This was a completely new experience for me and I was so interested in the proceedings that I prevailed upon my parents to allow me to return on my own the following morning to watch the play. And so my first direct contact with golf was established.

Tom Sanderson

(Peebles Golf Club)

Over the years the tournament had attracted entries from leading amateur players, many of whom had represented Scotland at international level, and it still retained its prestigious reputation upon my first acquaintance with it. I was not knowledgeable as to the players who were taking part and, when I returned on the Thursday morning, I simply attached myself to the small group of spectators who were accompanying a match that had just driven-off from the first tee. As to who were the players I have no recollection, but I do recall that I quickly attuned to what was considered as being good etiquette among spectators. After the second hole the players, their caddies and the spectators had to cross over the railway bridge to reach the third tee and it was there that I decided to linger and to observe some of the other competitors. For some reason long since forgotten, a particular player, whose wife (or so I assumed) was acting as his caddie, took my interest and I decided to follow the progress of his match. It transpired that he was T.T. Sanderson, and that name remained fixed in my memory from that day forth. I followed the match to its conclusion, which resulted in a win for my new-found hero, and I returned in the afternoon to see him tee-off against his next opponent. It was about twenty years later, courtesy of *The Golfer's Handbook*, I discovered that Tom Sanderson was well-known in golfing circles, especially in the Border area; that for several years he had held the course record at Peebles with a 68, that he went on to win the Border Golfers' Association Amateur Championship nine times, and that he won the Border Golfers' Association Champions Tournament in 1968. At the outset there must have been something about his personality, his style or his appearance that attracted me to follow him and, when afterwards I learned of the regard in which he was held and of the success he had achieved, I reckoned that I must have had an instinctive appreciation for a good role model. As to the 1954 Eden Tournament, I think he was beaten in the quarter-final, as I don't recall seeing him play against either of the eventual finalists. The final itself was over 36 holes on the Saturday and was contested between Ian Reid (St. Andrews New) and R.L. (Lindsay) Renfrew (Glasgow). Imagine the disappointment when my parents told me that we were going to visit relatives in Dundee that afternoon! However, I was allowed to watch the morning round and on its conclusion I joined with other youngsters in getting both players' autographs. It was much later in the evening before I learned from the radio that Ian Reid had become the new Eden Champion. In fact he won the tournament again in 1957, having been Fife Amateur Champion in 1955. For his part, Lindsay Renfrew won the Glasgow County Championship in 1963 and represented Scotland in the Home Internationals of 1964.

Thus upon the Eden links during a spell of particularly fine August weather, I was introduced to the game of golf. And three years later, no doubt influenced by the exploits and example of Tom Sanderson, I too joined the ranks of the golfing fraternity. Having experienced the fascination of the game for nearly sixty years and having learned so much relating to its history, how appropriate, indeed how fortuitous, that for me it should all have started at St. Andrews!

Chapter 2

April

Tuesday, 6th April: Meeting with Bill Andrew re luncheon

Back in November I had been invited to attend a meeting between Captain Bill Rae and Honorary President Bill Andrew at which the latter wished to discuss a number of items to which he had been giving some thought. Among these was his proposal to arrange a Celebration Lunch in recognition of the long service given to the Club by some of its older members, especially those with upwards of 60 years membership, of whom there were seven. By the time this matter was submitted for approval at the February management meeting, President Bill had already compiled a detailed account of the format which he envisaged for the function, and Committee duly agreed to his proposals. Now that I was installed as Captain, President Bill wished to meet with me at the earliest opportunity to discuss the arrangements; so we met the day following my return from an Easter weekend spent with relations in Lancashire. He had been informed previously that Committee was so supportive of his proposals that, rather than the event being self-funding as he had suggested, the Club was happy to welcome the long-serving members as its guests and to provide a pre-lunch reception for everyone in attendance.

Bill and I met in the Tom Morris Room and he spoke at length upon how he considered plans for the lunch should be implemented. I concurred with what he proposed but made it clear that, as the event was very much his own idea, I did not see myself as being involved in its detailed planning and was happy to let him deal through David Coid (Finance) and Grant Hood (Kitchen) regarding the catering and seating arrangements, level of pricing, method of payment, etc. with the proviso that he kept me informed as to what was happening. I agreed with him that the guests should receive a formal invitation from the Club and I acknowledged that I would attend to that matter. As to what would be required of me on the day, I would await his request. And so the wheels were set in motion!

Sunday, 11th April: Ayrshire Winter League final

Just over two weeks into my captaincy and the first opportunity arises to represent the Club in that role. In the preceding months our team of leading players had been competing in the Ayrshire Winter League and had succeeded in getting through to the final play-off, which was being decided over two legs. Our opponents were Troon Welbeck GC and in the first leg, which had been a home tie for ourselves, St. Nicholas had achieved a lead of 4 games to 2. Although notice of the team's progress had been reported sporadically at Committee meetings, and mention made at the AGM, no arrangements had been formulated, nor had discussion even taken place, regarding the team receiving support whilst competing in the second leg. At this juncture I was quite unaware as to the behaviour of previous captains in similar circumstances, but I considered it my duty to make sure that I attended the match in my capacity as Club Captain and to give tangible support to the team simply by being present. As events turned out, it was a decision which left me with one of the happiest memories of my time in office.

A gorgeous Spring morning was the perfect prelude to the final, which was being played over the Darley course in Troon and was due to begin about 11am. When I arrived at the Welbeck clubhouse both teams were already enjoying coffee and bacon rolls; nothing out of the ordinary for a team match, except that the culinary offerings had all been prepared and served by the Troon Welbeck Club Captain, David McMahon!

(Prestwick St Nicholas Golf Club)

Ayrshire Winter League Winners 2010: Prestwick St. Nicholas GC
Rear Row: Steven Bolland, Gordon Gilchrist (Club Captain), Kevin Brock, Alistair Belford
Front Row: Stephen King (Team Captain), Alan Poole, Gary Tierney

The atmosphere in the lounge exuded everything that is best in golf and, whilst David's actions may have passed unremarked, the spirit of friendly rivalry and of one man's commitment to the game shone through the whole pre-match proceedings. And that set the scene for an engrossing encounter in which five of the six games went to the 17th Hole or beyond. From my earlier years as a member of Troon Welbeck, I was well acquainted with the course layout and was able to cut across at various holes and thereby see something of every game. The Welbeck officials were apologetic as to the state of the greens, particularly when compared with those at St. Nicholas for the first leg. Its being a municipal course meant that the Welbeck Club had no responsibility for its condition and the St. Nicholas team was quite appreciative of that fact. In truth, the exceptionally severe winter had played havoc with many courses throughout the length and breadth of the country, but the greens on Darley were more reminiscent of 'brownies' as are found in courses in some of the world's desert regions. Nevertheless, although there was an almost total absence of grass on them, the greens did play relatively true and, considering how alien were the conditions, the St. Nicholas team adapted admirably to the challenge and more than held its own. The warm sunny weather, something of a bonus in mid-April, was ideal for myself as I perambulated across the fairways and through the heather as I sought out the various games. Every one of them was critical and, when asked, I was able to give some indication as to how the team as a whole was faring. For match play, few courses in their later stages can surpass the 14th and 15th Holes on Darley where a premium is put on well positioned tee shots and crisp, accurate approach irons into the greens. Absolutely nothing can be taken for granted over these two holes in which the bounce of the ball is often unpredictable amid the hillocks and steep slopes. The Darley Burn challenges nerves and judgement of distance to the 14th green no matter where the drive eventually settles, whilst the 15th green is equally dismissive of both the ultra-bold approach and the tentative pitch. But in the crucial games St. Nicholas got through these holes unscathed and went on to secure the three wins that were needed to ensure victory by an aggregate score of 7 games to 5.

Back at the clubhouse the Welbeck team and its officials were gracious in defeat and our team captain, Stephen King, spoke appreciatively of our opponents when presented with the Winter League Trophy. I declined Welbeck's generous offer to join the teams in the post-match meal, but returned to St. Nicholas to await the arrival of the victors and to enjoy with them their private celebrations in the casual bar. Everyone was in high spirits as details of the individual games were recounted and the team wallowed in well merited self-congratulation. On a personal note, being invited by the team members to be included in the winners' photograph was totally unexpected and a gesture for which I shall be forever grateful.

Monday, 12th April: Finance Sub-Committee meeting
One of the proposed innovations that Bill Andrew had brought to Committee's notice during the first year of his Presidency had been the possible introduction of a Past Captain's badge. Currently all past-captains are entitled to wear a special tie which is identical to the official Club tie save that it has an additional diagonal gold stripe which separates the navy blue and dark green colours. It is unlikely that many members are even aware of this small difference in the tie's design, or of its significance, and so President Bill thought it desirable that a suitably personal but unpretentious badge be introduced which would readily identify those who had previously been Club Captain. Upon his own initiative, and prior to his first raising the issue, Bill had made enquiries as to the manufacture and cost of the badges so that Committee would be in possession of the facts when considering his proposal; and Bill stated that, as a donation, he would personally bear the cost of producing the die for the badges' manufacture. Committee subsequently agreed to Bill's proposals and authorised purchase of the badges with the proviso that the past captains would only be charged the net cost of the manufacture. I was uncomfortable about the Club asking payment for the badges and resolved that it would be one of my first acts as Captain to set about rescinding that decision. So I convened a meeting of the Finance Sub-Committee with this specific item very much to the fore and persuaded my fellow members to recommend to the Management Committee that all Past Captains be presented with badges as a matter of entitlement and that the Club be responsible for the cost involved. The sub-committee also considered the financial implications of the forthcoming Celebration Lunch and agreed that Ian Wilson be invited as a guest of the Club in appreciation of his contribution towards providing presentation prints for the Guests of Honour.

Thursday, 15th April: Ayrshire Ladies' County Golf Championship

As had been approved by Committee more than a year previously, St. Nicholas hosted the venue for the Ayrshire Ladies' County Championship. The choice of date (April 15) struck me as being unduly early in the golfing season, especially for those competitors who are members of inland clubs and who will hardly have come out of winter hibernation before this important event is upon them. There is most likely some practical or historical reason behind this decision, but it is nevertheless unusual to have an important championship decided before the golfing season is barely underway. Due to my employment commitments I was unavailable to referee the Final of the Ladies Championship, nor was I able to spectate at the morning semi-finals but, having been invited as Captain of the host club to present the trophies, I made a point of leaving early from my office so that I would be in good time for the presentation ceremony. As events turned out, the final tie was completed rather sooner than had been expected and my arrival at the clubhouse was met with some relief by the officials. I was welcomed by the Secretary, Shelagh Young (Kilmarnock (Barassie)) who in turn introduced me to the Association Captain, Alex Glennie (Kilmarnock (Barassie)) and to the Vice-Captain, Sandie Streets (Largs). It was a pleasure to be greeted so warmly and enthusiastically, and I could hear the sound of animated voices emanating through the double door of the Mixed Lounge wherein all were gathered for the prize-giving – no doubt wondering as to when it would get underway! And so I was propelled immediately into my first speaking engagement.

(Ayrshire Ladies County Golf Association)

With Ayrshire Ladies' County Champion 2010: Lesley Hendry (Largs Routenburn)

Captain Alex, Ladies:

It is a great pleasure for St. Nicholas Golf Club to host your 2010 Championship. I hope that all of you have enjoyed the experience, both on the course and in the clubhouse. In particular, our greenkeeeping staff was anxious to present the course at its best and we trust that you found it to your liking. Just as St.

Andrews relies on the vagaries of the wind to protect it against the top professionals, so too does St. Nicholas. However, when wind is mixed with rain, playing over these links can be very miserable indeed. Thankfully the weather has been kind to you this week.

As many of you will already know, this championship was instituted in 1923. And St. Nicholas was its first venue. That was 87 years ago. In that first final, Jean McCulloch (West Kilbride) beat our own Miss Martin 2 & 1. Jean set a trend for future champions as she went on to win on subsequent occasions. The championship records are filled with names of multiple winners. Jean herself appeared in eight of the first eleven finals – winning six times. But this is 2010. Perhaps 50 years from now some of your names will be recalled with considerable deference on account of what you have achieved.

Finals Day is one of anticipation and expectation. So much can depend on the rub of the green. So much also on maintaining good form. The nature of match play means that the prize-giving ceremony is a mixture of elation, of pride, of disappointment, of what might have been. However, championship golf is all about competing and, when played over three days, the eventual winner is worthy of the accolade of Champion. As for the semi-finalists and the runner- up, there is the hope that next time they can progress one stage further.

Thank you for the courtesy afforded to me during this little speech.

I think it only remains for me to say, 'Let the prize-giving commence!'

Wednesday, 21st April: Portrait by Sandy Crawford

One of the most practical benefits enjoyed by the Captain is the provision of a reserved parking bay immediately adjacent to the clubhouse. This is of considerable advantage on competition days when, from mid-morning to mid-afternoon, spaces in the car park are at an absolute premium and one is often required to utilise the public seaside parking facility across the other side of the access road which, in itself, entails a 200 yards walk back to the clubhouse; not always the most pleasant of undertakings should it be raining at the time. Having one's own parking bay results in the fact that everyone within the Club becomes familiar with your car and, at the most unexpected times, places and circumstances, you encounter people waving from other cars or flashing lights to catch your attention – and you have not the slightest notion as to who they are; but you conclude that it must be someone who recognises your car from the golf club.

If knowing your car is one thing, knowing your face is yet another dimension in the unequal quest for mutual recognition between Captain and 600 members. Shortly after assuming the Captaincy, Secretary Tom provided me with the telephone number of Sandy Crawford, the photographer, and advised me to make arrangements for my portrait to be taken for display in the main entrance vestibule. Sandy knew exactly what was required of the study and, without even enquiring of me, instinctively set about capturing the image which I had hoped to convey. The informality of the surroundings and the professionalism of his manner contributed to a very relaxed and illuminating visit to his studio.

Monday, 26th April: Prestwick Rotary AM/AM

One of the most eagerly awaited dates in the local golfing calendar is the annual fund raising fixture organised by Prestwick Rotary Club in conjunction with Prestwick Golf Club. Each year the Rotarians nominate a deserving cause or charity to which all the proceeds from the event will be donated, and each year St. Nicholas Golf Club is invited to enter a team. According to custom, the Captain invites three members to join him in the team, and my first reaction was to extend an invitation to Vice-Captain Alan. Unfortunately he was unavailable on the day, but I knew of three other members who would appreciate an invitation to play over the Prestwick links and who could guarantee us all having a good day out. So I was accompanied by Douglas Bull, Gordon Taylor and Gary Tierney; and we had a great time together. The shotgun start decreed that we had to get ourselves out to the 7th Hole and, once there, we blended well as a team, gave of our best, chatted and laughed our way round the course, and finished with a creditable net score of 63; two behind the winners. How I rued, or perhaps more likely the team rued, my three putts on the 12th green and poor drive at the 15th Hole, when my contribution might have made all the difference! Such is golf! Back at the Prestwick clubhouse all of the teams gathered in the Smoke Room for the prize-giving ceremony and everyone was able to luxuriate in the atmosphere and unique character of that hallowed place.

With Douglas Bull, Gary Tierney and Gordon Taylor at Prestwick GC

(Prestwick Golf Club)

Thursday, 29th April: Committee meeting
A natural consequence of being elected Captain is that one is continually confronted with 'first time' situations. And so the last Thursday in April marked my chairing the first meeting of the new Committee. Unlike some other aspects of my duties, chairing a meeting was not something of which I was inexperienced, but it had been a few years since I had done so on a regular basis. Commercial business meetings require an element of *gravitas* to establish the necessary level of personal and corporate responsibility for all matters under discussion, so that nobody is under any illusion as to the introduction of light-hearted banter being quite inappropriate. In relation to recreational pursuits and the like, my maxim has always been to strike a suitable balance between formality and

informality, and that is the climate which I strove to promote at these meetings. By all means one must be business-like in one's deliberations; indubitably the present day golf club has numerous legal and financial obligations with which it must comply, but it must always be remembered that everyone on Committee is a volunteer and is giving freely of his time and talents on the Club's behalf.

I was pleased to learn from the new Conveners that there had been a successful transfer of responsibilities from their predecessors, and I was reassured that in making my appointments I had maximised the talents and experience at my disposal. Of the various matters under consideration by Committee, the most pressing related to the Ladies Convener's report. Following the AGM decision to admit ladies as Ordinary Members, and with the new subscription year due to commence 1st June, Tom Andrews had met with the ladies on 7th April and his report itemised the various points that had been raised by them. Committee members were already aware of the many issues involved and, after detailed discussion, consensus was reached as to the general protocol regarding membership numbers, priority of applications, procedures for transfer between grades and, where appropriate, entry fees.

(Prestwick St Nicholas Golf Club)

Prestwick St Nicholas Golf Club Commitee 2010-11
Back row, left to right: *MurrayBothwell (Marketing/Website), Tom Andrews (Ladies),*
John Errington (Match & Handicap), Bobby Hodge (Social), Walter Bryson (Juniors), Stephen King (Links),
David Coid (Finance). Not shown: *Robin Alexander (Membership) and Gary Tierney (House).*
Front row, left to right: *Tom Hepburn (Secretary), Gordon Gilchrist (Captain), Alan Poole (Vice-Captain),*
Bill Rae (Past Captain)

Colville Park Golf Club

Members of the original Motherwell Golf Club played over a nine-hole course on the fields of Riccardjohnston Farm, which was situated less than two hundred yards north-west of the 15th tee of the present Colville Park course. The club, which was open to gents and ladies, was instituted on 26th October 1894 but, because of compulsory agricultural cultivation schemes during the First

World War, the course became unavailable for play and the club was disbanded in 1917. It was three years later, when the steel manufacturing family of David Colville and Sons gifted Jerviston Estate to its workforce, that a sequence of events began which led to the reintroduction of golf in Motherwell. Jerviston House had been the residence of David Colville, Junior, son of the founder of the steel firm, but he had died in 1916, and the family's subsequent gift of the house and its extensive grounds to its employees provided workers and their families with hitherto unimaginable opportunities for recreational and welfare pursuits. In addition to the house itself – a creation of the renowned architect Robert Adam – there was also located within the estate, and only 150 yards distant, a much older building which was generally referred to as Jerviston Castle. It was actually a previous Jerviston House dating back to the 16th century, and attached to it were outbuildings and beautifully tended gardens. Among the sporting amenities which were introduced to the estate for the benefit of the workers were tennis courts, bowling greens and a football field; and David Adams, a well-known golf professional and clubmaker from Glasgow, was approached to lay out a nine-hole golf course. By today's standards David's was an unusual occupation in that he managed his own sports outfitters store in Glasgow whilst being non-resident professional at Douglas Park Golf Club in Bearsden. The new nine-hole course was constructed on the south-western section of the estate; and thus Colville Park Golf Club was founded in 1923. Within a relatively short time it was decided to extend the course by utilising the higher ground on the east side of the estate, and James Braid was commissioned to design an eighteen-hole course incorporating the original layout, together with any amendments which he might deem appropriate. Much of the groundwork was carried out by volunteers and the newly extended course was completed in accordance with Braid's plans in March 1926; work having begun the previous autumn with the construction of the new greens.

As I recall, locals in Motherwell tended to refer to golf being played at Jerviston rather than at Colville Park, but it was one in the same. It was towards the end of my third year at high school that a few of my classmates took up the game and I was invited to join them. But I did not have any clubs! No matter, that was quickly resolved. For anything between threepence and a shilling each, I was able to purchase a selection of hickory shafted clubs for which their fathers had no further use and, with the addition of an old canvas bag, I was able to go along to Jerviston with the other boys. It is only now, as I look back over the years, I realise that most of these fathers were employed in the steelworks, which accounted for their having had golf clubs in the first instance and their sons then taking up the game. Playing on the golf course was not restricted to Colvilles employees and anyone could play on payment of the green fee.

My most vivid, indeed nostalgic, recollections of the course at that time were the features which gave it its own unique character. The opening six holes were played among the wooded area of the estate but thereafter, and especially after crossing the railway bridge, the upper part of the course was of a very open aspect with no shelter from the prevailing south-west winds. Unlike any course to my knowledge the bunkers were not filled with sand, but with pulverised red blaes obtained, I presume, from the steelwork furnaces. They looked very pretty indeed, especially after rainfall when their colour turned a deeper shade of red. Recovery shots from Jerviston bunkers demanded a variety of speciality strokes; not something that could readily be gleaned from golf instruction books! In wet conditions the blaes tended to hold the water and become compacted so that the ball often sat as if on a paved surface, whilst in dry conditions only a very shallow top layer of blaes had any possible resemblance to sand, and underneath was firm and unyielding. When I hear some of today's players complaining as to the type of sand being used, or that the ball does not get gathered into the centre of the bunker, I become only too aware of how much perceptions as to the nature and vicissitudes of the game have changed. After all, a bunker is deemed to be a hazard and was never intended to be a place from which the ball should be easily extricated! If memory serves me correctly, it was not until the mid-1960s that sand replaced red blaes in the bunkers.

As for the greens, they were of the most variable contours imaginable. On at least five of them the greenkeeper was very restricted in finding a suitable pin position around which there could be a reasonably flat surface. To reach the green at the opening hole, a par three of just over 200 yards, required a good tee shot over an old curling pond but, having got there, the question was whether the ball would settle in the same furrow as that in which the hole had been cut; otherwise the first

Double Green at 11th and 13th Holes

putt of the round would be a challenging roller coaster across the furrows. Most likely as a result of subsidence caused by underground coal mining, the sixth and fourteenth greens were only level on the right-hand third of their surface and the remaining two-thirds sloped down steeply to the left; so that any ball played from the middle of the fairway and which landed in the centre of the green would not settle but could meander down to the left-hand fringe and possibly run off the green completely. The *pièce de résistance* was the short par three 10th Hole. Its green was situated on the shoulder of a sharp incline and was so convoluted in its layout that in dry conditions a ball struck purposely to land just off its top right-hand corner could sometimes run back down across the full width of the green and fall off on the other side. What with clumps of heather among the tussocks of thick grass, furrows gouged out by rainfall, a wicked drop on the left bank, and a steep bunker guarding the best line of approach to the green, the hole was aptly named Wilderness! The present day large flat inviting green must have new members and visitors mystified as to how this hole ever merited such a name. Alas, Colville Park followed the trend of so many other courses in levelling off the challenging slopes and borrows of the original greens and in so doing removed something of the course's inherent attraction.

There may not have been sand in the bunkers but each teeing ground had sand in the metal (or was it wood?) tee boxes. Wooden tee pegs, and also plastic pegs, were in general use by the members, but schoolboys like myself made use of this sand which was provided for the purpose of forming a small pyramid upon which to tee-up the ball. And golf balls themselves were at a premium; especially for juniors. When it came to purchasing a new ball from the Club Master's shop, Blue Spot was our preferred option; not on account of its quality, but because it was cheapest at around two shillings and sixpence. And golf ball casings, even on expensive balls, were prone to get cut and render the ball useless if a shot was thinned or topped when using an iron club. Coming across a Penfold Patented or a Dunlop '65' in pristine condition whilst ball searching in the rough was a moment for great rejoicing!

18th Hole with Ravenscraig Steel Works in the background

As if to confirm something of its individuality, Colville Park retained Bogey as the standard score for each hole; whereas at Wishaw Golf Club, only a few miles away and within the same burgh, Par was used as the means of rating individual holes – the distinction of which I was unaware until later years. Another quaint feature made its appearance at some of the longer holes on the course. These were white wooden stakes which protruded about 18 inches (450mm) above the ground and were sited just off the fairway. On them, in black lettering, was the number 215, which indicated the number of yards from the Medal tee. Not that many of us had cause to take much notice of these markers as a means of club selection for the next shot; rather they were a guide as to how far we had managed to drive the ball. Choosing the appropriate club for the second shot was a matter of sight and judgement; not the application of a yardage chart as is now the norm. If for any reason the actual distance to the green was required, this entailed an arithmetical calculation whatever the circumstances. With so much of today's emphasis on the exact carry achievable by the modern golf club, throughout the country yardages to the green are now to be found on sprinkler heads or on strategically positioned fairway discs; and even these are becoming superfluous with the advent and legalisation of hand-held measuring devices. One wonders as to what will be the next artificial aid invented (and approved) to further remove the game from its original concept!

Although Motherwell was an industrial town, and at the very heart of steel production in Scotland, it would be a mistake to assume that it was devoid of open spaces and greenery. Quite the contrary! There were several large parks, private estates, woodland walks, agricultural fields and even working farms within its boundary, and my abiding memory of the eighth hole at Colville Park is of the proliferation of skylarks that frequented the right-hand rough adjacent to the railway line. How ironic that, in the vicinity of the largest steel works in Scotland, skylarks thrived in their hundreds and today, with the demise of Ravenscraig, they are now something of a rarity. I suspect that the most likely reason for their decline in numbers is the removal of their natural habitat as a consequence, among other things, of the increased use of herbicides and pesticides in modern greenkeeping practices.

Jerviston House was an impressive, commodious edifice and a popular location for wedding receptions and other such functions. It was also the venue for the Club's annual dinner and prize-giving, but the actual golf clubhouse was a separate single-storey rough casted building located about 100 yards distant. It was an unpretentious structure, albeit having a large bow window on its front elevation, and comprised principally of the secretary's room to the front and, behind it, the locker room. The amenities were very basic indeed and, if I recall correctly, comprised only a WC, a wash-hand basin and a foot basin. If there were any other facilities, they were not something which I or my golfing companions had ever occasion to use. Of all the items that were on view in a small display cabinet on the wall of the locker room, the one which most interested me was a scorecard of the record score for the course. The signature on the card was that of Mark Seymour and his score was 69 strokes. His was a name with which I was totally unfamiliar, and it was many years later, courtesy of *The Golfer's Handbook*, that I encountered references to him. In my youth I had been impressed by those clubs whose record score had been achieved by D.J. Rees, S.L. King, A.H. Padgham, A.D. Locke and the like and, in a perverse kind of way, I rather regretted that Colville Park's was not held by a high-profile professional. However, one learns as one gets older – I hesitate to say 'gets more mature'! I was destined to discover that Mark Seymour was half-brother to the great Abe Mitchell and that he had represented both England and Scotland in professional international matches. He was twice runner-up in the 'News of the World' Tournament which, at that time, was second only in importance to The Open Championship. For the record, he was beaten in the 1931 final by Alf Padgham, and in the 1933 final by Percy Alliss, father of Peter, having earlier defeated the redoubtable Archie Compston in the semi-final. On three occasions he won the Scottish Professional Championship, twice won the Czech Open Championship and, whilst still an amateur player, the Golf Illustrated Gold Vase. No mean feat for any player; and a wonderful revelation to someone like myself who had been unaware of the story behind that mysterious name on the scorecard.

In my early years at the Club the outstanding player was Willie Redpath, who had just recently retired from a distinguished football career in which he made nine full-international appearances for Scotland, represented the Scottish League on seven occasions, and was an ever-present member of Motherwell FC's Scottish Cup winning team of 1952. To my mind Willie's golfing technique

Mark Seymour

was the personification of orthodoxy and he had the hallmark of a natural games player. His swing was neat and compact, rhythmical and balanced, and I never had the impression of his pressing or forcing a shot. As a playing partner he was reserved and unintimidating. I recall Davie Russell as being his nearest rival and, like Willie, he was a fine role model. But Davie's style was certainly not classical. He had a rather crouched stance, hands held low, dipped his knees at impact and appeared to sweep the ball away. He had a secure grip, and struck the ball with great authority. Henry Cotton always contended that a golfer was only as good as his hands and Davie was testament to that. The other leading player in the Club was Bob Henderson, but I never had occasion to play alongside Bob and only ever saw him when he was teeing-off at the opening hole. As for other notables who remain in my memory, no dissertation relating to Colville Park as I first knew it would be complete without at least mentioning the names of Matt Young, Willie Smart, Major E.C.Thomas, Willie Smith and Colonel Cox; together with John Williamson and the greenkeeper, Pat Innes. Were this a treatise on Colville Park Golf Club, there are dozens of names I recall with pleasure and whose exploits on and off the course I remember with great affection; but that is outwith the scope of these reminiscences.

I would wish, however, to record one other name that was well known throughout the membership, *viz*. Norrie Thomson, the clubmaker. If you happened to be thinking of purchasing new clubs, or knew of anyone who was considering the same, somebody was sure to suggest that a set of Norrie Thomson's could be obtained at a very reasonable cost and, in truth, many members must have taken that advice as his clubs featured extensively among golf bags at Colville Park. As I understand it, Norrie was then living in Motherwell, had joined Colville Park Golf Club, and was manufacturing these clubs locally in his own workshop.

Above: *Norrie Thomson, Elie*

Right:*Two other items of interest Mark Seymour 1-iron, and locally manufactured 3-iron by The Clyde Alloy Steel Co Ltd (a subsidiary of Colvilles Ltd)*

Chapter 3

May

Tuesday, 4th May: Learned of visitor injured on course

It is in the nature of any sports undertaking that the risk of injury is ever present; and golf is certainly no exception. 'Forewarned is forearmed' as the old maxim states; but no matter the precautions and warnings put in place, the risk factor cannot be totally eliminated. *The Golfer's Handbook* has recorded numerous incidents involving freak accidents and injuries occurring on golf courses; some quite bizarre as to the chain of events and coincidences that brought about the catastrophe. During my three years as Health & Safety Convener there had not been a single report of an injury being sustained on the course, but this morning I was confronted with the news that a very serious incident had occurred on the previous day. Its being a public holiday, there had been a number of visitors on the course as guests of members, and it transpired that it was a visitor who had been injured. Secretary Tom advised me of the circumstances as had been reported to him, *viz.* the visitor was seated on the timber bench adjacent to the lower tee of the 2nd Hole whilst the group of players in front were playing off the upper tee; and he had been struck on the head by a ball played by one of that group. The situation was extremely serious and an ambulance had been summoned immediately to the course. By all accounts it arrived very quickly and the patient was rushed to Ayr Hospital. On hearing this account I telephoned the member whose guest had been injured, and his wife informed me that the patient had been removed to Southern General Hospital in Glasgow for emergency surgery. Having expressed my concern, I then contacted my Links Convener, Stephen King, and my Health & Safety Convener, David Coid. Thereafter David and I met at the scene of the accident and we were of the opinion that, irrespective of what interpretation might be put upon our action, it would be irresponsible not to have the seat removed immediately from its current position, together with a similarly placed one at the 3rd Hole.

Friday, 7th May: Meeting with Bill Andrew re luncheon

With the Celebration Lunch due in just over three weeks, President Bill invited me to meet with him in order that I might be updated upon the current state of its planning with a view to finalising the arrangements. We met in the Tom Morris Room and discussed matters over a bowl of soup. Bill showed me a sample of the parchment scroll/menu which Murray Bothwell was designing for display on the luncheon table, and also some photographs which Ian Wilson was using as the basis for a commemorative print that he was preparing for each of the seven honoured guests. Just as I expected, Bill had everything in hand and it only remained that we establish our own individual roles with regards to the pre-lunch reception, the lunch itself and the presentations.

Monday, 10th May: Meeting with Robin Alexander

Since first becoming involved in committee business, I was aware as to how much the process of interviewing prospective new members had changed over the years. Unlike many other clubs, which in a period of financial recession were struggling to attract new members, St. Nicholas still had a lengthy Waiting List of almost 100 names. For expediency in processing these numbers, or so it appeared to me, the actual method of interviewing applicants on a personal level had been supplanted by a 'block-interview' type of approach. Indeed, to my mind, the method that was being employed could hardly be described as resembling an interview at all. Anything up to a dozen applicants and their proposers were initially invited to attend an 'interview' session at which officials of the Club said something as to its history and administration prior to each applicant being called upon to give a brief resume of his own background (not more than two minutes) to the assembled company. As to how such a procedure constituted a proper vetting of applicants completely eluded me, and the absence of any input from the proposers struck me as being a glaring omission. Furthermore, for applicants unused to speaking to an audience of strangers, the process was not only daunting – it was unnerving. Being dissatisfied with the current procedure, especially in regards to an applicant's first interview, I invited my Membership Convener, Robin Alexander, to meet with me to discuss amending the format. I had envisaged this action during my time as Vice-Captain and when Robin was elected onto Committee, and knowing of his managerial background in business, I determined that he would be my preferred choice to introduce the necessary changes. During our evening meeting in the Tom Morris Room, I outlined to him my misgivings as to the interview process and requested that he investigate the means by which my concerns could be addressed. In particular, I wanted responsibility put onto the proposer when introducing an applicant; the applicant being asked specific standard questions; and a means devised by which to make a rational assessment as to an applicant's suitability. We discussed the subject at considerable length, and I had total confidence in Robin's expertise towards achieving these ends.

Thursday, 13th May: Second interviews
Just like the inevitability of time and tide, so proceeds the ongoing business of a golf club. Whilst some innovations might conveniently be implemented immediately, others are at the dictate of the current procedures and require to be introduced gradually. At St. Nicholas the membership year is from June to May and, in anticipation of obtaining entry into the Club, those applicants at the top of the Waiting List were due to receive their second interview. In that regard, since the revisions which I had discussed with Robin were of more relevance to first interviewees, there was no requirement at this stage to alter the general format of the second interview sessions. As Membership Convener, Robin conducted what could best be described as an informative meeting rather than an interview, and my contribution was to present a suitable address to those present. Although I had chosen to say a few words when presenting prizes at the Ayrshire Ladies' County Golf Championship, this was to be my first speech among any of the Club's general membership and I was very conscious of the need to make a competent job of it. As it was, I was satisfied with the content of what I had prepared but nervousness, no doubt occasioned by lack of experience, meant that I tended to read off my notes and in so doing lost something of the confident presentation expected of a Captain. This interview session was held in the Tom Morris Room and Robin chaired the proceedings in a very efficient and informal manner.

Gentlemen:
I recall, whilst on the Waiting List, with what anticipation I looked forward to being admitted into

membership of this Club. Whenever I was in the vicinity of Maryborough Road and St. Ninians Road and looked over at the course, I thought how wonderful it must be to be a member of such a golf club, to delight in playing linksland golf and to enjoy spectacular views across the Firth of Clyde. I could hardly wait. And I presume that you all feel the same – and that is why you are back again this evening.

At your first interview, the Captain no doubt told you something of the Club and its history. He would have spoken of its formation in 1851, of Tom Morris being a founder member, commented on the course and the clubhouse, and would have referred to the champions and internationalists it has produced. Indeed, until well into the twentieth century, St. Nicholas was very much one of the country's foremost clubs in the development of the game. Tonight I do not propose to go into any detail on these matters. Rather I shall update you on the developments that have taken place within the Club since your previous interview.

The course has been extended so that it now measures 6044 yards when played from the championship tees. The Committee felt that 6000 yards represented a watershed if the Club hoped to continue hosting important competitions and attracting the attention of potential visitors as a worthwhile course. This extension of the course by about 100 yards was achieved by lengthening the 11th, 12th and 18th holes. However, for general play members will find that little has changed.

Due to the constricted nature of our links, bounded on one side by the railway, on the other side by the sea, and at both ends by public roads, we have not hitherto had a practice area. However, with a little bit of ingenuity we are constructing a practice hole in the area enclosed by the 5th, 6th and 7th fairways. You will note that I say a practice 'hole' and not a practice 'area', as the greenkeeping staff is desirous that it be of similar standard to the rest of the course. It will be about 100 yards long with a green incorporating four pin positions at any one time, a greenside bunker, a fairway bunker and a substantial teeing ground. It is hoped that this will prove to be a very useful facility for coaching junior members, and that members generally will find it of great advantage when practicing their short game and bunker play.

The new gents shower room was probably already completed when you were last here, but we have since started on a three-year plan for refurbishment of the clubhouse. The first stage involved the upgrading of the ground floor gents toilet, the Juniors Room, rear hall and staircase; and that work was completed earlier this year. The next stage will be the total refurbishment of the Mixed Lounge and the Dining Room. Most visitors comment favourably on these areas, particularly when comparing them with their own facilities; and there is no doubt that when we carried out our major extension works about twelve years ago they proved to be a vast improvement on the previous accommodation. However, the decor has become rather dated and the lighting is poor in relation to our current requirements, so that is why we are undertaking these improvements. That work will be carried out towards the end of this year. The third stage will be the refurbishment of this particular room, the Tom Morris Room. This is very much where the soul of the Club abides. It contains our memorial plaque and also the names of the past captains and club champions. Our intention when refurbishing it is to ensure that it retains its distinctive character compared with other areas of the clubhouse. In that regard we are very fortunate that Past Captain Bill Rae has agreed to act as the project administrator for these refurbishment works. With his professional expertise as an architect, he is ideally suited for the project and the club is indebted to him for his willing service on its behalf.

Just to show that we have moved into the 21st century, we now have our own website which has been a great boon in advertising our course throughout the world and in attracting visitors. We have also introduced an online booking system for entering club competitions. In past years an entry sheet for competitions was posted on the clubhouse notice aboard approximately one week in advance of a competition and members had to come down to the clubhouse to enter their names on the sheet. Now that process can be done online. When first introduced there was scepticism among some members as to whether it would be successful but, now that it is in place and being fully utilised, no one would wish to return to the previous arrangement.

A major change was made to our constitution at the Annual General Meeting when it was agreed that ladies would now be eligible to become Ordinary Members of the Club. Previously, ladies were only afforded Associate Membership, but with the current progress of equal opportunity legislation through parliament it was decided that this was the appropriate time to acknowledge that change was inevitable. Prior to the vote it was thought that there might be considerable opposition to the proposal but, in the event, only four members dissented. Should any of you find this change to be an issue as to your own application, I would direct you to Royal Troon and Prestwick Golf Clubs, both of which remain bastions of the male preserve.

As to your own future, you will find that generally speaking this is a friendly club. But as in any club of 600 members, there is a wide diversity of characters. From those who are quiet, to those who could only be described as ebullient. From those who are accomplished golfers, to those who are high handicappers. Gradually you will find your own niche within the Club. However there is nothing worse than that a new member should feel isolated; nor is there any excuse for such a case. The onus is on those of you who have supported applications to ensure that you initiate the new members into the life of the Club by showing them what is involved in entering competitions, introducing them to other members and making them aware of what facilities the Club has to offer. That should be the accepted way. Please don't leave it to the Secretary or the staff, helpful as they assuredly will be. It is important that everyone is made to feel welcome and part of the Club from the outset.

For my part as Captain, when you eventually become a member, I trust that everything will be just as you had hoped, and that you will derive much pleasure and enjoy many happy years golfing in such attractive surroundings – weather permitting!

Friday, 14th May: Irvine Rotary AM/AM

One of the great railway journeys in Scotland for golf enthusiasts is surely the last 16 miles of the trip from Glasgow Central to Ayr. Many eloquent words and evocative descriptions have been applied to the veritable string of fine linksland courses that are adjacent to both sides of the railway line shortly after the train leaves Kilwinning Station and the traveller gets his first sightings of the Isle of Arran and the Firth of Clyde. The modern railway carriage, with its broad windows and spacious interior, provides an excellent vantage point from which to survey the splendour of the Clyde coast; but for the golfer the scene is enhanced beyond measure by the mounds and hollows of rolling fairways and the stark brilliance of little red or yellow flags dotted about distant greens. The seasoned commuter will long since have established from which point in the journey the best views of individual courses can be obtained, and upon which side of the train to be seated; but the first-time traveller will find it a tantalising and exasperating experience as, almost too late, he catches but a brief sighting of a famous golf course as the train glides past. But blessed with a sunny day and a receptive disposition, the allure and anticipation evoked by the variety and sheer beauty of the links will transport him into the realms of enchanted dreams. And if he has been seated on the seaward side of the train, his most vivid recollection will surely be of Western Gailes. Of all the courses, it is the one that can best be seen to advantage from the railway carriage and which affords the greatest number of holes to the viewer. From the elevated position of the railway line the course, the dunes, the firth and the Arran peaks combine to produce a spectacle of rare beauty; one that is not just appreciated by the golfer, but by landscape artists, photographers, hill walkers and sailors.

With Robert Muldoon, Ricky Miller and Alan Poole at Western Gailes

Just as St. Nicholas always supports Prestwick Rotary Club's golf day, it also takes a tee-time for the annual Irvine Rotary AM/AM. Unlike the former, the venue for the Irvine event is variable and this year it was scheduled to be Western Gailes. Never previously having visited the course, I was delighted that my long-standing desire to play over it could at last be realised and it was with considerable relish that I looked forward to that happy day. On this occasion Vice-Captain Alan was available to play and I decided once again to invite two members from outwith Committee to make up our team, Robert Muldoon and Ricky Miller. In addition to being competent players, they are two of the most affable members in the Club, and I was quite sure that we would have an enjoyable round in the most pleasant of company. It so happened on the day that Robert was short of time and he missed out on much of the pre-match buffet and the evening meal, but this in no way diminished what was a memorable day for us. Just finding the access road to the course was an adventure in itself and an unmanned crossing over the main railway line demanded that a driver's attention should not be distracted in his eagerness to see the course. From the large car park we were welcomed into the clubhouse by one of our own members, Alex Lumsden, and were aware immediately of an unmistakable aura of history and traditional values. After registering with the officials, we were directed to the main area where an excellent buffet was provided, and thereafter we were transported to the extreme end of the course to commence our round at Hole 14. The format of the competition varied from the Prestwick event in that the two lowest net scores at each hole were to be counted. Endowed with fine golfing weather, it was a joy to play over this fine course which fully satisfied our expectations and, although we never threatened to win, our net aggregate score of 131 was quite presentable. Vanity prevails on me to record that I contributed a 2 for the team at the unforgiving par 3 7th Hole. The post-round dinner and prize-giving were held in the nearby North Gailes Hotel, followed by a charity auction on behalf of Malcolm Sargent House, Prestwick (cancer care for children) whose fund-raising manager, May Gilchrist, led the proceedings. Altogether a lovely day; and filled with happy memories.

Saturday, 15th May: Spring Meeting

In 1878 two new trophies were introduced to the Club for presentation at the Spring Meeting. Unlike most of the other trophies, these were not donated by an individual but were subscribed from among the general membership. The Ayr and Prestwick Trophy was presented by members resident in these two towns for competition in the First Class section, whilst the trophy for the Second Class section was presented by members from Kilmarnock. As has become something of a tradition, the prizes accompanying this event are donated by the current Captain. Having made a similar gesture the previous year for the Summer Meeting in my role as Vice-Captain, I needed to give serious thought as to what would be appropriate and acceptable for this year's winners. The questions arise as to whether the prizes should be practical or personal, golf related or general, for display or attire, household or pleasure; the list is extensive. Instead of trying to read anyone's mind, I decided to choose items which would have pleased me had I been a winner; and that became my quest. And so, for the winners in each class I ultimately purchased a crystal ship's decanter, and for the runners-up, a small clock.

As is customary on the day of the competition, the prizes for the Spring Meeting were put on display in the Main Vestibule for viewing by the members.

Thursday, 20th May: Meeting with Ladies' Club

Within the annals of Ladies' St. Nicholas Golf Club, the gentlemen's Club is quaintly, but correctly, referred to as the Parent Club. This status arose out of the circumstances whereby the Ladies' Club was originally formed. As far back as 1889 the St. Nicholas Committee had considered the possibility of admitting ladies into membership of the Club, but the matter had gone no further. When in 1892 the gentlemen's Club moved from its 12-hole course situated on grounds east of Ayr Road to its present location on the links, it nevertheless retained tenancy of these grounds. After considerable deliberation, the Club decided in June 1893 that the old course be modified to one of 9 holes and made available to ladies and to boys under 15 years of age. This was the background to the Ladies' Club being constituted in September 1893, and to the St. Nicholas Club Captain, Mr A.J. Larke, acting as its first Captain. It was agreed that lady members be permitted to play over the gentlemen's new links on one day per week. The following year, at the first Annual General Meeting of the Ladies' Club, Mrs. Larke was elected as Captain in succession to her husband. These playing arrangements, with some modifications, lasted until 1936 when the Club's lease of the old course was terminated; the Town Council having recently purchased all of the land from the previous owners. It was at this juncture that the Ladies' Club transferred to the present course, with all the attendant hours of play having to be agreed and alterations made to the clubhouse to accommodate the lady members. Each year the Ladies' Club is financed with a lump sum from the Parent Club to use at its own discretion for its general purposes and administration. From 1893 until 1964 it was standard practice for the Parent Club to have a representative present at all committee meetings of the Ladies' Club. Thereafter the format changed whereby the gentleman appointed as Ladies Convener on the Management Committee would meet on a regular basis with representatives of the Ladies' Club to report or to confer upon any matters which either committee wished to raise; but direct personal discussion was always the prerogative of the respective incumbent Captains.

The vote at the Annual General Meeting in favour of admitting ladies into Ordinary Membership was of historic significance within the Club. As to what the eventual consequences of this decision might be only time would tell, but in the meantime it was natural that the question of its implementation would be very high on the Ladies' Club's agenda. Three weeks previously the Management Committee had agreed upon the broad basis as to how the changes should be introduced and in the interval the Lady Captain, Eileen Munro, requested that a meeting be arranged to update the ladies on developments. I met with Eileen in the Ladies Lounge; she was accompanied by her Vice-Captain, Elaine Morran, whilst I was joined by Vice-Captain Alan and my Ladies Convener, Tom Andrews. The meeting was very amicable, but it emerged that the ladies were most unhappy about the prospect of a modified entrance fee being imposed for their upgrading from Associate to Ordinary Membership, and they asserted that they were not being fully informed as to Committee's intentions. At this stage the intricacies of the changes had yet to be finalised, and Committee was aware that unforeseen anomalies were bound to arise, but already discontentment was being expressed by the Ladies' Club.

. . . . 20th: Second interviews

Following the interview session of two weeks previously, the membership sub-committee re-convened to meet a further batch of applicants whose acceptance into the Club was imminent. Based upon the experience gained at the previous session, on this occasion I was able to deliver my speech in a more relaxed and informal manner. Having had time to become familiar with its content, I simply noted a few key words to get me started on the various sections and I dispensed totally with the written version. For me, once again getting used to speaking in public was a sharp learning curve, but I felt confident on the night and I was happier with my performance. Afterwards I had the pleasure of speaking in the casual bar with some of the applicants and their proposers, amongst whom was Bruce Patterson, the Scottish cricket internationalist and stalwart opening bat for Ayr CC.

Saturday, 22nd May: Ladies Day

Mixed foursome events confined to members of both St. Nicholas Clubs were a long established feature of the fixture calendar and, over the years, the May event was generally referred to as being 'Ladies Day'. In 1972 Mr. and Mrs. W. Chisholm presented a trophy for competition, and named it JT Smillie Memorial Cup in memory of Mrs. Chisholm's father. Traditionally pairings are formed whereby a Lady Member invites one of the Gentlemen Members to partner her on the day and, by custom, the Lady Captain will be partnered in the first match by the Gents' Captain. And so Captain Eileen and I were paired together, and the foursome made up by our respective Vice-Captains, Elaine and Alan. Ours was a very sociable match; made the more so by the ladies producing sandwiches and chocolate snacks at the turn, whilst Alan and I had come prepared with liquid refreshments for all. It was a most enjoyable round but, on reflection, a poor example to others, and especially unfair to those pairings actively competing for the trophy, since our progress got noticeably slower over the inward half. Needless to say our foursome did not feature among the prize-winners, at which ceremony I delivered a short impromptu speech.

In the evening we returned to the clubhouse along with our wives and husbands for the Dinner Dance, and Hugh and Kate McKail joined us at the 'top table'.

Wednesday, 26th May: Captain's Walk

It is in the very nature of a golf club that almost every member will have an opinion as to some aspect of the course or its layout that would benefit from its being altered. Unlike tennis courts and football pitches which have enjoyed decades of standardisation, all golf courses are in a continuous state of evolution and the character of each is totally unique. And that is one of the supreme attractions of the game! Just as a hill-walker finds exhilaration in unfamiliar country, or a mountaineer relishes the challenge of a new peak, so the golfer's appetite to experience new surroundings and to play on other courses is insatiable. His choice is wide and varied, and he is enticed by courses described as linksland or cliff top, downland or parkland, moorland or heathland, hillside or flat; notwithstanding that even a golfer of the most modest ability can often be accommodated on courses famed all over the world as championship venues.

In recent years it has been customary at St. Nicholas for the incoming Captain, within a fairly short time of his having taken office, to meet with the Head Greenkeeper and together walk round the course and discuss all relevant points relating to its layout and condition. In every golf club it is desirable that the Captain should have a good working relationship with all members of staff; but particularly so with the Head Greenkeeper. I was fortunate in that throughout my previous years on Committee I had been Health & Safety Convener; a position which had entailed my being in regular contact with John MacLachlan and through which we got to know each other very well. I was also fortunate in that there were no contentious issues with regards to the general condition of the course, or with the workshop facilities, since John had always been diligent in his attention to every aspect of his professional work.

Like all golfers I too have opinions as to how a course might be improved, but I am also aware that mine might be a minority view and I would not wish to foist my ideas upon a disapproving membership. Much depends upon how one assesses the role of Captain, especially in a club which has been in existence for almost 160 years. There are stories in some clubs of autocratic captains having introduced a feature which could be regarded as their legacy and a visible reminder of their period in office. Although they themselves may not have named the feature, the likelihood is that in future years they derived some satisfaction from hearing its being referred to as 'their' bunker or 'their' shelter. My philosophy was really quite simple; endeavour to uphold the Club's finest traditions, retain and promote its unique character, preserve what is genuinely historic, and always remember that a Captain's guardianship is but for just one year.

In terms of the course layout at St. Nicholas, I am satisfied that the best possible use has been made of the available land and its features, and to consider radically changing it would seem to me to be quite unnecessary. Ironically, if the course has a weakness, and even that is a matter of debate, it would relate to the very item which attracts the greatest number of compliments from visitors, *viz.* the superb condition of the greens. Indeed they are a joy to putt upon; but they lack the rolling contours and subtle borrows which are the hallmark of so many fine seaside links and, as such, can flatter the otherwise moderate putter. The one feature of which I had the greatest reservations was the incessant encroachment of gorse into areas of the course that formerly had been the preserve of heather and wispy rough; especially where the enjoyment of many ladies and high-handicap players was being spoiled by the severity of the challenge posed, whilst being of no consequence in making the course a more severe test for better players. Although I made my views known during the Captain's Walk, Vice-Captain Alan, who accompanied us, was not supportive of my suggestions for managing the gorse, and that for me was a great disappointment. Nevertheless, I still hoped that others on Committee might share my concern regarding its unrelenting spread over the links.

Captain's Walk with John MacLachlan (Head Greenkeeper)

. . . . 26th: Inter-club match v Kilmarnock (Barassie) GC

Friendly rivalry with other clubs, especially between close neighbours, is a hallmark of golfing life. Serious competition in the form of team matches involving each club's best players is the very essence of the golf experience but, thankfully, the nature of the game, with its handicapping system, allows golfers of varying abilities to compete on relatively equal terms. This is borne out by the method of team selection used by St. Nicholas for these inter-club matches; a sheet being posted on the Club's notice board and members invited to append their names should they wish to play. As a matter of protocol the Captain and Vice-Captain, if both are available, will play in the first game; usually against their counterparts in the opposing team.

In the course of the golfing year, St. Nicholas generally plays four inter-club matches and two committee matches; all of which are good fun. This year our first match was a home fixture against Kilmarnock (Barassie), and Alan and I had the pleasure of playing a four-ball against David Miller and his Vice-Captain, Douglas Orr. David was currently Vice-President of Ayrshire Golf Association and was playing off a handicap of 1. Everything about his play was neat, compact and totally unfussy, but it was the spirit in which he approached the game that made a lasting impression upon me; good golf, good manners and good company; encapsulating all that is finest in sporting traditions. The four of us had a super game together, and it was fitting that Alan and David vied with one another in producing a series of classic shots; but Douglas was on hand to come in with some telling contributions at vital stages in the round. Our finishing all square after eighteen holes was the appropriate result, and it was with the utmost satisfaction and good fellowship that we entered the clubhouse to await completion of the other games, before going through to the dining room for the post-match meal.

Captain David, Vice-Captain Douglas, Gentlemen:
I trust that all of you have enjoyed today's match in what turned out to be a fine golfing afternoon. We at St. Nicholas are very much in favour of these inter-club matches and, in particular, we welcome the opportunity of playing host to our friends from Kilmarnock (Barassie). There is a long standing association between our two clubs which dates back to 1894 when Kilmarnock Golf Club acquired 123 acres of land adjacent to Barassie railway station and commissioned our professional, Johnny Allan, to lay out a course for its members. Johnny had previously been attached to Westward Ho! and was mentor to JH Taylor who won the Open Championship on five occasions. In fact JH's first ever round in Scotland was played over the St. Nicholas links with Johnny Allan.

We were hoping for a keenly contested match, and Kilmarnock (Barassie) duly obliged. I must say that the first game was played in a most amicable manner and embodied everything that is best in the true spirit of golf. As for the match result, St. Nicholas teams never shrink from acknowledging the outcome and we congratulate our opponents upon their win by 3 games to 1 with one game halved. It has been a most pleasurable match, and we look forward with anticipation to meeting up again next year.

Thursday, 27th May: Committee meeting
Two months into my Captaincy and the chairing of monthly management meetings is now just part of my routine. The April meeting allowed fellow committee members to gauge the means by which I would conduct proceedings and it had given me the assurance that they were satisfied on that account. In retrospect, the most interesting item discussed at this meeting related to a Local Rule which permitted a short length of removable chain on the boundary fence at the 18th Hole to be unhooked if it interfered with a player's stroke. A relatively new member of the Club disagreed with the application of the R&A Rules and, without recourse to the St. Nicholas committee, contacted the R&A, summarised the circumstances, itemised his interpretation of the rules and sought advice on the matter. Upon receiving a reply, only then did he inform the Club Secretary of the action

which he had taken. In view of the fact that this Local Rule had been amended only three years previously following clarification obtained by the Club from SGU and R&A, Committee decided that it did not wish to re-open the issue and informed the member accordingly.

Saturday, 29th May: Nickson Trophy

For Prestwick golfers, especially those born and brought up in the burgh, the Links Championship (as it is popularly known) is of particular significance. The championship was instituted in 1956 when George Nickson, a local bailie, presented a trophy for individual competition open to members of the three private Prestwick Clubs and to any residents of Prestwick who are members of other clubs. Qualifying rounds of 36 holes are played over the St. Nicholas and St. Cuthbert courses; the leading 16 scratch scores then qualify for the match play stage which is contested over the links of Prestwick Golf Club. In 1988, in order to extend the number of entrants and to make the event more inclusive, it was decided to introduce a handicap section into the competition so that the leading 8 net scores of those who did not qualify for the championship would contest the Hugh Boyd Cup. Each year the presentation of prizes is made by a representative of Prestwick Golf Club, whilst the Captains of St. Cuthbert and St. Nicholas alternate in the duties of refereeing the final tie and of speaking at the prize-giving ceremony. This year it fell to me as Captain of St. Nicholas to deliver the Vote of Thanks and to announce the prize-winners. As always, I made every attempt to ensure that I was well prepared for the ceremony which was being held out-of-doors in front of the Prestwick clubhouse. As I emerged with the presentation party, and reassuringly checked that I had my notes in my blazer pocket, I was shocked to discover that they were not on my person. Without so much as a second thought I immediately about-turned, concentred upon retaining an air of composure, though inwardly in a state of extreme panic, and headed straight back to the locker room. In a turmoil of anxiety I rummaged through my holdall and, thankfully, unearthed the missing sheet. Returning to the scene, and conscious of being met with a wall of curious and expectant countenances, my sense of relief completely obliterated any other concerns I might previously have entertained and I was able to address the assembled throng of officials, golfers and spectators without the least trepidation.

Ladies and Gentlemen:

The Prestwick Links Championship is one of the highlights of our golfing year and attracts the very best of our leading players. Prize-giving speeches are of necessity short, but it is only appropriate that we should recognise how privileged we are to be associated with a town which has such a unique place in the history and development of golf.

Today marks the culmination of a full week of competition and we thank the 108 competitors who entered for ensuring the continued success and prestige of this event. Our thanks also to those of you who have supported the tournament by coming along to watch the matches. The presence of spectators creates an atmosphere and an added sense of importance to the proceedings, and this is appreciated by players and officials alike.

Our thanks to the three clubs, Prestwick GC, St. Cuthbert GC and St. Nicholas GC, for allowing us the courtesy of their establishments. For the use of their clubhouses, and the warm hospitality shown by their staff. For the use of their courses. We know what a pride each greenkeeping staff takes in presenting its course at its very best, and we compliment all of them for the very high standard achieved.

Tournaments do not organize themselves, and this is the appropriate time to acknowledge the contribution of those involved behind the scenes. Jim Picken, our efficient and affable Tournament Secretary who is the pivotal force behind the organization, and his fellow committee members, Jim Glass, Andy Peebles and Louis Thow. A particular word regarding Jim Glass who has announced that this will be his last year of active involvement in the event. Thank you, Jim, for your valued contribution over so many years. We are indebted to you, and your efforts have been very much appreciated. To anyone not named, but who has assisted in whatever capacity, be it on the course or in the clubhouse, our thanks also to you.

As regards today's proceedings, our thanks to our two intrepid referees, Billy Gibson and Graeme McGartland. Some people are blest when performing the duties of referee to give the impression of its being 'a stroll in the park', but those of us who have been in that situation know only too well that there lurks the constant fear of being called upon to express a decision on some finer point of the rules, and so we appreciate the enormity of the responsibility that you have had to bear.

And now I am happy to announce the names of the prize winners.

For the record:
Winner of the Nickson Trophy was Michael Smyth (Royal Troon); runner-up Gary Tierney (St. Nicholas).
Winner of the Boyd Cup was Frank Gardiner (St. Nicholas); runner-up Sandy Darroch (St. Nicholas)

Sunday, 30th May: Meeting with Bill Andrew
With preparations for the Celebration Lunch all but complete, President Bill and I had a morning meeting at which we clarified our respective roles on the day.

John Panton (1916-2009)

The Scots are a nation of great diversity, but in a perverse kind of way every Scotsman would like to believe that he and those fellow Scots whom he most admires embody something of the nation's essential character. Epithets such as 'dour Scots', 'canny Scots' and the like are but convenient stereotype caricatures used by those who don't appreciate the Scots' psychology. Perhaps ours could more accurately be described as a Celtic trait, rather than just Scottish, for there is little doubt that our Irish and Welsh friends are more understanding of our ways and of our thinking. John Panton's was just such a case. Often referred to as 'Dour John' by Sassenachs, who mistakenly interpreted his quiet modesty as akin to his being uncommunicative, he actually epitomised something of the heroic spirit of the Olympian. By nature a very reserved person, undemonstrative, reticent in speech and sober in his demeanour, he was the product of an environment in which respect for one's 'elders and betters' was considered to be a virtue. His great rival and Canada Cup partner, Eric Brown, who was his very opposite in temperament, stated that 'no finer gentleman ever walked the links'; and Peter Alliss described him as being 'one of his favourite people'.

The golfer whom in his youth he most admired was the great American amateur, Bobby Jones, and this facet of John's persona was revealed early in his professional career whilst competing in The

Open Championship at St. Andrews in 1946; at a time when all competitors required to play in a qualifying competition of 36 holes, held on the Monday and Tuesday, from which a maximum of 100 would gain entitlement to play in the Championship proper on the Wednesday. Having completed his first qualifying round on the Old Course, that same evening, after play was finished for the day, John went down to the New Course where he was due to play his second round and practised putting on one of the greens. Only afterwards did he discover that competitors were debarred from practicing on either of the courses between rounds and he reported his infringement of the rules. Pending consideration of the matter by the Championship Committee, John played his second qualifying round over the New Course and returned a score which would have gained him a place in the Championship. Needless to say, the committee members had no alternative but to disqualify him from the competition, but it was recorded that they 'greatly appreciated his conduct'. As it transpired, the last nine qualifiers were indebted to John's integrity for their securing a place in the championship. Among admirers, especially in Scotland, he was thereafter generally referred to as 'Honest John'.

I have no definite recollection as to why he, among all of the then current professional golfers, should have attracted my particular attention. Throughout the 1950s his name was much to the fore in golfing circles and I can only surmise that somewhere among *The Glasgow Herald* golf reports or in the Colville Park locker room I read or heard complimentary remarks concerning him. Yet, as I reflect on this matter, I recall a conversation in the clubhouse of Motherwell Cricket Club in the early 1960s when Doctor Jim Logan spoke deferentially of having seen John Panton play and of having been mightily impressed by him. That may indeed have been the catalyst; although I was certainly already aware of his reputation as a superb player and a much respected sportsman. When eventually I did see him play I was not disappointed. That was at Haggs Castle in Glasgow; and on a subsequent visit an incident arose which epitomised all of the personal qualities attributed to him. At one of the par-three holes his tee shot landed in a greenside bunker and, as he made his way up the fairway, there was a great deal of finger pointing and shaking of heads by a group of spectators standing around the green. It became evident that a thoughtless spectator had earlier clambered across the sand bunker and had left a deep footprint into which John's ball had dropped. The position of the ball made it inconceivable that a recovery shot could be played onto the green. All eyes were on him as he approached the bunker to discover for himself what all the fuss was about. Upon seeing what had occurred, his expression never changed; and without gesture or comment he took his sand wedge, blasted the ball in the only direction possible, which was back towards the tee. When a little later he walked off the green with a double-bogey five, he made absolutely nothing of his misfortune to either his playing partner or the assembled spectators. He remained composed and uncomplaining throughout and, if confirmation was needed as to his personal attributes, these few moments provided it for me.

When out on the golf course, John's headgear was as much a piece of his equipment as were his clubs. He invariably wore a cap and, with the sole exception of a posed photograph taken in his youth, I have never come across an action photograph without his being decked in one. The styles varied dependent upon the circumstances and the weather conditions, from lightweight cloth *à la* Ben Hogan to eight-piece Harris Tweed, but each in its own way was his hallmark and an unpretentious statement as to his identity. Upon returning from Portsmouth, Virginia in 1969, where he contested the World Senior Championship final with Tommy Bolt, he took to occasionally wearing a snapback baseball-type cap which had been produced as a memento of the match. It was a marked change from his previous mode and I rather suspect he enjoyed this latter-day flirtation with an alternative style. As to his golf sweaters, once again he tended towards unostentatious colours, generally varying shades of grey and blue; so much so that quite often he rather blended in with the spectators who were following him. *The Shell International Encyclopedia of Golf* quite erroneously described his physique as having been 'never less than portly' but, in fact, it was not until reaching fifty that he got noticeably heavier about the midriff. What did appear to increase over the years was the number of rule books and other paraphernalia that he stuffed into his right hip pocket! But in these later years when he had retired from the main tournament circuit, as his girth increased and his swing shortened, so his wonderful hand action and ball-striking were a delight to behold.

John Panton at Lundin Links 1964, aged 47.

In assessing John's playing career it is important to remember that he had already turned thirty years of age before he embarked on the British tournament scene and that he was essentially a club professional. He was not unique in that regard, since many other young promising golfers had also been involved in military service throughout the Second World War and, at that time, almost all of the British and Irish players had a club attachment; but it did mean that he missed out on those precious early years when players are in their prime and best equipped to attain tournament success. Nevertheless, he established himself as one of the country's leading professionals and a formidable challenger in the important competitions of the day. Similar to many of his rivals, his achievements are liberally sprinkled with second and third place finishes, but it is only tournament victories that posterity is likely to consider whenever his name is mentioned. And in that regard, bearing in mind the tournament conditions of that era, his was a successful career.

He was already Scottish Professional Champion when, in 1950, he achieved his first win on what could be termed the British professional circuit. That was in the Silver King Tournament at Moor Park, having motored all the way down from Larbert in Stirlingshire – something which he required to do throughout his career, for he remained attached to Glenbervie Golf Club all of his working life. The following year he won the Daks Tournament at Sunningdale, commencing with an opening round of 66 and leading the field all the way. His consistently good play earned him selection for the first of his three Ryder Cup appearances and he was awarded the Harry Vardon Trophy for the best average medal score in all major tournaments. In 1952 he not only won the North British-Harrogate Tournament, which was played over 90 holes, but partnered Norman Roffe (Coventry)

With Flory Van Donck (Belgium): Ayr Belleisle 1967

to victory in the Goodwin (Sheffield) Professional Foursomes Tournament. In 1954 the Yorkshire Evening News Tournament at Moortown was added to his growing list of successes, and two years later he gained his most prestigious title when he won the 'News of the World' PGA Match Play Championship at Hoylake, defeating Harry Weetman (Croham Hurst) by 1 hole in the 36-hole final. That same year (1956) he and his amateur partner, W.R. Alexander (Glenbervie) won the Gleneagles-Saxone Professional-Amateur Foursomes Tournament which was played over one of his favourite courses, *viz.*, the King's.

In three consecutive years from 1958 he won the Woodlawn Invitational Open at Ramstein, West Germany, and he held the British tournament record for nine holes with a score of 28 strokes. In addition, he won a host of national and minor championships, and was leading British player in the 1956 'Open' with a fifth place finish. Upon reaching 50 years of age he became eligible for senior competitions and twice won the British Seniors Professional Championship. In 1967 he defeated Sam Snead at Wallasey to win the International Senior Championship, and British golf correspondents were so impressed by his performance that they awarded him the Golf Writers' Trophy for that year. If proof were required as to the enduring quality of his play and of the soundness of his technique, it should be recorded that as late as 1968 he was runner-up in both the PGA Match Play Championship and the Shell Tournament; in 1969 was a semi-finalist in the Piccadilly Medal Tournament; and in 1974, at the age of 57, qualified for the final day's play in The Open Championship.

In the 1950s and 1960s inter-continental air travel was not the commonplace item which it is today but, despite that, golf took John to the farthest corners of the globe. In 1950 he journeyed to South Africa with Fred Daly, Harry Bradshaw and Ken Bousfield as part of a four-man British Isles touring team – and they travelled all of the way by ship! As well as playing on the continent of Europe, his selection for Canada (World) Cup appearances involved visits to Japan, Mexico, Australia, Puerto Rico, Brazil and Hawaii; and, of course, Ryder Cup and other events entailed trips to USA. On these journeys his luggage often included a cine-camera; not only to film these far-flung locations, but to record the styles and actions of many of the players he encountered. And when back home he gave willingly of his time to show these films and to speak of his experiences at social evenings in golf clubs and men's associations.

His cap (or 'bunnet') might have been his distinguishing feature when on the course, but it was widely rumoured that he had a penchant for driving Rover cars, putting a wager on 'the horses', and enjoying a glass of ginger beer and lime – and for being something of a tea jenny! For someone who was born and raised in lovely Pitlochry, and of such a modest and gentlemanly disposition – what with hazardous adventures during army manoeuvres in Asia and in Europe! – his was an intriguing story. He and his wife Betty, along with daughters Joan and Cathy, lived on the clubhouse premises at Glenbervie; so, one way or the other, life for his household was never far removed from the golf course. In middle age, when others might have contemplated taking up some sedentary pursuit, he became an enthusiastic curler and revelled in the banter and good-humoured ribbing of his team-mates.

Golf, with its abundance of statistics, is a sport which inevitably invites an analytical approach when making comparisons as to an individual's abilities and achievements. Unfortunately the yardstick employed is often so narrow, and the circumstances so diverse, that the conclusions can be somewhat misleading. John was quite simply a model professional who was a credit to himself and to the game which he played with such consummate skill. At his best he was the equal of any other golfer, and that was confirmed in the wind-strewn final round of the 1970 Open Championship at St. Andrews when, as the oldest competitor in the field, and amidst all of the world's finest players, he alone returned a score below par. In 1980 he was honoured with the award of Member of the Order of the British Empire (MBE) and, amongst several other honours bestowed upon him, his appointment in 1988 as Honorary Professional to The Royal and Ancient Golf Club of St. Andrews was further acknowledgement of the high regard in which he was held by his golfing peers.

John Panton deserves to be remembered as being one of golf's, and Scotland's, finest sporting ambassadors.

Chapter 4

June

How appropriate that Tuesday, 1st June, turned out to be a day of unbroken sunshine and clear visibility, which afforded excellent vistas over the Firth of Clyde to Arran and to Ailsa Craig, and also of the course as viewed from the clubhouse! Within the Tom Morris Room, where at noon about three dozen members and guests gathered for a Reception prior to the Celebration Lunch, sunlight streamed in through the bay window overlooking the first tee and the whole room was illuminated in a most spectacular fashion. If ever that room exuded an aura of hosting a special event, this was just such a time. No doubt other persons in the clubhouse would have been immediately aware of the somewhat elderly profile of the assembled company, of white hair and bald pates; but that was symptomatic of the occasion. Everyone was smart and well-presented;

Celebration Lunch: Reception in Tom Morris Room

(Prestwick St Nicholas Golf Club)

products of a generation when good form and personal pride in one's appearance were the accepted norm. Each new arrival through the door was met with startled recognition as the inevitable mask of the intervening years was stripped away, and handshakes and greetings were exchanged with genuine affection and pleasure. A welcoming glass of wine, spirit or juice was readily provided to mark acceptance into the fold and to put everyone at their ease. Initial welcomes were followed by introductions, and without the need for prompting or direction, the Reception simply blossomed of its own accord as friendships were renewed and new acquaintances formed. The room was filled with the resonance of intimate chatter and an air of anticipation pervaded the proceedings; it was as if the success of the forthcoming afternoon's event was already assured.

From the Reception, the assembled company made its way through to the Dining Room where Grant Hood and his staff had everything arranged and presented in a most attractive fashion. The communal table extended the full length of the room and at each placing was a parchment scroll wrapped in a blue ribbon and bearing the names of the honoured guests. The white tablecloth was adorned with poses of red flowers, ornate cooling buckets, bottles of wine, pitchers of water, sparkling glasses, polished cutlery, bread rolls and individual menus; the whole scene beckoned approval and whetted the appetite. And the meal which followed was worthy of the setting.

As had been pre-arranged with President Bill, I contributed a few opening remarks to get the post-lunch formalities underway.

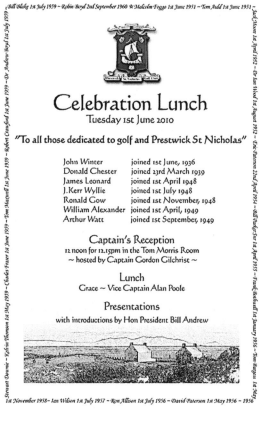

(Prestwick St Nicholas Golf Club)

Gentlemen:

I trust that you enjoyed your lunch.

Golf clubs enjoy having celebrations, under whatever pretext. In recent years there has been a spate of clubs celebrating their centenary, and this year there are celebrations to mark the 150th anniversary of The Open Championship; there are retiral dinners for popular professionals; dinners to recognise the long service of clubhouse stewards; dinners to celebrate any notable success or achievement.

But today's event is a little different. Today we are celebrating the members; but not just any members. In particular those who have held membership of our Club for more than 50 years. It is by way of expressing a 'Thank You' to them for providing the continuity that every club requires; and a recognition of their lifelong attachment and commitment to the Club and of the regard they have for its well-being. This is a time for renewing acquaintances, for recalling names, for reviving memories. It is a time for unashamed nostalgia.

It was Honorary President Bill who first suggested this event, and it is he who planned its format and has made it happen. And so, I shall now pass the remainder of the formal proceedings into his capable hands.

(Prestwick St Nicholas Golf Club)

Standing: *Robin Alexander, Ronald Gow, Eric Paterson, Alan Poole, Stewart Downie, Malcolm Foggo, Tom Burgess, Alan McKinlay, Willie Alexander, Arthur Watt*
Seated: *Kerr Wyllie, Bill Andrew, John Winter, Gordon Gilchrist*

President Bill then took charge of the presentation element of the function and guided it through the various stages, all of which he had planned so meticulously. Each honoured guest was introduced to the company by a personal friend and, as can be imagined, whilst the agenda might have been formal, the various introductions (other than my own) were full of humour, reminiscences and anecdotes, which generated good-natured banter and unbridled merriment as befitted this joyous celebration. For my part, as Captain, I had the honour of introducing the principal guest, *viz.* John Winter.

Gentlemen:
To a young man like myself, the concept of continuous membership encompassing eight decades is a daunting prospect. When considering this fact yesterday, I calculated that by the time I emulate John's period of membership I shall have already celebrated my 126th birthday.

I hope, John, that you are a devotee of PG Wodehouse's golf anecdotes. As you will know, the narration is by the Oldest Member as he sits in his rocking-chair on the terrace of the clubhouse and observes all that is happening around him. He has not played since the rubber-cored ball superseded the gutty. Such a description of the Oldest Member certainly doesn't apply to yourself. What you do not know is that only four weeks ago I was in the Main Lounge at Royal Troon, looking out onto the eighteenth hole when you appeared up the fairway. Your pitch to the green pulled up about 30 feet from the flag and I watched as your approach putt was hit with perfect weight but ended up about two feet wide of the hole. I was so hoping that you would sink the next putt – and you did!

John, you were already a member of St. Nicholas for over 20 years before I first played golf. Most of my early clubs were hickories and, at that time, I was still unaware of the need to apply raw linseed oil to the shafts, nor did I know of the old trick of steeping the clubs in a bucket of water when the iron heads began to get slack. One of my favourite clubs was a Maxwell mashie – the one with the perforations in the hosel. The theory was that the holes helped lighten the head but, in fact, unless care was taken in looking after the club, the holes could provide a source for water to rot the bottom of the shaft. I vividly recall the whistling noise which the club made whenever it was swung.

The privilege is mine to introduce you to the company, but there is the distinct drawback in that until today we had never met. So, of necessity, any information which I have obtained is second-hand, but I am sure, John, that, if needs be, you will put matters right.

John joined St. Nicholas on this very day in 1936. He was educated at Glasgow High School and later graduated from the University of Glasgow. The first teaching post allocated to him was here in Prestwick. He struck up a golfing friendship with Fred Smith; and one of his star pupils at school is here with us today, Drew Adam. Drew's father was Club Master at St. Nicholas and Drew succeeded him in that position. However, John's career in teaching was cut short when circumstances dictated that he should

(Prestwick St Nicholas Golf Club)

Stan Stevenson, with Ian Wilson's commemorative print as a backdrop

take over the management of the family's curtain making business in Darvel. John, I shall leave it to yourself to fill in the blanks relating to your golfing exploits, and to recall the names of those with whom you were closely associated. For my part, it is my very pleasant duty as Captain to congratulate you on 74 years continuous membership of the Club and to invite you to accept in recognition of that fact this commemorative print specially produced by Ian Wilson, together with a facsimile of the front page of The Glasgow Herald of 1st June 1936.

Each guest made an appropriate reply and was presented thereafter with the limited edition print specially produced for the occasion by one of our members, Ian Wilson, together with a facsimile of the front page of *The Glasgow Herald* on the day of his joining the Club.

Sunday, 6th June: Inter-club match v The Irvine GC

Due to family commitments I was unavailable for the second inter-club match of the season, which was against The Irvine Golf Club. That weekend Jeanette and I were in England attending a wedding near Birmingham on the Saturday, and our great-niece's christening in Lancashire on the Sunday; so Vice-Captain Alan took on the mantle of captaining the St. Nicholas team.

Tuesday, 8th June: Portrait in Vestibule

Upon entering through the front door of the clubhouse into the vestibule, one's eye is naturally drawn to the adjacent wall upon which are hung a photograph of the Honorary President and an oil painting of the Club's first Captain, David Smith. Until now my own portrait had not appeared beside them but, although I dared to pause only briefly, I must admit that I was filled with an inner glow when I saw that it was now being displayed. Vanity is not a trait which attracts admiration, and rightly so, but I must confess that I was pleased with the result and hoped that others would approve of it. It must be extremely irksome to a Captain if he is confronted every time he enters the clubhouse with an image of himself of which he is less than comfortable.

The Captain's Wife and 'Hubbie's' Portrait

. . . . 8th: Invitation to Cocktail Party

Of all the pleasurable moments in life, the unheralded receipt of an invitation to an exclusive social event must surely rank high on the scale. Be it to a royal garden party, the opening night of a theatre production, the inauguration of a dignitary – whatever the occasion – the initial thrill to the invitee, especially to one who generally does not move in such circles, is a joyous moment. Back in January, whilst I was Vice-Captain, Secretary Tom had informed me that an invitation to attend the Sesquicentennial Celebration of the First Open Championship had been received from Prestwick Golf Club and that he had responded on the Club's behalf. Still musing upon the appearance of my photograph in the vestibule, I was handed by Tom an unopened envelope which, as I was about to discover, contained the formal invitation for Jeanette and me to attend a cocktail party as part of Prestwick's 150th anniversary celebrations. The very act of holding the invitation card and reading our names thereon was a unique sensation which conjured up an immediate flood of anticipation and excitement as to the event; and an awareness of the fortuity and great privilege that had befallen me as Captain. Jeanette was similarly enthusiastic when I showed her the invitation and our elation was unbounded. What a pleasure it would be to share the experience together!

Wednesday, 9th June: Roger Casket

In monetary and historical terms, the most valuable trophy in the Club's collection is the Jubilee Casket. To commemorate the Diamond Jubilee of Queen Victoria's reign (1897), it was presented to the Club by one of its members, Mr. James Henry Roger, for annual competition among amateur golfers who are members of a Scottish golf club and who have attained 50 years of age. The inaugural competition was held in 1898 and Mr. D. McLagan of Torwoodlee GC, Galashiels had the distinction of being the first winner. The silver casket is ornately engraved and was initially augmented by a gift of £100 as a fund to provide prizes. Since 1931, by which time the fund was fully expended, all prizes have been supplied by the Club. The competition now forms part of the extensive programme of seniors' competitions that has emerged throughout Scotland in recent years as a consequence of many gentlemen obtaining early retirement from employment and of their enjoying much better levels of health than previous generations. I played in this year's competition and was accompanied on my round by Gordon Turnbull (Louden Gowf) and by John Goodwin (Shotts) who, incidentally, was originally from Prestwick. Due to the lack of attendance of the various category-winners following the close of play, our Match Secretary, Malcolm Foggo, decided to dispense with a prize-giving ceremony, and I concurred with this decision. For the record, the winner of the Jubilee Casket was a St. Nicholas member, Hugh Cameron. This was yet another example of the impracticality of arranging a prize-giving ceremony in circumstances where many players have travelled from afar; and when an early starter can hardly be expected to return to the clubhouse awaiting the outcome of rounds that commenced six or seven hours after his own.

Friday, 11th June: David, Henk and George

The hospitality provided by Troon Welbeck GC at the conclusion of the Ayrshire Winter League final back in April, together with the dignified manner in which its players and its officials congratulated members of the St. Nicholas team on their success, was a most rewarding experience and epitomised all that is best in the true spirit of the game. In the course of speaking with my counterpart, David McMahon, I ascertained that he had never played over the St. Nicholas links and, therefore, I invited him and the Welbeck Treasurer to join with me in a four-ball over our course sometime in the near future. As it happened, the latter was unavailable on the day, but David secured

Past Captain Henk Tor as his partner and arrangements were finalised. I invited George Hunter to partner me in the four-ball and, in keeping with the occasion, the weather was warm and sunny. Following morning coffee in the Tom Morris Room, we enjoyed a fine round together and, appropriately, our match was halved. Afterwards, over lunch in the clubhouse, it emerged that we had much in common. David had originated from Lanarkshire and was well acquainted with many of the dancing establishments that I had frequented in my youth; Trocadera Ballroom in Hamilton (locally referred to as 'The Troc'), Cedar Ballroom at Lanark Loch (generally referred to as 'Lanark Palais'), and Hamilton Town Hall (where the leading jazz bands of the day made regular appearances). For his part, Henk had actually played in a jazz band; so, in retrospect, it was plain to see how we had all taken to one another from the outset. Conversation was easy and spontaneous as we reminisced about our mutual interests and our respective golf clubs, but my abiding memory of the day was a poignant moment in which David told me that this visit to St. Nicholas was one of the highlights of his captaincy. How generous of him to have expressed such a sentiment; a day to be cherished!

With Henk Tor, George Hunter and David McMahon

Saturday, 12th June: Summer Meeting
The Club Medal, awarded to the winner of the Summer Meeting, was instituted in 1870; the first winner being John W. Boyd. After playing this event as a one-class competition for more than eighty years, it was subsequently divided into two classes, with the winner of the Second Class becoming the recipient of the Club Medal. A small commemorative bowl, which had been presented to Gordon Lockhart upon his winning the Jubilee Bowl in 1906, was gifted to the Club and was thereafter awarded to the winner of the First Class. By tradition the Vice-Captain donates prizes for the winner and runner-up in both classes, and Alan duly obliged. As Jeanette and I were receiving guests from Cambridge, domestic arrangements precluded my playing in the competition.

Monday, 14th June: E-mail re out-of-bounds ruling
Every golf club is an entity in its own right and, quite naturally, is possessive of its independence and

traditions; albeit it will be affiliated to a regional association and will adhere to the dictates of golf's governing body, the R&A. However, individual committees have the authority to introduce local rules as befits their particular circumstances as long as these are in keeping with official guidelines and *The Rules of Golf*. By the same token, if the R&A or a regional association utilises the course for one of its championships, it can suspend or introduce whatever local rules it may wish for the duration of the event. So in 2007, after seeking guidance from SGU and R&A, and having deliberated at great length as to defining the out-of-bounds situation relative to the playing of our 18th Hole, the incumbent Committee had reached a conclusion and had incorporated it into the local rules. Having reflected upon that conclusion at the May Committee Meeting and having informed the disputant of the outcome, it was with some surprise that Secretary Tom received an e-mail from the member stating that he intended taking the matter further and would be contacting both SGU and R&A.

Wednesday, 16th June: Committee match v Turnberry GC

The happy prospect of playing in the annual committee match against our friends from Turnberry Golf Club is one of the rewards of serving on Committee; but when it coincides with their acting as hosts, the pleasure is all the greater. Turnberry Hotel is one of Scotland's most celebrated establishments and attracts visitors from all over the world. The international traveller regards it as a 'five-star' complex in the most spectacular of locations and, to those who are so inclined, it is a golfer's paradise. Through the medium of television broadcasts from The Open Championship, even those who have never ventured within sight of its environs are familiar with its imposing appearance, its golf courses and its iconic views of Ailsa Craig, Firth of Clyde and the famous Turnberry lighthouse. Indeed, there is so much more that could be expounded as to the range of its attractions and to the luxury of its accommodation; but that in itself would merit a lengthy dissertation!

As always, both committee teams met in the clubhouse for an introductory coffee before setting out on the links. This year the match was being played on the Kintyre course which, paradoxically, is rated two strokes more difficult than the Ailsa course upon which The Open Championship is contested. Alan and I played in the first game against Peter Wiseman and Norrie Stevenson, respectively Turnberry's captain and vice-captain. Both play off single-figure handicaps and can prove to be a very formidable pairing; as I was well aware of from previous encounters. This was amply demonstrated once again, as Alan and I found ourselves standing on the 13th tee and five holes down. Undaunted, Alan won the next three holes; I put my tee shot at the short 16th to within 2 feet of the hole for a birdie, and then secured a net three at the 17th with a lofted pitch to the side of the hole. So, from being on the verge of a comprehensive defeat, we arrived on the 18th tee with our game all square. Eventually everything hinged on the final putts. Alan was closest to the hole and only about 4 feet distant. Norrie, however, resolutely held his nerve and holed his putt to ensure at least a halved match for Peter and himself. Thereupon Alan's putt was conceded and we shook hands upon what had been a memorable tussle. The concession was a sporting gesture in the spirit of the game, and much appreciated by me, but I rather suspect Alan would have relished the opportunity to knock in that final putt. As for the team match, it resulted in two wins apiece with two games halved. Following refreshments, both teams were provided with an excellent buffet meal; the whole event very ably organised by Graeme Rennie.

Captain Peter, Vice-Captain Norrie, Gentlemen:

At the corresponding match last year, Turnberry members were looking forward to hosting the 2009 Open Championship. This year the members at Prestwick Golf Club are looking forward to celebrating the 150th Anniversary of The Open Championship. But what have the committee members of St. Nicholas been looking forward to? They have been looking forward to coming here today! This is an event in which, whenever a member telephones to intimate that he is unavailable to play, one can detect genuine disappointment in the voice. Earlier this year I had occasion to be in Turnberry Hotel when a group of golfers from England was in the main lounge. One of them said that they had played in all the famous venues in the British Isles; that they had played in America and in South Africa – and Turnberry was best of them all!

But today is not just about the course; it is about meeting up with fellow golfers and renewing friendships. It is an opportunity to get to know one another, and it was as a result of such contact that I learned previously of Vice-Captain Norrie's love of cricket, a game which I also enjoy very much. And today we have included in our team our own cricketing legend; a scourge to batsmen and bowlers alike, Bob Ellis. Indeed, among our new intake of members is another Scottish internationalist cricketer, Bruce Patterson, for so long Scotland's premier opening batsman. It strikes me that, for contests like today's which have ended in a tie, we should consider having a single-wicket cricket match to determine the outcome.

Captain Peter, I thank you for the warmth of your welcome and the generosity of your hospitality. For my part, the nature of my own modest ability precludes my commenting in any detail as to the match, but we of the St. Nicholas team are very appreciative of the respect afforded to us as evidenced by the quality of opposition which you provided.

There has been a long and happy association of our two clubs. Long may it continue!

We look forward to welcoming you to St. Nicholas next year.

Tuesday, 22nd June: Rescheduled Club Championship Final

In 2008 a decision was made to introduce a Finals Day. Prior to that date the various championships within the Club had been arranged on an *ad hoc* basis, but the incumbent captain, Donald Morgan, proposed that the final ties for all of the championships be played on the same day; thereby providing a focus for the matches and enhancing awareness among the membership. From a practical point of view, considering that the finals are normally played during the weeks traditionally utilised for summer holidays, the potential complications inherent in such an arrangement were self-evident. Whilst acknowledging the drawbacks, Committee agreed nevertheless to the introduction of a Finals Day with play commencing at noon; and that was the situation for the current championships. By implication, having established at the outset the date upon which the final ties would be played, members who knew that they were unavailable on that date were dissuaded from entering. In reality, the lure of playing in a club championship is understandable, and the dilemma of reaching the final in these circumstances is a consideration which many consciously defer until such time as it may arise. And so it arose in this instance; and, of all people, to Vice-Captain Alan! Gaining one of the fifteen available places to qualify for the match play stage, and then progressing through three ties against the best golfers in the Club, was not something which Alan had thought likely. In truth, others had superior handicaps and he was not considered among the favourites for the championship but he knew, as others did too, that he was capable of putting up a good challenge and that it would be of interest to see how far he could progress. In the qualifying rounds and in the knockout ties he struck a rich vein of form and duly won his place in the Final. But months previously he had booked a family holiday in France to commence on the day of the championship finals, and now he was torn between family obligations and his commitment to contest the match. An additional embarrassment lay in the fact that, as an office bearer, it was expected of him that he should show a good example by adhering to Committee's directives and, of course, he was exposing himself to justifiable criticism from anyone who had refrained from entering the championship due to their being unavailable on Finals Day. Jeanette and I had been down in London for a few days previously and, when I looked in at the clubhouse, I was confronted with the news of Alan's success in the semi-final. What was to be done? Oh, the responsibility of Captaincy! Without going into all the details of the affair, suffice to say that I decided ultimately to allow the tee-off time to be brought forward to 10am; Alan having offered to delay his holiday departure to the last possible moment and his opponent, Scott Mitchell, graciously agreeing to the earlier start. So the date scheduled for the Final remained unaltered, albeit with some modification as to the intended timing.

Wednesday, 23rd June: Second interviews

The subscription year at St. Nicholas begins on 1st June and a little time is needed following that date to establish just of how many places are available for offer to new members. The Membership Convener, Robin Alexander, concluded that 13 places still remained after account was taken of the number of resignations that had been intimated to the Secretary. So, for the third time, I was required to deliver my Captain's contribution to a gathering of second interviewees.

Thursday, 24th June: Committee meeting

Further to Committee's decision not to re-open the debate as to the status of the removable chain at the 18th Hole, Secretary Tom told the meeting that the member concerned intended to pursue the issue with both SGU and R&A. Committee was of the opinion that the matter was outwith the member's jurisdiction and that he be instructed to desist from approaching any outside bodies without firstly having obtained Committee's approval.

In connection with the likelihood of additional changes being required to membership conditions as a consequence of the proposed Equality Bill, I obtained approval to create a Membership Development Sub-Committee with a remit to thoroughly investigate the issues as they related to the Club. I was very aware that the sub-committee's task would necessitate a considerable degree of focussed concentration and it was obvious to me that there were already too many demands upon my time to allow my being involved in the day-to-day intricacies of its deliberations. Accordingly, as the subject would have repercussions beyond my period in office and, as a means of enunciating its importance, I invited Vice-Captain Alan to act as Convener and I appointed those whom I considered most appropriate to sit with him, *viz.* Membership Convener, Match & Handicap Convener, Ladies Convener and Club Secretary; with the proviso that they consider inviting two ladies to join the sub-committee once the parameters of its deliberations had been established.

There is no limit as to the circumstances whereby individuals find themselves serving a term on Committee. Some by their very nature actively seek to be involved, others perhaps feel under an obligation following approaches having being made to them, whilst a few perhaps see it as a means of satisfying personal ambitions. No matter the motivation, serving on Committee at St. Nicholas entails at least three years of commitment, both in time and in endeavour. It is desirable that the general membership recognises and appreciates the effort being made on its behalf, but it is equally important that Committee functions in the best interests of the Club. To that end, management meetings should be vibrant affairs in which views are expressed openly, and debates conducted in a respectful manner. Whatever diversity there may be in opinions, personal relationships should remain harmonious in order that the work of Committee might be constructive and fulfilling to each of its members. With that in mind, I put forward the suggestion that we organise a Committee golf outing later in the year, to which the response was favourable and enthusiastic; so much so that possible venues and dates were tendered immediately. In fact, several of the proposals were on a much grander scale than I had envisaged. However, it was agreed that it be left to Secretary Tom and myself to make appropriate arrangements.

Friday, 25th June: Inter-club match v Prestwick St. Cuthbert GC

If there is such a thing as local rivalry in the context of golf clubs, of the two other clubs in Prestwick, St. Cuthbert would probably be afforded that appellation by St. Nicholas members. Both clubs have much in common and I would venture to suggest, in terms of attracting new members, each is seeking to recruit from a similar pool of applicants. And of course, both clubs have lady members, whereas Prestwick Golf Club remains a 'Male Only' establishment. This year's fixture was at St. Cuthbert, a course of quite different character to St. Nicholas; its being flat parkland with lush underfoot conditions and tree-lined fairways. The present course was opened for play in 1963 and has matured into a most attractive place at which to play one's golf; affording easy walking and very pleasant surroundings. The club's original course was located to the north of Prestwick, but was closed to accommodate major development of the adjacent international airport. With Vice-Captain Alan being unavailable (due, I suspect, to an obligation to assist in packing for the forthcoming family holiday in France), I invited Robin Alexander to partner me in the first game against the St. Cuthbert vice-captain, Graeme McGartland, and his partner, Craig Gemmell. As events turned out our game was re-scheduled to go out last. Conditions could not have been better for an evening round; the air was mild with only the slightest hint of a breeze, and the course itself was in lovely condition. Robin and I blended quite well in the contest but, after a close and sporting tussle, we eventually lost by 2 and 1. As to the match result, St. Cuthbert won by three games to two. St. Cuthbert Golf Club is rightly acclaimed as being a most hospitable venue and, afterwards in the clubhouse, both teams became the beneficiaries of that reputation.

Vice-Captain Graeme, Gentlemen:

Once again we have enjoyed an exhilarating evening's golf amongst our friends at St. Cuthbert. There is so much that unites our two clubs, and we all have friends or workmates who are members of the other club. And whilst we are united in friendship, we are also united by name. Saint Cuthbert, Saint Nicholas, St. Andrew's, Royal St. George's, Royal St. David's – we are in august company. But just to emphasise that we are egalitarian in outlook, we also associate ourselves with St. Boswells, St. Fillans, St. Medan and St. Michaels Golf Clubs.

Following last year's drawn match at St. Nicholas, we decided to select a team based upon age and experience rather than upon current form. And here I must apologise to my team members when I say that we were outmanoeuvred tactically. The master plan was that Robin and I should lead from the front but, on arrival at the clubhouse, we were informed that ours would be the last game out. I suspect that St. Cuthbert reckoned that age would be a factor and that by 8.30pm our energy levels would be so depleted by dehydration and lack of food that our performances would suffer. And so it proved to be. At 8.30pm our match was indeed all square after 15 holes, but thereafter we succumbed at the next two holes and lost our game. And in so doing our team lost the match.

On behalf of the St. Nicholas golfers, I thank you for your welcome and for the generosity of your hospitality both out on the course and in the clubhouse. Congratulations also upon your winning the match.

We shall look forward to meeting up again next year for your return visit to St. Nicholas.

In the course of the evening the St. Nicholas party was informed of the recent death in Spain of Jim Glass, who had for many years been a stalwart of St. Cuthbert Golf Club and to whom I had paid tribute at the Prestwick Links Championship only four weeks previously.

Sunday, 27th June: Finals Day

By custom, the current Captain acts as referee at the Final of the Club Championship and, so, the responsibility fell upon me to officiate in this instance. Not for the first time I required to refresh my memory with regards to some of the finer points of the rules; especially those upon which the character of our links might invite a query, *viz.* water hazards, immovable obstructions, unplayable lies and the like, and also local rules relating to out-of-bounds, taking relief, etc. With the intention of increasing awareness among the general membership, and of endowing the occasion with a proper recognition of its importance, Committee had agreed to continue with the experiment of organising a Finals Day in which all of the Club's major championships would be decided, *viz.* Gents Championship, Ladies Championship, Junior Championship, and Coila Cup (Gents Handicap Competition). Unfortunately both the Ladies and the Junior Championships required to be postponed. By prior arrangement, the final of the Gents Championship took precedence and by tee-off time a few dozen spectators had gathered around the clubhouse to see the two finalists play their opening shots. Irrespective of the weather, I decided to wear my navy blue blazer, dark grey flannels, white shirt and club tie in the performance of my refereeing duties. By so doing I hoped to indicate my respect for the players, and to convey to the spectators something of the event's significance. It was with some pleasure, and satisfaction, that I beheld Honorary President Bill Andrew similarly attired.

There was a tangible air of expectancy, even curiosity, surrounding Alan and Scott as they awaited the commencement of their game. Neither player having previously progressed to this stage, there was no past record upon which to assess how each would react to the challenge, and there was a general feeling that the tie could be decided either way. How refreshing from a spectator's point of view that there was no suggestion of a particular player being considered as favourite to win! It promised to be an intriguing encounter and hopes were high that both finalists would do themselves justice on the day. As was my wont on the first tee, I congratulated both players upon having reached the final, hoped that each would play well, and advised them that I was there to give any rulings that might be requested of me, but that they should simply conduct the match in the same manner as they had with opponents in previous rounds when no referee was present.

A par four was sufficient for Alan to win the opening hole, but any suspicions that Scott was overawed by the occasion were promptly dismissed when he secured a birdie two at the 2nd Hole to square the game. From that point the match continued to be closely contested, holes were exchanged and, by virtue of a birdie three at the 8th Hole, Alan was one up at the turn. Both players scored pars at the next two holes, and standing on the 12th tee the match was delicately poised. And quite suddenly the defining moments appeared. Having the honour, Alan struck his ball to the very heart of the green at this 208 yards hole. By contrast, Scott blocked his tee shot out to the right and perilously close to the boundary fence which runs the full length of the hole. After a fruitless searching amongst the rough adjacent to the fence, Scott conceded the hole rather than electing to play a second ball; and so Alan went two up with six holes to play. The 456 yards 13th Hole was halved in four, but a par four at the 416 yards 14th Hole, followed by a birdie three at the 15th Hole, enabled Alan to win by 4 and 3. Allowing for the conceded put on the 12th green, he was 3 under par when the match finished. After spending a short time with the finalists back in the clubhouse, I returned to the course and caught up with the Coila Cup final at the 12th Hole. In a closely contested match Brian McRobert came from behind to pip Chris Rigby by one hole. As was only to be expected, both finals were played in a very sporting manner.

With Club Championship finalists, Scott Mitchell and Alan Poole

(Prestwick St Nicholas Golf Club)

.... 27th June: Gift from David McMahon
In any aspect of life, unsought favourable comment upon one's actions or behaviour is a most welcome bonus. This is particularly true in business whenever a party with whom one may have had contentious dealings nevertheless recognises, and acknowledges, that you have acted with integrity and in a spirit of fair-mindedness. That same integrity and willingness to do what is right, in my opinion, is an absolute requirement of Captaincy. A fine balance needs to be struck on occasions when the apparent right of a member may have a detrimental effect on the Club, but these

are exceptional cases and need to be treated with circumspection. However, I digress, and now return to the matter of favourable reactions. When I arrived at the clubhouse for my refereeing duties I was informed that a small package addressed to myself had been handed in at the bar, but I had absolutely no idea as to what it might relate. Imagine my surprise and delight when I discovered that it contained a boxed set of jazz cds with the compliments of David McMahon; a much appreciated gift from the Captain of Troon Welbeck.

Monday, 28th June: Removal of unsolicited portrait

Back in May, prior to my own portrait being displayed in the entrance vestibule, a photograph of the current Club Champion had been hung surreptitiously in the space reserved for that of the Captain and, with my approval, Secretary Tom had removed it from the wall. Although it has not been the Club's custom to display a photograph of the current Club Champion, any proposal to institute such action would certainly have received my support. When calling in at Tom's office this morning to countersign 'end of the month' cheques, I observed that the same photograph had re-appeared in the vestibule, albeit upon another wall. Ironically the subject of the photograph was no longer Club Champion, the new champion having been installed only yesterday, but Sigmund Freud himself would have been hard pushed to explain the motivation behind this compulsion to have that particular photograph put on display. The crux of the matter was the unauthorised action by a prominent member of displaying material on the walls of the clubhouse without first consulting the House Convener, far less seeking Committee's approval. Without further ado the photograph was again removed but, rather than make an issue of it with the perpetrator, it was decided simply to remind the general membership that all furnishings and fabric within the clubhouse were the prerogative of the House Convener and that nothing could be installed or removed without his approval.

Wednesday, 30th June: Cancellation of inter-club match with Troon Portland GC

Prior to first serving on Committee, my experience of playing private courses in South Ayrshire was extremely limited. I had played on all of the municipal courses, Troon Darley being a particular favourite of mine, but as to playing the private courses I recall only having golfed at Brunston Castle and on the former Arran course at Turnberry. So the prospect of visiting Troon Portland was something to which I had being looking forward with considerable anticipation. But it was not to be! By the oddest of quirks there was a mix-up between the respective Club Secretaries as to the date of the fixture. Secretary Tom had recorded the date as being Friday, 2nd July, but it turned out that Troon Portland had noted it as being the following Friday. This only came to light when Tom telephoned to confirm the fixture and, as Portland considered it too short notice to play on the earlier date, and St. Nicholas found the later date to be unsuitable, it was decided to cancel the match. It was all a wonderful parody of Fred Astaire and Ginger Rogers: 'I say Friday second of July: You say second Friday of July – Let's call the whole thing off!'

Antiquarian Golf Books

There was a time, not yet distant, when the acquisition of historical facts and anecdotes on the subject of golf was the province of those who were prepared to delve through second-hand book shops, public reference libraries and old newspaper cuttings. Searching in the two latter categories was invariably with a particular topic in mind; some item of specific interest that demanded research and which had the prospect of producing a satisfactory conclusion when once uncovered. Newspapers in particular provided the most diverse, and diverting, information. From adjacent columns to the one being studied, the eye could so easily be drawn to advertisements, football reports, photographs, picture-house film times, court reports and goodness knows what else. Unless focussed, much valuable research time could drift away; albeit in the most pleasurable of circumstances. And what researcher has not been thrilled in that *eureka* moment when all his efforts have been rewarded with success! Modern technology has certainly made research less demanding than of yore and, in public libraries and heritage centres, local history books and local newspapers can be accessed readily; each catalogued on a computer spreadsheet and meticulously indexed as to location, date and page number. What could be more convenient! In truth, compared with the hours of laborious, if not frustrating, diligence that was once required in dust-laden surroundings, the current high-tech environment is a godsend. The sense of achievement may be diminished, but the end result can be just as satisfying.

In recent times I have benefited from the use of the Internet in uncovering facts and downloading books which hitherto might have involved years of searching with no guarantee of success; not to mention the question of expense that might be entailed. Nevertheless, perverse as it may seem, uncertainty as to the outcome contributed to the fascination of the physical search and provided the stimulus whereby its fulfilment was an ever-elusive possibility. The downside from a personal, if not selfish, perspective is that little gems of information which one unearthed and thereafter cherished as valued items in one's repository of knowledge can now be accessed by anyone at the pressing of a few keys on a personal computer. It is now commonplace for a speaker's introductory remarks to be laced with dates and names which have obviously been lifted straight out of Google or some other similar search engine. Farewell to the era of painstaking research!

The acquisition of facts is but a by-product of the delights to be found in reading and studying old golf books; and I recall quite vividly the first time I bought a second-hand book. It was 1967, when I was employed in a surveyor's office situated near to Charing Cross in Glasgow. One lunch-time, whilst strolling down North Street, on the side long since obliterated to make way for the M8 underpass, I ventured in to an unpretentious second-hand book shop and cast my eye around to see what might be of interest to me. And there, among the huge variety of books spanning the gamut from hardback classics to paper-back thrillers, I came across a couple of golf books that caught my attention. One was *The First Golf Review*, edited by Willie Allison, which cost me two shillings and sixpence, and the other, *Golfing Technique in Pictures* edited by Tom Scott, which required the princely sum of eight shillings and sixpence. As chance would have it, although both books were essentially contemporary in character, together they provided a potted history of golf's evolution and a wide variety of reminiscences from golf correspondents. Little did I realise, as I handed over the eleven shillings for my purchases, that I had just embarked upon a lifetime's fascination with golfing literature and the frequenting of antiquarian bookshops in quest of knowledge regarding the Royal and Ancient game, its personalities, tournaments, courses, clubs and its means of playing. Not that these two items marked my introduction to the world of golf books, since I was already a regular purchaser of *Golf Monthly*. I rather suspect that it was Henry Cotton's book, *My Golfing Album*, which first alerted me to the pleasure that could be derived from any number of topics pertaining to the game if written authoritatively and with flair by someone who had a passion for the subject. Unlike many books of that time, Henry Cotton introduced his reader to facets of golf and its development which were a joy to discover and, in the midst of his analytical study of golfing technique, his accompanying photographs and perceptive narratives were so captivating as to beg further enquiry. And I found Patrick Smartt's *Golf Grave and Gay* to be a fitting introduction to the category of light reading.

But it was in the realm of second-hand books that I was most interested, and my favourite haunt for pursuing this quest was John Smith and Son's bookshop in St. Vincent Street, Glasgow. The top floor comprised entirely of the antiquarian section, and to me it was a veritable Aladdin's cave filled with books of every description. At that stage I had no notion as to any book's importance or rarity value; my interest was purely in the subject of golf writings and I chose whichever books attracted my attention. It would appear that I arrived on the scene just before there was a massive awareness of golf books becoming a collector's item, for I purchased W.W. Tulloch's *The Life of Tom Morris* for just £6, and *Golfer's Guide Annual 1899* for only £2.50! Whilst there is a certain satisfaction in possessing a book which is considered to be of special interest to a collector, its monetary value is of no consequence compared to the pleasure of simply owning it. Many of the classic books are now out of copyright and I welcome the reprints that have recently come onto the market and are available to all at a reasonable price; some can even be accessed without cost on a personal computer.

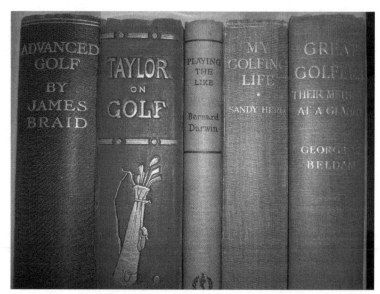

Some interesting reading from a bygone age

What for me started out as a natural curiosity into the history of golf and its past celebrities, very quickly evolved into buying just about anything that related to the game. I too had caught the collector's bug and, whilst in that phase, purchased many books that were primarily of an instructional nature. Just about every champion, or so it appeared, had collaborated in writing a book explaining how he believed that the game should be played and in it provided ample photographic evidence to illustrate his theories. Interesting as these books often were, only a very few are of any lasting significance and many others have been rendered totally obsolete by the changes made in the development of golfing equipment. In my estimation, the classic instruction books are those which go beyond the mechanics of a golf swing and which shed light on the multifarious elements that contributed to the golfing experience of the era in which they were written; books that give an insight to the conditions under which the game was played, the clubs employed, the clothes worn, the characters encountered, the challenges faced, the courses played, and all manner of other interesting facts and anecdotes that give credence to the advice and opinions contained within their covers. *Taylor on Golf*, that superb 1902 production of J.H. Taylor, and Harry Vardon's *The Complete Golfer*, of 1905, are two fine examples of this type of book.

Within any sphere of human activity there will always be those who would wish to chronicle its progress, and those who would wish to investigate its past history – and often the twain shall meet! From its earliest days there have been golfing enthusiasts who felt compelled to put pen to paper to reminisce on past events, to record the history of their club, to extol the champions of their day, to explore the origins of the game – the list is considerable. Some publications were only a few pages in length, printed privately and as limited editions, whilst many others were of voluminous proportions. *Golf: The Badminton Library* by Horace G. Hutchinson is encyclopaedic in its range and contains contributions from several other distinguished writers but, as a testimony to one man's diligent research and unflagging commitment to preserve, record and celebrate golf in all its aspects, I can think of no greater achievement than that of Rev. John Kerr in his magnificent volume, *The Golf Book of East Lothian* – a truly remarkable piece of work!

There is a veritable treasure trove of work by essayists and journalists awaiting discovery by those so inclined and, thankfully, over the years several excellent anthologies have been compiled which provide a wonderful introduction to that aspect of golfing literature. Many of these anthologies are readily available, and contain items which, although not having attained the status of being antiquarian, are exceedingly rare and difficult to obtain in their original publications. Through such compilations countless readers have discovered the delights to be savoured in the writings of Horace G. Hutchinson, Bernard Darwin, P.G. Wodehouse and Herbert Warren Wind, to name but a few, and to enjoy the photography of George W. Beldam and Bert Neale, and the watercolours and sketches produced by Thomas Hodge.

No mention of antiquarian books can ignore the importance of early Golfing Annuals and Handbooks, for they are filled with an inexhaustible supply of incidental facts relating to Clubs and their courses which, with the passing of time, have survived to become data of absorbing interest. These annual publications are one of the first points of reference when researching anything of historical significance, and lure the reader into a convoluted maze as every detail uncovered almost invariably triggers yet another line of enquiry. Course layouts, competition results, subscription rates, green fees, course records, hotel accommodation and all manner of detailed information is provided for individual clubs, and the accompanying advertisements are an invaluable source of even more illuminating background knowledge.

Anything of rarity will always command interest amongst specialist collectors, but the motive behind the acquisition of the rarer golf books strikes me as being the measure of the collector. If one has a genuine interest in the subject of golf, then the searching out of old second-hand books can be a fulfilling and enriching pastime, but if the primary objective is simply the acquisition of anything that is considered to be desirable to a collector then, I would suggest, a disservice is being done to the genuine student of the game when these books become priced at grossly inflated rates. I must confess that I have been thrilled on occasions to purchase a book at below the collector's market price, but the satisfaction lies in securing the book and not in having made a financial investment.

Long may the purchase price of books be related to the worth of their content – rather than to their monetary value as a collector's item!

Chapter 5

July

Friday, 9th July: Cocktail Party

When seventeen months previously I had been pondering over Captain Bill Rae's invitation to become Vice-Captain, I was fully aware of the significance of 2010 in relation to The Open Championship and of the fact that any celebration of its 150th anniversary would occur during Bill's successor's term of office. As to whether St. Nicholas Golf Club would be involved in any capacity was quite unknown, but I must confess that the thought crossed my mind as to how I would react were I to decline Bill's invitation and to discover afterwards that the St. Nicholas Captain was indeed asked to represent the Club at a commemorative function. Although the 2010 Open Championship was being played at St. Andrews, Prestwick Golf Club arranged a weekend of events to mark its own primary role in the inauguration of the competition in 1860; and the St. Nicholas Club duly received correspondence requesting the Captain's attendance at these celebrations – starting with a cocktail party. It so happened that Lady Captain Eileen and her husband, Wilson, were attending the event in another capacity, and Jeanette and I shared a taxi from Ayr with them. A large marquee had been erected adjacent to Prestwick's 14th green and we were directed there upon our arrival at the clubhouse. Past Captain Morton Dewar and Secretary Ian Bunch welcomed us to the party and we were offered glasses of champagne as soon as we entered the main arena. A large number of people were already in attendance, and the buzz of conversation which assailed our ears let it be known that the festive nature of the evening was already well established. It was a colourful scene, with the ladies in all manner and style of cocktail dresses, whilst most of the gentlemen were in lounge suits. Any misgivings I had of my ability to break into conversations were immediately dissipated upon my seeing several acquaintances whom I recognised and, with Jeanette at my side, I knew that I could relax and enjoy the evening.

Formal introduction of the Prestwick Captain, Brian Morrison, to the assembled guests was made by Alan Cook, and thereafter Brian extended to everyone a very warm and friendly welcome on behalf of the Club. In addition to a seemingly endless supply of champagne, waitresses were constantly offering a large selection of delicious *canapés* to the whole assembly; lobster in pastry shells, smoked salmon, roast beef, king size prawns in garlic, mini-bruschetta, cocktail sausages, haggis with mustard dip. It was a sumptuous affair and typical of the generous hospitality for which Prestwick Golf Club is well-known. As to its format, the evening was spent mingling among the company, chatting with friends and acquaintances, making and receiving introductions, conversing about current golfing issues, and generally luxuriating in the magnificence of the occasion. I was particularly happy to meet up with my fellow captains and their partners from the other local clubs, several Prestwick members, some St. Nicholas members and also Drew Adam, the former Club Master at St. Nicholas, whom I had met for the first time only a few weeks previously at the Celebration Lunch. One of the great delights of the evening occurred when Alasdair Malcolm informed me that Professor David Purdie wished to be introduced to me in my capacity as Captain of St. Nicholas Club. That in itself was a thrill, simply because it reminded me of the honour of my being Captain and of the responsibilities entailed in holding that office. David had been a guest speaker at St. Nicholas Club's 150th Anniversary Dinner held in Brig o' Doon Hotel, Alloway in 2001, and I was aware of his having been a Junior Member of the Club in his youth. He was attired quite strikingly among the gentlemen in that he was wearing plus twos; and he called over the official photographer to have us snapped together!

Saturday, 10th July: Anniversary Competition
Following the cocktail party of the previous evening, the 150th anniversary celebrations continued with a golf competition on the Saturday. As one might expect of hosts whose Club tradition is the playing of foursomes, the competition was among teams comprising of three twosomes, with the best score on handicap counting at each hole. The field was split into two sections, each with a shotgun start. For those of us on the outer fringes of celebrity golf, it was pleasing to look through the draw sheet and to note that among such names as Peter Thomson and Sandy Lyle, ours were there also. Not that these celebrities were part of our team; but how stimulating just to be in the same field! The morning players teed off at 9am and the afternoon section, in which I was drawn, was programmed to start at 1.30pm. Any hopes of enjoying a day's golf basking in July sunshine were dispelled from the outset, for the morning arrived overcast and with the threat of rain. When I arrived shortly before noon, the Prestwick clubhouse was positively jumping with activity and animated conversation.

The caddie master, Stan Craig, meticulously turned out in his green jacket and dark grey flannels, was a familiar personage to me and, as always, he made me feel welcome and at ease as he directed me to the board indicating the seating arrangements for the buffet lunch. I noted that our team of six was allocated a table in the upper lounge, and no Oscar winner ever mounted a staircase with greater rapture than I did at that moment. At the top of the stairs my eyes beheld a multitude of people, all engrossed and chattering in an atmosphere of good fellowship and high spirits. It was a great joy to enter that company and to be part of the overall experience. There we made our introductions and were matched up with our respective partners. Our team comprised Norman McLean, Tim Sale, Jock Howard, Michael Denny, Ian Thomson and myself. I had the pleasure of partnering Jock as one of the twosomes and, whilst not achieving anything of great significance when out on the course, we did at least make some contributions to our team's overall score. I found out from Jock that, although his family roots were in Ayrshire, he now lived in Leicestershire, and that he was on the editorial staff of *Golf World*. Our team as a unit scored rather poorly and, much to our disappointment, we got thoroughly soaked in the latter stages of the round. That aside, it was good to be involved in such a historic occasion but nevertheless, like several others who lived nearby, I forsook the comfort of the clubhouse and made straight for home to dry-off and prepare for the formal dinner.

. . . . 10th: Anniversary Dinner
Just to have attended the cocktail party and to have played in the anniversary golf competition was an experience of sheer delight; and had that been the extent of my involvement, the memory of those two events would have forever kindled fond recollections of a magical weekend. But the highlight of the celebrations was yet to come, and it was a measure of the long and harmonious

relationship which our two clubs enjoy that, as Captain of St. Nicholas, I had been invited to attend the 150th Anniversary Dinner. In addition, Jeanette had been invited to a celebration dinner for wives and partners which was being held simultaneously in Troon.

We booked a taxi to take us from Ayr to the dinners. I alighted at Prestwick Golf Club and Jeanette was taken onwards to her destination. Thankfully, by this time the rain had ceased and we did not need to be concerned about the possibility of getting our clothes wet or, in Jeanette's case, her hair. As with the cocktail party, the Anniversary Dinner at Prestwick was held in the large marquee and, prior to taking our seats, a Champagne Reception provided ample opportunity to exchange pleasantries with the Prestwick members and their guests. Just like the cocktail party, the scene was absolutely stunning. The table arrangements were magnificent, all beautifully presented to receive more than one hundred and fifty diners each suitably dressed for this 'black tie' occasion. This was indeed a very special event.

(Ayrshire Post)

Sir Bob Charles, Lee Trevino, Brian Morrison, Peter Thomson, Colin Brown,
Tony Jacklin, Sandy Lyle

I was seated in close proximity to the top table beside Jimmy Wilson, Past Captain of the Prestwick Club. Jimmy proved to be a most engaging companion, and conversation with him throughout the evening was relaxed and entertaining. Regrettably, Graeme Simmers, Past Captain of R&A, who was due to be seated on my immediate right, was unable to attend the function. Initially this was rather a disappointment, since it meant that there was a vacant seat between me and the next diner but, as events turned out, I benefited greatly because several Prestwick members courteously took time to come round from the other side of our table and introduced themselves to me. The excellence of the meal cannot be conveyed adequately in a few words but, in summary, it comprised a shellfish starter (lobster, crayfish and crab) and a main course of Ayrshire lamb, both accompanied by appropriate wines, followed by a savoury of smoked pancetta, and a selection of Scottish cheeses, all supplemented with vintage port and Kummel.

Following the prize-giving for the 150th Anniversary Competition, Colin W. Brown, Captain of The Royal and Ancient Golf Club of St. Andrews, resplendent in his red jacket, proposed the toast to Prestwick Golf Club. He recalled Prestwick's hosting of the first twelve championships prior to its being shared with St. Andrews and Musselburgh. Brian Morrison replied on behalf of the Club and proposed a toast to the assembled guests. Bruce Critchley, former Walker Cup player and current broadcaster, paid a generous tribute to each of the five Open Champions who were present at the dinner; Sir Bob Charles, Tony Jacklin CBE, Sandy Lyle MBE, Peter Thomson CBE and Lee Trevino. Peter Thomson replied for the players and, to the amusement of the company, pointed out that Lee did not really require anyone to speak on his behalf. Peter provided some interesting and entertaining anecdotes reflecting upon how much the status and organisation of the championship had changed since his initial victory in 1954 and of the vast increase in the financial rewards available to the modern professional golfer. The formal proceedings were concluded with a Vote of Thanks by Harry McCaw, one of R&A's members from Ireland. Everyone present was gifted a replica of the original Challenge Belt in the form of a red Moroccan leather napkin holder, together with a commemorative bag tag bearing one's own name; two very special keepsakes!

As to the means of returning home from this superb event Peter Wiseman, Captain of Turnberry Golf Club, informed me that his partner, Barbara, had telephoned to say that Jeanette and she were on their way back by car from the Ladies' Dinner at Troon and that she would collect us at Prestwick Golf Club. What could have been more convenient!

When back at our house, Jeanette and I were curious to learn what each of us had to say about our respective dinners. I had had the most wonderful evening but, I suspect, somewhat conservative compared with Jeanette's time at Troon. Although she did not describe it as such, it sounded to me more like an adventure full of unexpected twists and enthralling encounters. From the moment she and the taxi driver arrived at the clubhouse of Royal Troon Golf Club, only to be informed that it was not the venue for the dinner, she appears to have experienced something reminiscent of Alice descending into Wonderland. It was suggested to them that the clubhouse of Troon Ladies Golf Club, which is less than three hundred yards distant, was most likely to be the place they were seeking, and they were given directions as how to reach it. Not being familiar with the surroundings, and not seeing any signboard outside the building, they were unsure if they had arrived at the right location. In fact, at this stage they could not even be sure that this was indeed where the dinner was being held. Upon ringing the doorbell at what looked like a side entrance, they were met and welcomed by Mrs. Freda Bunch, wife of Prestwick Golf Club's secretary. Having established that she was at the correct venue, the taxi driver then took his leave of her, and she ascended the stairs with Freda.

Jeanette was attired in all her finery as befits attendance at a formal dinner; suitably made-up with hair coiffured and looking her very best. She was immediately aware that her hostess was dressed in a rather casual style, and when she was introduced to the room where the other ladies were assembled she was mortified to find that everyone was dressed in a similarly casual fashion. Nothing had been intimated in the invitation to suggest that the function would be informal! And of course she was not acquainted with any of those present save Barbara; and Barbara was pre-occupied in conversation at the far end of the room! As chance would have it, a lady seated nearby invited Jeanette to sit down beside her and her daughter. She introduced herself as Jolande, and it turned out that her husband was Sandy Lyle; a name with which even a non-golfing addict like Jeanette was familiar. The two of them got on famously and Jeanette really enjoyed being in her company.

The meal which followed was similar to that served at the gentlemen's function, and each lady was also gifted the two commemorative keepsakes. Whilst my range of contacts at the Anniversary Dinner was obviously somewhat limited, Jeanette was engaged, as only women can be, with the wives and partners of many of the male dignitaries. Not only had she spoken at some length with Jolande Lyle, but she had conversed freely with several of the ladies whose partners were representing those clubs which had hosted The Open Championship.

Wednesday, 14th July: Letter of thanks to Ian Bunch
Composed and sent a short letter of thanks to Ian Bunch relating to Jeanette and my attendance at the 150th anniversary celebrations. Ian's planning and organisation of the weekend was absolutely superb and this was reflected in the undoubted success of each of the events.

Thursday, 15th July: The Open Championship
Over the years I have been fascinated by the aura surrounding The Open Golf Championship and have spent many pleasant hours reading accounts of past championships and researching the scores and statistics of individual players. For the enquiring mind there is a plethora of information to be unearthed and sifted through; odd facts and coincidences, tales of triumph and disaster, defining moments, heroic failures, spectacular recoveries – the list is endless. But in spite of this consuming interest, it will no doubt come as a surprise to learn that my enthusiasm does not extend to my actually joining the thousands who flock to spectate at the championship – even when it is played in Scotland! Whenever I have attended a golf tournament it has invariably been with the intention of following the fortunes of a particular player or players, rather than focussing upon the leading contenders or of finding a suitable vantage point from which to view a scoreboard and watch the players pass by. Over the years I have been present at a wide variety of sporting events, many of which I recall with great pleasure, but, in reality, my passion for sport has always been one of personal participation, at whatever level of ability, rather than finding satisfaction in spectating. However, with my captaincy came a ticket for The Open; not just any Open, but on its 150th Anniversary – and at the Home of Golf itself! I was acutely aware as to how highly this complimentary ticket from the R&A is appreciated by the affiliated clubs, and I considered it only polite and proper that I should make a point of attending. Consequently, I decided that I would make the pilgrimage to St. Andrews and I chose to go on Day 2 of the championship. And so, forty years after my only previous attendance at a St. Andrews Open, I was about to make a return visit.

I set off from home in Ayr at exactly 7am with the intention of going via Stonehouse and Newmains before joining the M8 motorway at Newhouse. Unfortunately, there was a major road diversion at Strathaven and I had to travel by way of Kirkmuirhill and Carnwath before reaching the M8 motorway at Livingston. From there I crossed over the Forth Road Bridge and followed the designated route for golf traffic to St. Andrews, which was via Lundin Links. The last ten miles or so of the journey proved to be rather congested and I arrived at the temporary parking area in the University playing fields shortly after 10.30am. After having a snack in my car to ensure that any pangs of hunger would be kept at bay, I walked down to the Old Course and entered it in the vicinity of the tented village. I made my way along to the seventeenth hole and was just in time to see John Daly play an awkward recovery pitch off the path immediately behind the green. I remained there until he and Andrew Coltart drove-off from the eighteenth tee, and I then negotiated my way through the spectators who were gathered in The Links and I cut across to the far side of the first fairway at the controlled crossing off Grannie Clark's Wynd.

My first action was to purchase an Official Programme, prior to making straight for the Golf Museum, which (R&A forgive me!) was my principal point of interest. My immediate objective was to view the driver that had been fashioned by John Allan, St. Nicholas's first professional, but I knew that there would be a multitude of other artefacts which would attract my attention; and so there proved to be. It was not until 1.20pm that I emerged from the museum and decided to occupy a seat in the grandstand adjacent to the first fairway, from where I could see players driving off the first tee and others approaching the eighteenth green. I sat there for just over one hour, during which I saw 'Tiger' Woods putt out of the Valley of Sin, Justin Rose putt through the Valley of Sin and, would you believe it, Tom Watson putt into the Valley of Sin! I stayed there until 2.30pm in order that I might see Colin Montgomery make his opening drive and then, for me, it was time to head for home. I had enjoyed the experience of being present (no matter how briefly) at such a milestone in The Open Championship's history, but within me there was a sense of detachment – I was a voyeur among the throng of golfing enthusiasts. My attendance was something which I considered to have been a privilege, an oddly personal obligation that I most willingly undertook, a day which I would recall with pleasure but, in truth, as to who might be the champion, I was only mildly curious; unlike the passion that Tom Watson's challenge had aroused within me in 2009.

Tuesday, 20th July: Tee-time booked at Wallasey
Ever since I had been to Wallasey Golf Club in 1967 to watch that memorable Teacher's Seniors International Final between Sam Snead and John Panton, it had been my ambition to return to the Wirral peninsula and to play the course myself. As with so many good intentions, the years slipped past without my having taken any positive steps towards fulfilling that dream, for that is probably the status to which it had receded; but being elected as Club captain was the spur which prompted me towards making it a reality. I requested Secretary Tom to contact his counterpart at Wallasey and, if possible, to book a tee-time for me five weeks hence, which would coincide with my summer holiday arrangements in the Peak District.

Wednesday, 21st July: Meeting with John MacLachlan
Thanks to the excellent management of the course by John MacLachlan and his greenkeeping staff, the St. Nicholas links have been in first-class order for many years, during which period numerous compliments have been expressed by visitors, especially in relation to the condition of the putting surfaces. As a consequence of my own awareness of the ever increasing spread of gorse over the course, I had noticed that the heather-clad mound to the right of the first fairway and the central mound which dominates the sixth fairway were both covered in gorse seedlings and, if left undisturbed, would soon be engulfed by them to the detriment of the heather. Accordingly, I had a word with John and he agreed to make sure that the gorse did not take hold in these two areas.

Saturday, 24th July: Evening meal at clubhouse
Jeanette and I had dinner at the clubhouse with Vice-Captain Alan and Immediate Past Captain,

Bill, together with their wives, Gail and Liz. In the course of the evening I handed over to Alan a framed copy of my Referee's scorecard as a memento of the Club Championship final.

Sunday, 25th July: Tom McCaffer Trophy

The Club's annual Tri-Am competition used to be considered as being a very good vehicle for introducing members to others with whom they would not normally play or with whom they were unfamiliar. The general format was that members would enter for the competition as individuals and the Match Secretary would then form them into teams each of three players, and of mixed abilities, whereby they would play together and the team's score for each hole would be the best net score among them. It was a very good means of widening one's acquaintance with fellow members, and was of great value to new members in assimilating them into the life of the Club. The inclusive nature of the event was further enhanced by means of each competitor being encouraged to donate a prize (of modest proportion) so that everyone could be a recipient at the evening's presentation of prizes. In 2009 it had been decided that, instead of teams being randomly selected by the Match Secretary, members would have the option to make up their own teams of three, without restriction on handicap categories, but others could still enter their names individually and await the outcome of the selection process. Needless to say, the vast majority formed teams made up of their regular playing partners and only a small number put their names forward for the Match Secretary's selection. To my mind, this new format rather detracted from the essential character and spirit of the competition. In the knowledge that it would be my responsibility to present the prizes in the evening, I decided against putting my name forward lest my participation should subsequently prove inconvenient were I to be faced with Club commitments earlier in the day. As fate would have it, when the draw sheet was displayed on the notice board, the final group was one man short. What could be more suitable than that I should play at the tail end of the field! So I duly appended my name to the sheet.

Neil Bremner and Fabian Greenan were already on the first tee and ready to drive-off when I joined them after my having been delayed in the clubhouse for a few minutes by Committee business. After a quick handshake among us, we got our round underway and Fabian's net 3 on the first green saw us off to the perfect start. Indeed, this type of competition necessitates that the team blends well together at the very outset as early momentum is the key to success. Having been in poor form myself for quite some time, I was a bit apprehensive lest I should be the weak link in the three-ball. Thankfully, I notched a birdie 3 at the third hole, and then played a superb pitch to the sixth hole to secure a net 3; and that did wonders for my confidence. After eight holes we were scoring well, but the ninth was to prove the pivotal hole of the round. Neil and Fabian both found trouble with their tee shots and, after having struggled to recover, each had picked up his ball. I was standing further up the fairway as these events unravelled and just at that moment our score could have collapsed. It rested with myself to play out the hole; and if ever I needed to keep my nerve and to play a Captain's role, this was the moment. A well struck pitch over the large bunker to nine feet from the flag left me with a fairly slick downhill putt; which I holed for a birdie 3. With a stroke on handicap it converted to a net 2; and we had reached the turn in 27! The three of us were elated, combined really well to play the inward half in 28, and upon walking off the eighteenth green were informed that we had won the competition by one stroke. In Neil and Fabian I had found the ideal partners, and I had them to thank for ensuring that I would be among the prize-winners at the Annual Dinner.

Winners of Tri-Am: With Neil Bremner and Fabian Greenan

Monday, 26th July: Junior Open 2010

Since its inception in 2002, the Junior Open has developed into being one of the principal events in the St. Nicholas year. How things have changed over the past six decades! There was a time in many clubs, although I cannot comment with regard to St. Nicholas, when juniors got scant encouragement to progress in the game and whose presence on the course was often considered by older members to be something of an inconvenience. In many cases this was reflected in the restricted times accorded to them for play, minimal rights on the course and a total absence of even the most basic tuition. Of course there were many exceptions to this disregard of juniors but, generally speaking, good young players tended to develop of their own accord and only when their aptitude became apparent did a club's hierarchy take notice of them.

Once again the competition was well supported with over 100 players in the field. Alas, weather conditions for the early starters were absolutely appalling; heavy rain falling continuously until 10.30am. For many of the juniors, contending with the rain was in itself an ordeal, but the added challenge presented by the gorse bushes at the opening holes proved more than some could endure, especially when trying to play with wet grips, and No Returns became the norm among those at the top of the starting sheet. After the rain subsided, I made my way out to the far end of the course and took up to watching as many games as I could. In that regard I was amply rewarded at the fourteenth hole where I witnessed one of our leading junior players, Sandy Darroch, holing-out from about 180 yards for an eagle two. In view of the fact that he had played through much of the foul weather during the early part of his round, his net 69 was a very commendable score and was itself deserving of winning; but it was not to be.

Back in the clubhouse I met up with Honorary President Bill, where we had an informal chat in which I updated him on the business of the Club. Bill informed me that he regularly monitors attendances at the Committee meetings and was pondering as to whom Alan might invite to be his successor as Vice-Captain. He also said that there were a couple of matters he wished to discuss with

(DMC Photo Gallery)

With Junior Open prize-winners – and standing at a suitably lower level!

me in the near future, *viz.* the current role of the Club Secretary with regards to the scope of his management responsibilities, and membership issues consequential to the introduction of the Equality Act.

In the early evening, having prepared what I was going to say at the prize-giving, I returned to the clubhouse and watched the last few competitors complete their round. When it came to the ceremony I was surprised to see just how small were many of the boys. In an era when teenagers are noticeably taller and broader than their predecessors, I was rather expecting to be faced with many of my own height until I realised that those to whom I referred as being 'small boys' were actually relatively young and hardly into their 'teens. On this evidence of so many youngsters playing in the competition, future prospects for sustainable levels of club membership, if properly managed, might indicate grounds for optimism.

President Bill, Vice-Captain Alan, Past Captains, Ladies and Gentlemen, Competitors:
Today's Junior Open is one of the major events in the St. Nicholas golfing calendar, and this is evidenced not only by the large entry of players from throughout Central and Southern Scotland, but by the great number of our members who assist on the day by checking-in entrants at Peter's shop, or who act as starters, ball spotters, stewards and scorecard scrutinisers. Others, too, assist in setting out the prizes for display; and the catering and bar staffs who have provided food and refreshments all day. We have also to remember that for several weeks, if not months, the Secretary's office has been busy with all the correspondence in arranging the event. And, of course, the greenkeepers have been busy in ensuring that the course is presented in its best possible condition. Our thanks are due to all of those involved.

However, one person epitomises this event, and that is our Junior Convener, Walter Bryson. Walter has planned this competition from its inception, has obtained generous sponsorship, and has been meticulous in his attention to every detail – and all the while exuding an air of calm and of being in control. The success of this event is attributable to Walter and we offer him well-merited thanks and congratulations on a job well done.

One thing over which Walter has no control – and you will all already know to what I am about to refer – is the Scottish weather. I offer my commiserations to everyone who had to endure the unpleasant conditions of wind and rain in the early part of the morning. To those of you who were most affected, I hope that you will not be discouraged and, if you are still eligible, that you will come back next year. But despite the adverse weather there were several meritorious performances. I won't go into any detail save to say that I was fortunate to witness Sandy Darroch holing out for an eagle '2' at the 14th Hole. That is something which will remain in my memory for a long time!

I know that many of you will be anxious that we get on with the prize-giving. So I shall now call on Walter to announce the results of the competition.

. . . . 26th: Letter of complaint from Ladies

I had rather hoped that the recently appointed Membership Development Sub-Committee would have been allowed a period of grace in which to consider its remit and to determine how best to proceed before being subjected to negative comment. However, Secretary Tom drew my attention to correspondence received from the Ladies' Club which, among other things, was critical of the fact that it did not have a lady representative on the sub-committee; albeit the Ladies Convener was a constituent member. I could quite understand the ladies' views on the subject, but I was disappointed as to the timing and vehemence of their response. To someone not acquainted with the Club's Constitution, the first reaction would probably be to say that, at the very least, it was insensitive not to have had a lady co-opted from the outset (and I sympathised with that opinion) but, in reality, the situation was more complex and open to challenge from Ordinary (i.e. Full) Members should that route have been taken. The ladies were Associate Members of the Club, paid a reduced annual subscription, had no voting rights and, as such, had no authority to make alterations to the existing Constitution. But alterations were the very thing that was under consideration – and power to enact change was vested in the Ordinary Members! Not until it had established the appropriate procedure for initiating the proposed far-reaching changes was Committee in a position to involve the Ladies' Club in formal discussion or negotiation. Having set up the sub-committee and having expressed my personal opinions to its Convener, Vice-Captain Alan, I quite intentionally did not interfere in the running of its affairs; it was for the sub-committee to decide how it wished to communicate with the Ladies' Club and when, or whether, to co-opt ladies into its number.

Thursday, 29th July: Committee meeting

In the course of conversation it had been put to me that, during his year in office, the Captain should arrange his holidays in a manner which ensures that he can be present at every monthly Committee meeting. This struck me as being rather an extreme viewpoint, although I recognise that behind it lies the question of one's commitment to the office and of one's reasons for having accepted it. Dates for Committee meetings are not cast in stone, but at St. Nicholas the last Thursday of each month is generally considered as being the norm. It is not unknown for meetings to have been re-scheduled to suit the Captain's personal arrangements, and that can often be justified, especially if contentious items are due for debate, but in the normal run of business I would much prefer that the Vice-Captain be given the opportunity to take the chair and to benefit from the experience. It was with this in mind, and knowing that I would be on holiday the following month, that I did not deviate from that principle when arranging the date for the August meeting.

Friday 30th July: Betty Singleton Trophy

When a competition invariably attracts a large entry, those who organise the event have the satisfaction of knowing that its popularity not only reflects their own enthusiasm, but that their efforts are being appreciated. One event which comes into that category is the Ladies' Club's open competition for the Betty Singleton Trophy, which is played over one round as a twosome and draws entrants from all over the West of Scotland. Just as members and officials give readily of their time to help at the Junior Open, the same applies to this annual event. And so, for two hours in the morning I acted as Starter; taking over from Past Captain Bill Walker and being succeeded by Past Captain Stan Stevenson. Having been invited by Lady Captain Eileen to present the trophy to the winners at the evening prize-giving and to add some personal comments, I took time during the afternoon to consider what words might be appropriate. It had been arranged that Honorary President Bill would speak on behalf of the Club at the outset of the prize-giving ceremony, so anything I required to say would be of no great length. As events turned out, Bill addressed the company and thereafter Eileen announced the results, whilst I duly presented the trophy and prizes. But when the last prize was handed over, Eileen took the opportunity to make some observations upon equality issues before drawing the proceedings to a close. Upon moving away from the table, she remembered that I had been invited to speak; and she immediately offered to rectify the situation. With some of the competitors already getting up from their seats, I thought it best to leave matters as they were. Afterwards President Bill said that he considered Eileen's mention of equality issues to have been totally inappropriate in the circumstances, especially as many of the ladies present were members of other clubs; and I agreed!

The Open Golf Championship 1970

Memorable rounds of golf evolve in their progress; whereas golf reports, by their very nature, are condensed and do not always communicate the diversity of moods that prevail, or the vagaries of chance that present themselves, as a round develops. Players know that even the most diligent of preparation does not ensure that birdies can be produced to order; only with that elusive blend of skill and good fortune can a near perfect round be achieved. But being memorable does not just apply to successful outcomes; many otherwise brilliant rounds are now rooted in golfing folklore as a result of just one wayward drive or one unkind bounce of the ball which, in an instant, undid all of the previous good work and consigned the golfer's name to the list of those unfortunates who had the prize within their grasp but saw it slip agonisingly away. Saturday, 11th July 1970 was destined to be one of those memorable days that will forever be recalled as having produced one of golf's most dramatic moments.

Mine was a late decision to attend the final day's play of The Open Championship at St. Andrews; not on account of any indecision on my part but simply because it depended upon whether John

Panton qualified for the final round. Until then I had never been at 'The Open', but if John was going to be involved I was desirous to see him play. Having opened with rounds of 72 and 73 he was comfortably inside the qualifying limit of 149 for the third round, but a further cut was to be made for the fourth round. So it was early on Friday evening before I learned that he had scored 73 in his third round and was inside the qualifying limit of 223 for the final day's play. I was still living in Motherwell at this time, and that meant an early start for my drive to St. Andrews; a much slower journey in pre-motorway days, and one which involved travelling via Kincardine Bridge and Crook of Devon. Just outside Milnathort I gave a lift to a young Australian hitch-hiker who was headed for St. Andrews with the intention of following Peter Thomson. This was in the days when it was still possible, with a little ingenuity, to keep relatively close to the players and to follow a single pairing all of the way round the course. I naturally told him that I would be following John Panton, but the name meant nothing to my Australian friend. We parted in the vicinity of the course and agreed that we would look out for the scores of our respective heroes. I strolled round to the area of the public putting greens adjacent to the first fairway and observed a group of people on the West Sands who appeared to be very interested in some activity that was taking place. On closer observation I could see that a golfer was utilising the beach as a practice strip and had obviously attracted the interest of some spectators. I wandered over to see what was happening, and immediately recognised Roberto De Vicenzo as being the golfer who was engaged in striking a succession of balls with what appeared to be a 3-iron or 4-iron. His caddie was positioned about 180 yards along the beach and was gathering the balls on their first bounce. It was a phenomenal exhibition of controlled shot making by the big Argentinian, and his caddie was only required to move a few steps to the right or left to catch each ball.

Thereafter I sat in the grandstand adjacent to the first fairway and watched the early starters as they teed-off, and I vividly recall seeing Eric Brown play that first hole in what were very blustery conditions. At length Bob Charles and John were announced as being the next game and, after watching both of them drive-off, I picked up my haversack, descended from the grandstand and mingled with the two or three dozen spectators who were obviously intent upon following them on their outward journey. Once down on the course, and out of the relative shelter of the buildings and grandstands adjacent to the 1st and 18th fairways, the wind was noticeably stronger and fairly ruffled the players and spectators as they became exposed to its full force. The flexing of the pins on the greens and the violent fluttering of the flags were ample evidence as to just how challenging golf was going to be for players caught up in these unfavourable elements. John was safely onto the first green with his approach pitch and two putts secured a reassuring par. On to the second hole; at over 400 yards a formidable par four at the best of times, but this day one of real menace in these adverse conditions. A solid drive saw John's ball well positioned on the fairway, and he followed up with a glorious shot to within 12 feet of the hole on the distant double green, and sunk his putt for a memorable birdie. He was off to the best start possible. There was no mistaking the fact that the wind had increased by another notch as the players stood on the third tee; and, whilst he found the green with his second shot, he took three putts to get down. The fourth hole was out of his range in two shots and another bogey five went onto his card; but at the long fifth hole he was on the green with his third shot and holed out for a par five. The sixth hole found him on the green in two and his approach putt finished about four feet from the hole. At this juncture the skies were overcast and the wind was gusting at an alarming rate. John stood over this short putt for an inordinate length of time as he was buffeted by the elements and, almost inevitably it seemed, he failed to hole it and recorded a fourth consecutive five. In total contrast, Bob Charles, a more slender figure than John, twice addressed his putt only to step back as the wind tore into him and upset his stance; but at the third attempt he secured his par. Throughout the round it was noticeable just how often Bob, having taken up his stance, did not go on to execute the shot but came away from the ball until he felt more comfortable in the gusty conditions.

The skies cleared as both players made their way down the seventh fairway, and the number of spectators following the game was greatly increased by those who were making their way out to the far end of the course, where they would find a suitable point at the Loop from which to view the remainder of the field playing those four shorter holes. There was a controlled crossing over the seventh fairway and immediately upon letting the players pass through the ropes the marshals closed off the crossing to those spectators who were following the game. As both drives had disappeared over the ridge which traverses the fairway, it was not possible to see the approach shots to the green and it required a little haste to catch up with the game to find out how the second shots had fared. John got his par four and followed it up with a steady par three at the eighth hole. At this stage he was playing very well and I rather hoped that he might be able to get round the course in 74 or 75. His drive at the ninth hole found a bare lie on the fairway and he played a low pitch and run shot which saw the ball scuttling its way onto the green; he holed out in four, and his outward score of 38 was just two over par. Although my attention was principally on John, I was very aware that Bob Charles was also recording a commendable score. I was enjoying my day at The Open!

A tidy four was obtained at the tenth, and then onto the par three eleventh which is renowned as one of golf's great short holes. The grandstand immediately behind the tee provided spectators with a classic elevated view of the hole and I duly found a seat from which to see the tee shots. Even allowing for the wind, which incidentally had abated slightly, I suspect that few players in the field considered selecting other than an iron to play this 170 yards hole. John, however, took out a wood and manufactured a beautifully flighted ball which covered the flagstick all of the way and somehow finished above and beyond the hole when logic decreed that it should have rolled back closer to the cup. I was quite sure in my own mind that he had employed a No 4 wood for that stroke, but one contemporary newspaper referred to it as being a brassie. The gentleman beside whom I was seated said that he had been positioned there for the previous one and a half hours, and John's was the finest shot he had yet seen. Nevertheless, after such a superb tee shot, John was confronted with the most delicate of downhill putts of about seven or eight feet. He barely set the ball in motion and it dribbled down the slope only to stop tantalisingly short at the very edge of the hole. After my experience of failing to get past the controlled crossing on the seventh fairway, I was already ahead of the players as they walked towards this second crossing, which would lead them to the next tee.

It is an odd phenomenon that even in the greatest throng there can be pockets of tranquillity. The previous spectators who had been making their way out to the Loop were now left behind and, I suspect, a few others who intended following this game had probably been delayed at the controlled crossing or had elected to move further down the fairway, for just three of us were in the company of the players and their caddies as they stepped onto the twelfth tee. At that moment we were completely divorced from the crowds, the activity and the tension of a major championship.

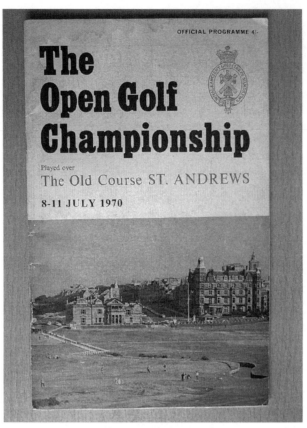

Official Programme

It was as if we had been transported to some minor competition which had attracted only a few diehard enthusiasts, some of whom were to be seen dotted about in the distance. John played a good pitch onto the green at this relatively short par four hole and sunk his putt for the second birdie of his round. On the thirteenth, which was a demanding hole of 427 yards, John drove his ball to the right of all the bunkers on what would be considered as being the conventional line. Bob on the other hand (he being a left-hander!) cut his drive away out to the left beyond some scrub and rough ground. That is how I perceived it at the time, although I later discovered that some players prefer to play out in that direction as it provides them with a better view of the green for their second shot. So it is quite possible that what I thought to be a loose drive by Bob was in fact just as he had intended. What I do know is that this led to a considerable delay in their completing the hole. For his part, John played the most glorious iron shot to the elevated green; but from the fairway only the flag was visible and not the putting surface. Everything about the shot looked perfect from the moment the ball left the club face, and this was confirmed a few seconds later when applause could be heard emanating from the grandstand overlooking the large double green. As to whether it was a long or a medium iron he used I could not be sure, for John had a whole armoury of manufactured shots in his locker, but this stroke was one of the highest quality. Bob Charles and his caddie were not to be seen, and John and the spectators made their way up the slope eager to see the outcome of the shot. And the ball was lying just two feet to the left of the pin on a green whose area exceeds

4000 square yards! There was still no sign of Bob Charles, and a game playing the 5th Hole on the outward half had also reached the vicinity of the double green. Peter Thomson was in this latter pairing and it looked as though his playing partner was having to chip-on from somewhere to the right of the green. John and Peter stood in the middle and chatted together whilst their playing partners executed their shots. Ultimately it was the outward game which putted out first, and all of this time, which must have been close upon 10 minutes, John had this little putt waiting to be dealt with. But deal with it he did, and a third birdie went onto his card. He was doing very well, and was now level par for the round and two over for the championship.

The wind was coming across the players from their right, but the long par five fourteenth hole was quite reachable with a short-iron third shot, provided the drive and second shots eluded trouble. A great stream of spectators, travelling against the direction of play, was making its way out to the far reaches of the course; and considerable surprise was expressed upon seeing the numbers as displayed on the hand-held scoreboard which accompanied the game. One of these spectators remarked that all of the games in front were indicating scores of at least five or six strokes more than John; so the quality of his play in the difficult conditions was becoming evident. A good straight drive had removed the threat of the 'out of bounds' wall along the right-hand side of the fairway and John's second shot was directed to the left of Hell bunker. From there he produced a lovely deft pitch to four feet from the hole and a third consecutive birdie beckoned. And he missed the putt! What a disappointment after having played the hole in copybook style! 'That was always Panton's problem; he canna putt' said a spectator beside me, and he turned away to continue his trek towards the Loop. It was a cruel observation in the circumstances but, in truth, there had been many times in the past when John's superb play from tee to green was undone by indifferent putting, especially from under six feet.

If there had been only a few spectators lining the twelfth fairway, the opposite was now the case as the players played the fifteenth hole. In addition to those who were making their way outwards on the course, others had turned about to follow this game after having seen the scoreboard. John's second shot was safely onto the green but the ball finished at least thirty feet from the flagstick. After the missed putt on the previous green, a nice approach putt was essential to avoid heaping any undue pressure upon what was proving to be a very good round. I was standing behind and on a slightly lower level from where John putted and, as such, could not see the hole itself. However, I was able to follow the run of the ball as it made its way across some minor undulations on the green; and then it disappeared – into the hole! The putt probably did not merit the old St. Andrews' expression of being 'a lang steal,' but it certainly felt like it. It was the perfect response to the lapse on the previous green. How I wished that the spectator who had commented on John's putting had been there to see it all! He was now one under par for the round. The sixteenth hole was negotiated unerringly for another par and both players moved onto the next tee to confront what is probably the most intriguing hole on the course; the 17th or Road Hole. John cleared the artificial profile of the old railway sheds with his drive and his ball landed neatly on the fairway. Once there he obviously elected to play the hole conservatively, for he resisted the challenge of taking-on Road Bunker with his second shot. Instead he played slightly short and to the right of the green hoping that he might get down with a pitch and single putt for his par. As things turned out he needed two putts, which meant a bogey five and back to level par for the round.

Bob Charles had the honour on the eighteenth tee, and John followed him with a good drive well beyond the road which crosses the fairway at Grannie Clark's Wynd. With the huge grandstand as a backdrop to the final green, John played a superb wedge shot which cleared the Valley of Sin and pitched to a halt within a few inches of the hole. Huge applause greeted the shot and John was given a great ovation as he walked onto the green. The tap-in which followed was indeed a formality and John had got round the course in 71 strokes, one under par. Bob Charles, who had been runner-up only twelve months previously at Royal Lytham & St. Annes, secured his par and finished on 74. John's final aggregate score for the championship was 289 and his name was destined to remain for some considerable time at the top of a subsidiary scoreboard which recorded completed rounds or, as is commonly referred to, 'leaders in the clubhouse'.

There was a large scoreboard situated behind the grandstand which flanked the first fairway and which displayed all of the players' names and their respective scores at each hole as they progressed round the course. Unlike modern computerised systems, the cards bearing the numbers were all inserted by hand onto the board following, or so I believe, portable radio communications from out on the course. It must have been at least half an hour after John finished his round that I was studying this board, when I noticed him coming down from the direction of the clubhouse. He was dressed in a brown suit, was wearing his cap, and not a soul took any notice of him nor, I suspect, even knew who he was. To the people round about he was just another middle-aged man making his way among the other spectators. And he came up and stood beside me! I remarked on his having played very well and he told me that he had found putting in the strong wind to have been the most difficult part of his round. At this stage I was aware of how well he had played but had no inkling that his score would prove to be the best of the day. As matters turned out, not only had he carded a sub-par round but no one else in the field even succeeded in matching the par of 72.

Having caught up with the scoring, I then made my way around the back of the eighteenth green and down The Links with the intention of watching all of the leading games approaching the Road Hole. I managed eventually to get positioned behind the infamous stone wall and obtained an unobstructed view across the seventeenth green and right down its fairway. It also provided me with a clear view of the players driving from the eighteenth tee. And there I remained whilst the rest of the field played out these last two holes. All of the players were familiar to me from either photographs or television broadcasts, but this was the first time I had actually seen some of them in the flesh. At this juncture the likely winner appeared to be either Doug Sanders, Harold Henning or Jack Nicklaus, but as the drama unfolded Doug Sanders had the destiny of the Championship in his own hands. Dressed in what for its time were garish colours, bright plum or the like, he could be seen coming down the seventeenth fairway with Lee Trevino in the final game. Never having watched Doug previously, I was fascinated by the number of backswings he made (was it six or seven?) prior to executing his approach to the green. He certainly could not be accused of rushing his shots. However, after all of this extensive pre-strike routine he proceeded to pull his ball into the Road bunker; considered by many as the most fearsome hazard on the course – if not in the entire world of golf! As to whether Jack Nicklaus, playing in the game ahead, had holed-out on the eighteenth green before Doug entered the bunker to play his recovery shot I cannot recall, for the last game had certainly lost ground on the game in front. No matter, the fact was that Doug Sanders had contrived to put himself into one of the most unenviable situations possible. Not only is the

Road bunker deep, but the hole was positioned in the narrow waist between it and the road. Nothing short of a perfect explosion shot, assuming a reasonable lie in the sand, would provide him with the possibility of scrambling the par four he so desperately needed. Words cannot convey the extent of the pressure he must have been under as he considered his options, for his challenge rested on a knife-edge. And, quite literally, he played the shot of a lifetime! The ball was lofted beautifully out of the trap and it flopped down to within twelve inches of the cup. Right there and then it was the shot that had won The Open Championship – and I had witnessed it at first hand! No doubt symptomatic of the crisis he had just endured, Doug wrapped his arm around Lee's shoulders as they walked off the green to the nearby eighteenth tee.

By this time everyone knew that Doug Sanders only needed to get a par four at the eighteenth hole and the championship would be his. The eighteenth hole at St. Andrews; the most benign finishing hole imaginable for a championship, and Doug drove safely across the road to within pitching distance of the green. He was about to have his name engraved on the Claret Jug! Spectators started dashing up the fairway, as is something of a tradition, to get a good vantage point from which to see the closing moments around the final green. As for me, I had enjoyed a wonderful day at The Open. John Panton had provided me with memories of a round that would be marked indelibly in my mind; he had even spoken to me afterwards; and I had seen the shot that had won the championship for Doug Sanders. I could wish for nothing more! My car was parked about half a mile away from the course and I decided that I would dispense with watching the remainder of the play and would make an early exit from St. Andrews in advance of the roads becoming congested with departing spectators. Back at the car I switched on the radio to catch the final action – and the rest is history! Within twenty minutes, the fabulous shot that had won The Open Championship had been superseded by one of the most famous three-putts of all time – and I had missed it!

In the final analysis John Panton and Peter Thomson tied, along with Tommy Horton, for ninth place in the championship. I often wondered whether my friend, the Australian hitch-hiker, had picked up on that particular statistic!

Chapter 6

August

Since coming onto Committee four years previously, I was aware that there appeared to be little involvement between it and the Club's Honorary President. The only instances of direct contact that I could remember had arisen when Committee considered it prudent to use him as an informal 'sounding board' to gauge the opinion or sentiments of Past Captains in matters which it considered might be either sensitive or controversial; and that was a rare occurrence. As for private dialogue between the incumbent Captain and the Honorary President, that may very well have taken place but, if so, was not common knowledge within Committee. Whatever the situation may have been hitherto, I resolved to keep in fairly regular contact with our Honorary President, not just out of common courtesy in recognition of his position, but so that I might benefit from his knowledge and experience of past times and circumstances. I was very conscious that behind some of the rules and regulations contained in our fixture booklet, former Committees had probably, with good reason, been engaged in intense debate regarding the background to some particular issue or incident the genesis of which was no longer immediately apparent. Concurrent with my intention to have periodical dialogue between Captain and Honorary President, I was also aware that Bill had his own vision as to the role of President and that his was more proactive than had formerly been the case. So one way or the other, the chemistry was right to allow a free exchange of thoughts and aspirations.

Tuesday, 3rd August: Meeting with Bill Andrew
In the evening I met with President Bill in the Tom Morris Room for an informal, but confidential, chat during which he informed me of the two subjects that were uppermost in his mind. The first was the question of the entitlement of male members to seek Associate Membership should the Club decide to implement certain aspects of the proposed Equality Bill which was currently being debated inside and outside of parliament; and the second matter related to the day-to-day management of the Club, particularly in relation to the duties and responsibilities of the Club Secretary. For my part, I enquired as to the protocol expected of myself on Past Captains' Day to which I had recently been invited, and also of the possibility of arranging a putting competition involving all age groups within the Club as a means of acknowledging and celebrating the 150th Anniversary of the institution of The Open Championship at Prestwick – principally on account of Tom Morris and Charlie Hunter's participation in the first Open Championship, and of their both being members of St. Nicholas Golf Club.

Wednesday, 4th August: Ladies' Texas Scramble
Secretary Tom had received a request from the Ladies' Club to re-schedule its Texas Scramble from Thursday 9th September to Sunday 12th September to accommodate a previous re-arrangement of its fixtures. As the latter date was already booked for the Junior Medals Final, with a ballot at 12.45pm, and as Sundays are not normally considered for ladies competitions, we contacted the

Match & Handicap Convener, John Errington, to establish if there were any reasons against our approving this request. The outcome of our discussion was to allow the Texas Scramble to be re-scheduled, subject to there being no disruption of the juniors' competition.

Friday, 6th August: W.S. MacDonald woods

Over the years I was occasionally in the company of older members when their conversation turned to reminiscences and anecdotes relating to characters who had added some 'colour' to the Club in former times. One name regularly mentioned with great affection was that of Willie MacDonald. He had been our golf professional for a period of 34 years, and stories of the patience that was required from members who had ordered clubs from him were legendary; but there was universal acknowledgement that he was an excellent clubmaker. Willie had come to St. Nicholas in 1946, by which time the clubmaker's art bore no comparison to that of the hickory era, but he acquired a reputation for producing first-class steel-shafted persimmon woods. The balance and feel that he attained were considered by members to be second to none (*nulli secundus!*) and it had for some time been my ambition to acquire an example of his work. So it proved to be quite a 'find' when I came across five of his woods in a charity shop, and I purchased all of them for just five pounds. I have always been a great admirer of the Master Model clubs which John Letters & Co manufactured throughout the 1950s but, I must say, there is something very special about possessing clubs with an individual pedigree; actually knowing the name of the craftsman who fashioned a particular club provides a unique attachment to it and enhances one's appreciation of the clubmaker's skill.

Spoon (No 3 Wood) hand-made by W.S. MacDonald
Pillar-box red with gold lettering

Sunday, 8th August: Blochairn Trophy

It had been at least seventeen years since last I played at Colville Park and in the intervening period I had often relished the thought of returning for a game. So it was with this in mind that I decided to enter my name for its annual open competition, the Blochairn Trophy; and I drove up from Ayr on what was a very pleasant Sunday morning. I was prepared for the fact that many alterations would have taken place both on the course and in its surroundings, and I did not anticipate that I would come across many members whom I had known from the past. The prospect of wallowing in my own piece of nostalgia, and of reliving the pleasure of walking over fairways which were once so much part of my school days and early adult life, was for me something of a spiritual journey. And indeed, the alterations were quite considerable; much too many to itemise, save to say that the panoramic views which the upper parts of the course formerly afforded over the Clyde Valley from Dechmont Hill to Tinto Hill are now substantially restricted by the multitude of trees that have been planted in the intervening years. Am I alone in lamenting the loss of the individual character and open aspect of so many inland courses in the pursuit of tree-lined fairways? Be that as it may, it was good to be back at Colville Park. To say that I played poorly would be an understatement; in fact I played miserably. That of itself was so disappointing, but no more than a continuation of my very poor form. Such was my embarrassment at having returned a score unworthy of any club captain, I desisted from lingering about the clubhouse any longer than was necessary. All rather sad I must confess, but perhaps I shall return one day to lay the ghost of an unfortunate experience. But I had absolutely no regrets about my decision to play; playing miserably did not equate to being unhappy in the company of my playing partners; and my fond attachment to Colville Park remains intact.

Wednesday, 11th August: John MacLachlan re gorse

Within every golfer, from the highest handicapper to the top professional, there exists a course architect; and, by right, so there should be! It is the most stimulating of mental pastimes, in the comfort of a favourite armchair, to redesign one's home course but, when introduced into company as a topic of conversation, it can result in vehement discussion and even violent disagreement. How different it all appears to have been in golf's formative years; or so we are inclined to believe. As I have already stated, my principal concern regarding the condition of the St. Nicholas course was the steady encroachment of gorse, especially at the second and third holes. I have heard it said that the measure of a good golf hole is one that is in the player's mind before he even gets around to playing it. If the comments made on the first tee by many of the ladies who were taking part in the Betty Singleton Trophy are anything to go by, then the second hole at St. Nicholas comes into that category. Not only has the gorse swallowed up much of the heather, which was a feature of the hole, it has now become established upon the straight line between tee and green so that even the shortest of fluffed tee shots is most likely to end up with the ball being in an unplayable lie, if not lost altogether. The presence of three, and sometimes even four, games waiting on the second tee was not an unusual occurrence on Medal Days, and a constant source of complaint. To my mind the hole had become unreasonably penal, especially for many ladies, older members and the less accomplished player, and was a major factor in the extended time being taken to complete a round of golf. Knowing how sensitive the issue was, since many of the better players within the Club are ill-disposed to see any gorse removed, I asked John MacLachlan if, in an unostentatious manner, he could trim back the intimidating growth immediately in front of the tee and also reclaim some of the heather areas that were being invaded.

. . . . 11th: Boys' Amateur Championship

From previous conversations with David Miller, Captain of Kilmarnock (Barassie) GC, I knew just how much it meant to his club that it had been selected to host the Boys' Amateur Championship of 2010, and I was resolved to show my support by going along to see some of the play. Therefore, after my meeting with John MacLachlan, I drove up to Barassie and followed a few of the three-balls during the second qualifying round. It soon became apparent to me that parents of the boys were excluded from caddying and, on enquiring, was informed that the R&A had stipulated that during his round parents had not to approach within 50 yards of their son. This struck me as being an eminently sensible ruling although, even with my limited involvement in golf administration, I would be surprised had it received unanimous approval from those concerned. As to the ability of the boys, I was not in the least surprised; but as to the physique and deportment of many I could hardly believe my eyes. They bore absolutely no resemblance to the boys who had competed in our Junior Open. Had they been involved in an Assistant Professionals' event, they would not have looked out of place! I followed the group consisting of Ryan Davies (Aberdare), Paul McPhee (King James VI) and Conor O'Neil (Pollok). That turned out to be a really good threesome and I was impressed by the obvious camaraderie displayed among them. Conor returned a score of 70 and, when added to his previous round of 74 over Dundonald Links, tied for second place among the qualifiers for the match play stage; in which he progressed to the semi-final.

Kilmarnock (Barassie) 4th Tee: Ryan Davies, Conor O'Neil and Paul McPhee

. . . . 11th: Junior/Senior Competition

Of necessity I had to curtail my time at Barassie that I might return to St. Nicholas to participate in the annual Junior/Senior Competition. From past experience I knew this to be a very enjoyable event and one with a character all of its own. I struggle to define just how this unique atmosphere attaches itself to the fixture, but I suspect for the Seniors it revives latent memories of school days when golf was played unencumbered by yips and theory. The format of the competition is stroke-play in which a Junior and a Senior are partnered to play as a twosome. I remember so clearly how, as a boy, the influence exerted by older members made a lasting impression upon my attitude to the game and to the manner and spirit in which it should be played. Whether my appreciation of these members' golfing abilities and ethics would have been endorsed by their contemporaries is a moot point, but it does emphasise the importance of setting a good example to younger players. Robbie McCulloch was paired with me for this competition and, whilst he will have no reason to recall the quality of my play with any sense of awe, we had a most enjoyable round together.

Friday, 13th August: David and Marion Duncan

I had the great pleasure of introducing as visitors to the Club my office colleague, David Duncan, and his wife, Marion. They are members of Caldwell Park Golf Club at Uplawmoor and were enthusiastic about playing over the St. Nicholas course. Fortunately it was a fine sunny day for their visit, and Jeanette walked round the course with us. On occasions like this the St. Nicholas welcome

Jeanette with David and Marion Duncan at 12th green

is absolutely superb. Being Captain no doubt encourages staff to be particularly attentive to one's guests, but it has been my experience over the years that, whenever I have introduced visitors to the clubhouse, the attention and friendliness extended to them by the staff has been exemplary, and they have left with nothing but the most favourable impression of the Club.

Saturday, 14th August: Mixed Foursomes

The Mixed Foursomes Competition could be described as being the reciprocal of Ladies Day in that it is organised by the Gentlemen. Once again the fixture is restricted to 'Members Only', but in this case pairings are arranged by ballot and not by invitation. Since my game was completely out of sorts, I would normally have refrained from putting my name forward for a foursome competition. However, as Captain, I felt obliged to give the event my support and was drawn with an excellent partner in Moyra Withycombe. Almost inevitably, and embarrassingly for me, I was the weak link in the pairing and we never threatened to accumulate a respectable score. None the less, I had to put a brave face on things, as did poor Moyra, and was required afterwards to present the prizes in the Clubhouse.

Sunday, 15th August: Troon Week Mixed Foursomes
As if my golfing woes were not already near to breaking point, I was prevailed upon to partner Lesley Ness in the Troon Golf Week Mixed Foursomes over the Fullarton course; an attractive layout of only 4800 yards. Lesley's partner had been forced to withdraw and I was brought in as his replacement. The inevitable outcome replicated my exploits of the previous day, although my game did improve over the last ten holes; but not sufficiently as to prevent us from being at the bottom of the list. I had let down two ladies very badly in the course of two days!

Wednesday, 18th August: Visit to Kirkhill GC
When Jeanette and I got married in 1971, we took up residence in Cambuslang and I applied for

With Ian Barnstaple (Colville Park) 1984

membership of Kirkhill Golf Club, which was situated little more than half a mile from our house. My proposer was Tom Hamilton, whose family was related to former next-door neighbours of mine in Motherwell. There was a waiting list for entry and I eventually joined in 1976. At its New Members' Night I made the acquaintance of Stewart Crichton, and we have remained the firmest of friends ever since. Last year Stewart had been a guest of mine at Turnberry and he had invited me, along with Andrew Taylor and Hugh McKail, to a return game at Kirkhill. And we had a super day out!

For many years I have partnered Stewart in Kirkhill's Annual Invitational Greensome Competition. In 1984, whilst I was still a Kirkhill member, Ian Barnstaple (Colville Park) and I won the inaugural event. Due to my attending a Ruby Wedding Celebration in Cambridge I was unable to partner Stewart in this year's competition and, when he enquired if I knew of anyone who might take my place, I suggested to him that he consider inviting Vice-Captain Alan. I am pleased to say that Alan obliged by accepting the invitation, and duly subjected himself to the rigours afforded by James Braid's uncompromising layout.

Thursday, 19th August: Committee v Greenkeepers

It is beneficial to any club if the Head Greenkeeper is himself a golfer, and the more so if his assistants are similarly involved. There was a time in many clubs when the positions of professional and greenkeeper were held by one and the same person, but that is now something of a rarity and probably applies only to a few smaller clubs. In terms of *The Golfer's Handbook*, that paragon of information, one of the consequences of accommodating the ever-increasing volume of statistics has been the removal from the Club Directory of any reference to the greenkeeper. There is no doubt that the enhanced status of the modern greenkeeping profession, involving so much technical knowledge and specialist expertise, is something which all thoughtful golfers recognise. It is also of paramount importance that a good working relationship should exist between the greenkeeper and Committee. Each has an important role to play in the well-being of the club and it is preferable that their contributions should dovetail rather than one feel that it is being dictated-to by the other.

Most club golfers have no knowledge whatsoever of the finer points of greenkeeping; they only judge a course by the general condition in which they find it, but unfortunately there are sometimes those who venture into the province of the greenkeeper and expound at length upon matters which professionally they are ill-equipped to comment. This is surely every Head Greenkeeper's nightmare. No person employed as a professional, in whatever capacity, wants to be subjected to scrutiny of that kind. By all means he must be accountable but, being employed on the basis of his professional competence, he should be free to exercise his own judgement. Having secured the services of a first-class Head Greenkeeper, it is surely obvious that, unless he is encouraged and made to feel valued, no one should be surprised if he becomes dissatisfied with his position and either seeks other employment or is enticed away by another club.

As I have alluded to previously, St. Nicholas has been well served by its current greenkeeping staff, and the annual match between Committee and the greenkeepers is a great opportunity for the Club to show its appreciation of the excellent service it receives. The format of the afternoon is similar to that of any club or team match in that the golf is preceded by a short reception, and is followed afterwards by refreshments and a communal meal in the Dining Room. In my experience these have always been jolly affairs and are an ideal means of letting both sides get to know one another on a personal basis. For the record, Vice-Captain Alan and I lost by 2 and 1 to Head Greenkeeper John and his assistant Stephen McBlain. When I say that Stephen is a scratch golfer, and that John is an 8-handicapper, you will understand why I feel sensitive about the possibility of their being subjected to ill-informed criticism. As to the overall match result, Committee won by three matches to two.

Tuesday, 24th August: Committee v Ladies' Committee

Due to my wife and I being on holiday in the Peak District, I was unable to play in the annual match between Ladies' Prestwick St. Nicholas Golf Club's Committee and our own Management

Committee. Vice-Captain Alan assumed my responsibilities on the day and by all accounts everyone enjoyed a very pleasant afternoon's golf. The fact that the match resulted in a comprehensive victory for the ladies was not lost upon those who take an interest in such statistics!

Thursday, 26th August: Wallasey

I would be deluding myself were I to suggest that I drove into the car park at Wallasey Golf Club free of any apprehension as to how the day would unfold. Had I arrived as just another visitor who had booked a tee time, I would probably have felt a little discomfited simply due to my being unfamiliar with the club's protocol and not knowing anyone around me but, nevertheless, inwardly I would have been relishing the prospect of playing over this fine course and discovering just how much of it coincided with my recollection of 1967. However, a few days after Secretary Tom had

Dick Eccleshall, Mark Williams and Roy Bulmer: Wallasey Golf Club)

Portrait of Bobby Jones: Wallasey Golf Club

made the booking on my behalf, he received word that Roy Bulmer, the club's archivist, had kindly invited me to make up a four-ball with him and his friends. That unexpected invitation made things so much easier for me as it ensured that someone would be on hand to meet me, to introduce me to the clubhouse and to keep me right as to the playing arrangements. So why should I have been the least apprehensive? Two reasons really. One, my form of late had been at rather a low ebb and, two, I was aware only too well that, due to the altered circumstances of my visit, I was now representing St. Nicholas Golf Club and did not wish to give an unfavourable impression of it. Jeanette accompanied me to the clubhouse with the intention thereafter of making a personal reconnaissance of the district's retail facilities.

We were welcomed most cordially by Roy and he introduced us to Dick Eccleshall and Mark Williams, the other members of the four-ball. After a coffee in the Main Lounge, we changed into our golfing gear and met up on the first tee. Dick and I were partnered for the match, and Jeanette waited just long enough to see us drive-off before she did likewise – in the car! For my part, the situation in which I found myself could not have been bettered; the sun was shining, there was only a slight breeze, views out to the Irish Sea were crystal clear, the course was in lovely condition, and I was in the best of golfing company. In the course of our round I discovered that Roy was retired from the merchant navy, that Dick was a Past Captain of Wallasey Golf Club, and that Mark had been a marine engineer in the oil industry; three very interesting backgrounds and the pleasantest of companions. We enjoyed a good game and Dick was the mainstay of our little partnership. I was impressed by Roy's putting and this was confirmed on the eighteenth green when he holed from about nine feet to get his four leaving me with a six-footer to secure my par and to halve the match. Being the perfect host, he conceded my putt.

Jeanette was already back at the clubhouse when we finished our round and she was being entertained by Past Captain Alan Bott and Gordon Fullerton, which was yet another testament to the friendliness of the Club. Before taking lunch Roy gave me a tour of the clubhouse and out of his collection, having noted that I was still playing with traditional woods, he gifted to me a carbon shafted Citation 'Power Bilt' driver which was in pristine condition; complete, of course, with a genuine persimmon head. Jeanette and I lingered to take photographs of the trophy room and were mightily impressed by the oil portraits of Bobby Jones and Dr Frank Stableford. My long dreamt-of visit to Wallasey had now been fulfilled, and it had exceeded my wildest expectations thanks to the thoughtfulness and generosity of Roy and his fellow members. From Wallasey, Jeanette and I drove into Hoylake and West Kirby, and took time to view the exterior of Royal Liverpool Golf Club's clubhouse and, of course, its championship links.

Saturday, 28th August: Past Captains' Day
Whilst I had always known through reference to the Fixture Card that the Club had a Past Captains' Day, I was unaware of its format. Not having been advised to the contrary, I assumed that the current Captain would not be involved in the proceedings and I had arranged my summer holidays without consideration of the event. So it came as something of a surprise to me, when I learned only a few days prior to setting off on my holiday, that it was traditional for the current Captain to be invited to participate in a round of golf during the afternoon and for him to address his predecessors at the ensuing dinner. My holiday arrangements made it quite impossible to play in the golf competition since Jeanette and I were not due to leave Wirral until the Saturday morning. Nevertheless, I thought it only proper that I should endeavour to attend the dinner in the evening; so I ensured that we made an early morning start to get back home in sufficient time. I enjoyed the experience of being among the Past Captains, a few with whom I had had little previous involvement, and I recall especially the long conversation I had with Stewart Downie and the words of encouragement which he imparted to me.

Sunday, 29th August: Members and Guests Competition
The prevalence and popularity of Members and Guests competitions is something that has increased considerably in recent years; and St. Nicholas is not an exception. The inaugural event was held in 1997 when, if memory serves me correctly, the tee was booked for about 3 hours to accommodate

the players. In the intervening years the tee-times have been extended to such a degree that the whole day is now virtually taken up by the competition and a reserve list is often introduced due to its being oversubscribed. My first awareness of such events occurred in 1984 when Kirkhill Golf Club decided to hold an Invitational Greensome whereby each member invited a partner from another club; and the prizes on offer were unquestionably more attractive, and more valuable, than was the norm in club competitions. By an odd coincidence, not only had I been successful in the inaugural competition held at Kirkhill in 1984, I was also the winner of the first St. Nicholas Members & Guests Competition in 1997. On that occasion I was partnered by my good friend Stewart Crichton (Kirkhill) when, quite literally, we played the round of our lives and won by 6 strokes. When I ascertained several months later that the Club intended to make the competition an annual fixture, I offered to donate a trophy for future years. My offer was accepted and Malcolm Foggo, our Match Secretary, said that Stewart's and my name should be engraved on the trophy as having been the first winners. This was duly done, but I refrained from entering any of the subsequent competitions. And this year, as Captain, I was in no position to continue with my avoidance of the previous twelve years. So I invited Stewart to partner me on the day, and we were joined by Vice-Captain Alan and his father, Billy. Neither pairing proved to be serious contenders, but we had a very pleasant game and, on completion of our round, dined together in the Mixed Lounge. As the day unfolded the competition ran progressively behind its schedule and Malcolm had eventually to cancel the prize-giving ceremony due to its being impractical for many of the guests to wait any longer before heading home.

With Stewart Crichton (Kirkhill) 1997

Tuesday, 31st August: Scottish Area Team Championship
Having been absent from the August meeting of the Management Committee, fate decreed that a controversial issue had arisen on the night and its outcome left unresolved. It concerned an approach from the Scottish Golf Union (SGU) for St. Nicholas to co-host with Prestwick Golf Club the 2011 Scottish Area Team Championship. Committee members had been informed in advance of the meeting of this enquiry, and also of the fact that the Joint Match Secretaries were opposed to

accommodating the event on the grounds that the date requested (May 14th) was one of the very few Saturdays still available to members which had not been scheduled for medal play; and, furthermore, that it would inconvenience those members who were preparing seriously for the Club Championship. It transpired that Committee was almost equally divided as to whether or not to accommodate the event, and it had been decided that the views of the three committee members not present be taken into account before making a final decision. Upon being informed of the situation by Secretary Tom, I contacted Vice-Captain Alan, who had chaired the meeting, and advised him that I considered the possibility of a vote being overturned by those not privy to the original debate to be inappropriate. Alan explained the reason behind Committee's deferring the decision, and I fully understood its predicament, but he agreed with me that only votes cast at the meeting should determine the outcome. In accordance with the majority vote, we agreed to co-host the SGU Championship.

Highland Open Amateur Golf Tournament

First impressions often prove to be lasting, and that applies to my introduction to the golf course at Pitlochry. It is only now, as I recall the circumstances of that first visit, that I realise the similarities between it and my discovering the Eden Course at St. Andrews back in 1954. Once again it was during a summer holiday spent with my parents. We were on our return journey from a motoring holiday in the far north-west corner of Scotland, in the course of which we had travelled from Durness to John O'Groats and had then proceeded down to Inverness. The year was 1966; my father was driving our maroon-coloured Ford Zodiac (with bench front seat and column gear change), and we had taken photographs of the royal yacht Britannia as she steamed along the Pentland Firth. The last stop on our holiday was to be an overnight stay at Pitlochry; and by this time, when on holiday, I had my golf clubs in the car boot. Upon arriving in the town on the Friday afternoon, my first action was to seek out the local golf club and to enquire whether visitors were allowed on the course the following morning. Somewhat to my surprise, the course was not located in the vicinity of the river which flowed through the floor of the valley but was reached by a road which emanated directly off the town's main street and then proceeded at a steep gradient up the hillside. I was intrigued to discover what kind of course would present itself to me considering the challenging nature of its approach road – a far cry from the gentle tree-lined avenue to Colville Park or the readily accessible footpaths to the St. Andrews links. Whatever preconceptions I might have entertained as to a golf course laid out on the side of a hill, these were jettisoned the moment I reached the upper section of the road. Upon my coming over the valley shoulder was revealed the most idyllic picture of an Edwardian clubhouse set amongst pine trees, a backdrop of manicured fairways amidst more trees, a gurgling stream, pastoral fields, and the whole scene overlooked by a rugged mountain. The course simply beckoned to be explored! I was informed that if I wished to play the following morning (Saturday) I would require to tee-off before 9 o'clock; and that is just what I did!

On that sublime Saturday morning in August, the conditions were absolutely exquisite; clear skies, warm sunshine and hardly a breath of wind. Standing on the first tee, unaccompanied, and wallowing in the majestic vista before me, the green appeared as a very distant objective far beyond and above the burn which traversed the fairway. The actual distance to the hole proved to be somewhat deceptive, because the opening drive was all downhill towards the burn. Once there, the green was not quite so far off as had seemed from the tee; but it still required a very challenging longish second shot to reach it. And so I set off on my round. After crossing the burn it was a steady climb all of the way to the third green, much as was to be anticipated as seen from the first tee; but from that point onwards the pleasure of the round was unbounded. The panoramic view down the Tummel Valley was beautiful and, after the exertions of the opening three holes, I was rewarded with easier walking midst glorious scenery, a course layout full of interesting features, attractive birch and pine trees, wild flowers and birdsong; all to be enjoyed in the soft Highland air. It was absolutely wonderful; one of the most exhilarating mornings I have ever spent on a golf course. On completion of my round, I learned that the club hosted an annual open competition with scratch and handicap sections, the Highland Open Amateur Tournament, and I resolved to compete in it the following year.

And so, in 1967 I sent off my entry form and booked bed and breakfast accommodation in Pitlochry for three nights. My ambitions did not extend beyond qualifying for the match play stages of the Handicap Section, but I was excited about competing in my first-ever golf week. I was now the owner of a Yukon grey Morris Oxford, registration no. YFS 324, and on the Sunday afternoon I drove up from Motherwell to Pitlochry via Muthill and the Sma' Glen; and was very conscious of being on my own. The actual tournament was preceded by a Sweepstake on the Monday, and I made my way to the Starter's Box to enquire about getting a tee-time. As chance would have it, I was slotted in with a two-ball that was just about to drive-off and, unbeknown to me, I was destined to commence a friendship that has lasted ever since. On that first tee I was introduced to Michael

Michael Scobbie (Thornton) and caddie
Pitlochry 1970

Scobbie and to his playing partner, Derek Lee, both of whom were members of Thornton Golf Club in Fife and who were part of a group of players entered from that club. An enjoyable round was followed by introductions in the clubhouse to the other members of the Thornton contingent, and over the next few days I was made welcome in their company. The tournament attracted some prominent players of the time and the winner that year was Andrew Brooks (Carluke) who, within a couple of years, was destined to play in the Walker Cup before joining the professional ranks and then, in his late forties, being appointed professional at Royal Saint George's GC, Sandwich. The following year's tournament was won by the Scottish Internationalist, W.B. (Bill) Murray (Downfield), and on both occasions I failed to qualify for the Handicap Section. Mike Scobbie was a gifted player, with a particularly good short game, and was very much in the equation when it came to qualifying for the match play stages of the scratch competition. He and I became good friends over these two years and it was a pleasure thereafter to meet up with him at Pitlochry for 'The Highland'.

After two failures I decided to make a concerted effort for the 1969 tournament and so, for a few weeks beforehand, I made regular visits to the practice area at Colville Park and worked on my game. And the practice paid dividends! Just a few weeks before the Highland Open I won the Coleman Trophy at Carnwath and in the process gained third prize in the scratch section; played away above my normal game for sixteen holes – but finished with two sixes! This time I was in better shape for Pitlochry than I had been on the two previous years and was hopeful of putting up a reasonable show. Alas, things did not go well! After 27 holes of the qualifying competition my hopes were receding fast and, to compound my plight, it started to rain and gradually developed into a steady downpour. My two playing partners and I got utterly soaked, and our scorecards were reduced to a soggy pulp – and yet I played the inward half in 33 gross, thereby qualifying for the handicap section by three strokes. What a recovery! I reckon that fate must have decreed that this was to be my year for, with the exception of the first round, all of my games went to the home green or beyond – and I managed to ease my way through each time! In the final against Les Wright (Downfield) I was one up playing the 18th Hole, having never been behind in the game but, from a downhill lie on the fairway, I completely thinned my approach shot. The ball hardly got airborne and went straight into the burn guarding the green, flipped off its surface like a pebble, cannoned into the bank, shot up in the air and landed on the putting surface. A long approach putt to within two feet of the hole was sufficient for Les to concede the match. 'You've been holing these a' day' he said, 'and you're no' likely to miss that one'.

The final of the Handicap Section was played over eighteen holes on the Saturday morning, and followed immediately behind the main event which was over thirty-six holes. On completion of my game I was congratulated by my first round opponent, J.S. Deane (Luffness New) and he kindly agreed to take a photograph of me and my young caddie, Alan Robertson. The family with whom I had boarded implored me to let them know how I fared; and accordingly, in a most relaxed manner, I walked down to their house (no mobile telephones in these days) in the knowledge that the principal finalists had still to play their second round. Inwardly I was overjoyed at my success, and I ambled back to the clubhouse in a similar fashion – only to find that the presentation ceremony was already underway. Another few minutes and I would have missed it altogether! The final had been completed much quicker than I had anticipated. Not that it had finished far out on the course, for A.H. Campbell (Troon) had only beaten the local favourite A.J. (Sandy) Scott (Pitlochry) 3 and 2; but I had obviously lost all track of time. Thankfully, I was able to take my place among the crowd and to step forward, when my name was announced, to receive my engraved tankard from the Mr. T. P. Stewart of the Atholl Estates Office. Talk about nearly missing the boat!

With my prize-voucher I purchased a car travelling rug; and for my mother and each of my aunts and uncles, as a memento of my success, a miniature copper coffee pot bearing the Pitlochry coat-of-arms. Such innocent times!!

Pitlochry 1969, with my caddie, Alan Robertson

Chapter 7

September

Thursday, 2nd September: Request from Arthur Maxwell

One of the benefits afforded by the Club to its members is the availability of its premises for private functions. Consequently, throughout each year many requests for the use of various rooms for birthday celebrations, christening parties, funeral receptions and the like are approved by Committee. Sometimes use of the course facilities is requested and just such a one, albeit of modest proportions, was made by Arthur Maxwell for a fund-raising event on behalf of the local Rotary Club. Members of the public had been invited to estimate how many golf balls Arthur would be able to hit in a 10-minute period, and Arthur enquired as to whether it would be possible for the first fairway to be closed for a short time one evening whilst he set about the task. It was envisaged that the total closure time would be about half an hour since, as a retired gentleman, he wished to attack the challenge in a series of short bursts rather than as one continuous effort and, naturally, helpers required to be on hand to serve and collect all of the balls. And the outcome of Arthur's endeavours? On the evening of Tuesday, 28th September he played 228 strokes and raised £333 for the Marie Curie Foundation; to which sum the Club donated a further £100 towards his fund-raising effort.

Tuesday, 7th September: Selected team for Prestwick Rosebowl

The history of this fixture is of fairly recent vintage, its having been inaugurated in 1975 by the then Captain of Prestwick Golf Club, Mr. J.A. Rutherford, who presented a rosebowl trophy for competition among the three Prestwick clubs. The ethos of the competition is to foster the harmonious relationship that exists among the clubs and to provide a forum for their meeting and playing together on an annual basis. To that end the venue rotates from year to year. Secretary Tom advised me that it was the Captain's prerogative to choose the St. Nicholas team and that this is normally done in conjunction with Malcolm Foggo, the Match Secretary. Malcolm then informed me that the eight-man team usually comprises the Captain and three Committee members, plus four others from among the playing membership, and that within the Club it is considered as being something of an honour to be selected for the Rosebowl team. With this in mind, he produces a list of non-committee members whom he considers worthy of consideration on account of their recent good performances in the Club's competitions; and from these the Captain chooses the four who will accompany his personal choice of Committee members. Tom handed me Malcolm's list; and I selected the team!

Friday, 10th September: Captains Board

In the course of my regular meeting with Secretary Tom, he informed me that my name had been added to the Captains Board in the Tom Morris Room.

Sunday, 12th September: Lunch with Archie and Bunty Fulton

During my first year on Committee the Immediate Past Captain, Jim Pettigrew, with the assistance of Bob Ellis, Valerie Stephen and Tommy Maxwell, was engaged upon compiling an updated history of the Club. The kernel of this work had its inception about six years previously, when the Captain had commissioned one of his colleagues to produce a book for publication to mark the 150th anniversary of the Club's foundation. After getting off to a promising start, involving a considerable amount of time and research, the work had come to a halt and it rather appeared as if the book would never be completed. Jim was of the opinion that too much effort had already been expended on its production to allow its demise and he had set about resurrecting the project. I too had been conscious that nothing had been forthcoming in the intervening years and was disappointed on that account. In the course of providing Committee with an update on the progress being made, Jim had let it be known that he would welcome further assistance from anyone who was sufficiently interested in the project and, at the conclusion of the meeting, I offered my services to him.

Within the next few weeks the original manuscripts of Mr. Ian Hall, together with some additional sections produced by Jim's team, were collated and presented to the printer; but the latter

Archie and Bunty (Kinnell) Fulton with Jeanette in the Conservatory

informed Jim that the text was of insufficient quantity to justify the production of a book and that its content was more akin to that of a booklet. This news came as a disappointment to the production team and it was evident that some means would need to be devised whereby the original concept of the publication could be realised. The printer suggested that we insert lists of office bearers and trophy winners as a way of increasing its volume, and I offered to compile a chapter upon some of the better known professionals and clubmakers who had been associated with the Club. Those whom I had in mind were Tom Morris, John Allan, John Gray, Charlie Hunter, Jimmy Kinnell and Tom Haliburton, and I was confident that I could glean sufficient information from my own collection of golf books to fill a few pages. Little did I realise the by-ways I would be led into as my researches progressed. The most significant item which I unearthed was the fact that Jimmy Kinnell had been succeeded as the St. Nicholas professional by his brother, David, and that the latter had been in the post for almost 34 years, from 1902 until 1936; and not a single current member knew anything of him! It soon became apparent that from 1890, with the appointment of John Allan, until the retirement of Willie MacDonald in 1980, the Club had employed only six professionals during those ninety years. So I decided to seek information about all of them.

I knew that Jimmy Kinnell had originated in Leven, and that was where I commenced my investigations relating to both him and David. After an extremely convoluted journey I eventually discovered that David's daughter, Bunty, was still alive and was living in Ayr. Although she was hesitant initially about discussing her father with me when I first made contact, she proved subsequently to be very helpful; and her husband, Archie, was very supportive throughout. This investigative work took place during the summer of 2007. On being elected Captain three years later, I resolved that I would invite Archie and Bunty to be my guests at the clubhouse, and this I arranged. Bunty did not want any fuss made of the occasion and I respected her wishes. Jeanette and I collected them by car at their house and we entertained them to Sunday lunch; having requested the corner table in the conservatory. We had a lovely afternoon during which they, but especially Archie, gave us a vivid résumé of their family backgrounds and of their married life together. It was a very precious time, and both of them showed great interest in the Club's photographs and name boards when I gave them a conducted tour of the clubhouse. Several names caught Bunty's attention as she recalled her father having spoken of them when she was a girl. The entire afternoon was a joyous experience for all of us, and Bunty and Archie were most appreciative of their visit. Everything about the day was delightful!

Monday, 13th September: Refurbishment works commence
In accordance with the Club Constitution, the immediate Past Captain serves on Committee throughout the following year. No specific role is accorded to him although he automatically becomes one of the Club's four Trustees. I assume that the purpose of his being on Committee is to ensure a degree of continuity in Club matters and to provide a source of experience and knowledge of which the new Captain and Committee members can avail themselves. During my time on Committee none of the Past Captains was appointed to a convenership, although Jim Pettigrew had taken upon himself the task of resurrecting the project to publish an updated history of the Club. As anyone involved in golf administration is aware, maintenance of the course and of the clubhouse is a constant requirement and, as part of a three-year programme to improve the clubhouse facilities, an upgrading and refurbishment of the Mixed Lounge and Dining Room areas had been planned for implementation during my time in office. This work was obviously of a specialist nature and beyond the normal scope of a House Convener's duties; so I decided that, rather than burden the House Convener with additional responsibilities, I would create a temporary convenership to oversee the upgrading works and would embody it under the all-embracing title of 'Special Projects'.

The immediate Past Captain, Bill Rae, is a qualified architect, and in recent years he and I had worked in a professional capacity on various construction projects. I had formed a very high opinion of his professional expertise and I knew him to be fastidious in his attention to detail and of sound judgement in matters of decoration and furnishings. And so at the outset of my captaincy I enquired of Bill if he would consider acting as the convener for Special Projects, and he readily agreed. As to how he interpreted that role I left entirely to him, and he duly reported at the monthly committee meetings upon the progress being made towards implementing the upgrading works. Needless to say Bill fulfilled the role admirably and today marked the commencement of the works on site. The critical factor in relation to completion of the project was the Annual Dinner & Presentation of Trophies which was scheduled for Friday, 22nd October. In order to achieve that completion date,

Bill informed Committee that, in the intervening weeks, the programme of works would entail phased closures of both the Mixed Lounge and the Dining Room.

Wednesday, 15th September: Meeting re wall hangings

Now that the refurbishment works were underway, Bill Rae requested that Secretary Tom and I meet with him in the Committee Room to discuss possible wall hangings for the Mixed Lounge and Dining Room. Bill and I had talked on this matter previously and we were of the opinion that retaining the existing prints and paintings would not be in keeping with the proposed new surroundings. When the three of us met, Bill said that he wanted our reaction to the possibility of commissioning a painting by one of our own members who was a professional artist and who had made some valuable comments to him on just this subject. The artist had provided examples of the type of picture which he had in mind and had intimated a four-figure sum for his fee. Upon viewing the pictures, which to the uninitiated might loosely be described as abstract, modern, *avant-garde* or the like, we agreed that members were likely to object to such a sum being expended in this manner and we were of the opinion that a more traditional display would better promote the ambience which we were seeking to create.

. . . . 15th: Letter to Bob Craig and Iain McCall

Every year within the fixture list there are usually two or three competitions which act as qualifiers for national events in which the winners from each club go forward to a regional qualifier. Except for the members concerned, and perhaps also their regular golfing partners and the Match Secretary, their progress is not normally accorded a great deal of interest within the Club. For them, needless to say, it is a great experience and one which most members would readily welcome had they themselves managed to qualify. However, progressing beyond the regional to the final stage certainly increases awareness among the Club generally. Bob Craig and Iain McCall, two members with the reputation of being a formidable partnership, qualified for the Grand Final of the Scottish Club Handicap Championship which was due to be played over The Duke's Course at St. Andrews. Although neither Bob nor Iain were known to me on a personal level, I thought it appropriate to write letters congratulating them upon reaching the final and offering my best wishes for the day.

Friday, 17th September: Speaker for Annual Dinner

Unlike adjacent parkland courses only a mile or so distant and susceptible to the vagaries of harsh winter weather, links courses in the south-west of Scotland are usually open for play throughout the twelve months of the year. The sandy underfoot conditions which provide efficient drainage of rainwater, and the temperate climate associated with the coastal location, ensure that golf can be enjoyed on the links at times when inland courses are either waterlogged or frostbound. The main golfing season is generally recognised as being from April to mid-October, and my thoughts were turning to what Past Captain Jim Pettigrew described as being the 'cholesterol season', *viz.* the Captain's attendance at prize-giving dinners. Over the years there has become established a fixed rota as to when and where each club in our vicinity holds its annual dinner; as to who is invited to which function; and as to who is expected to speak on such occasions. As matters have evolved, it so happens that the St. Nicholas dinner is the first one in the cycle and is held traditionally during the third week of October. So it came as a surprise to me when Tom Hepburn enquired as to whom I would be inviting to be my guest speaker that evening. This was something that had never previously crossed my mind and, whilst on hindsight it is a very obvious scenario, I was taken aback at the prospect. Had I been aware at the outset of my captaincy, I could have reflected upon whom I might approach on the subject and would have taken time over my deliberations. But with the dinner little more than one month away, I was immediately under pressure to procure a suitable person for the event – and at very short notice! Tom mentioned a couple of members within our Club who might be approached, but I determined that I would first of all see whether I could engage someone of my own choosing from outwith the Club; even although I had no obvious contact in mind. I considered it important that my guest speaker be golf-orientated; my having attended numerous so called Sportsmen's Dinners at which the speakers simply performed a standard routine which had nothing to do with the context of the dinner, and the content of which, in many cases, was less than edifying. But who to invite?

. . . . 17th: Discussion re opening of practice hole

The passing of time inexorably heralds change, and golf is no exception. The omission after 1925 of Prestwick from The Open Championship rota is a prime, indeed a poignant, example of how the ever-increasing popularity of an event elicits a corresponding upgrading of all the attendant facilities. The Prestwick course was still of championship standard but, short of radically altering the layout of the holes in the vicinity of the clubhouse, which as a consequence would have entailed utilising hitherto unused areas of the links and substantially altering the character of the course, there was no way it could adequately accommodate the huge influx of spectators that the championship was beginning to attract. Until 1986 Prestwick St. Nicholas was a final qualifying course for The Open Championship, but it too succumbed in that respect to the march of time. Confined by the Ayr/Glasgow railway extending the full length of its eastern boundary, and bordered by the Firth of Clyde to the west, there was no scope for expansion and almost every square metre of the links was taken up by the course, so much so that there was no space for a practice area – an absolute requisite for the modern professional golfer and, of course, a much needed and much desired facility for the ordinary club member.

Two years previously David Breckenridge, as Links Convener, had initiated proposals to incorporate a practice area in a triangular portion of ground enclosed by the 5th, 6th and 7th Holes. The length of the range could only be about 100 yards, but it would undoubtedly add to the Club's amenities and simultaneously provide a suitable location where tuition of Juniors could be undertaken. On discussing his proposals with John MacLachlan, David found the latter to be very supportive of his plans; but John recommended, rather than simply creating a practice area which incorporated a bunker, that a practice hole be constructed complete with tee, green, fairway bunker and greenside bunker, and that it be maintained to the standard of the course in general. David obtained Committee's approval of the scheme and, after deliberating upon the details of its construction, it was forecast that the practice hole would be ready for play in Autumn 2010.

At the August Committee meeting, Stephen King (Links Convener) had advised that work on the practice hole was almost complete and Committee agreed that there should be an opening ceremony to commemorate the event, and that David Breckenridge be invited to play the first shot.

When I discussed the timing and form of the proposed ceremony with Past Captain Bill Rae and John MacLachlan, they told me of David's aversion to any fuss being made of his involvement and that he would prefer everything to be 'low key'. With that in mind, I left Bill and John to make the necessary arrangements with David, and made it clear to them that I would be happy to comply with whatever was agreed.

Saturday, 18th September: Arrol Cup

In terms of what is generally considered as being the most prestigious trophy to be won at St. Nicholas, few would dispute that the Arrol Cup holds pride of place. Presented to the Club in 1893 by the renowned civil engineer, Sir William Arrol, the trophy is put forward for annual competition among members of clubs in the West of Scotland. The competition is a one day 36-hole scratch event with an entry handicap limit of 5. Among its previous winners are James Robb (Amateur Champion 1906), John Wilson (Scottish Amateur Champion 1922, 1931; Walker Cup player 1923), Hamilton (Hammy) McInally (Scottish Amateur Champion 1937, 1939, 1947), W.C. (Cammie) Gibson (Scottish Amateur Champion 1950), Paul Girvan (Walker Cup player 1987), and several other International players, including such as Robert Andrew and Gordon Lockhart who subsequently established themselves in professional golf. I followed some of the play during both the morning and the afternoon rounds, but was rather dismayed to find that a substantial number of players, whose first round score had put them out of contention for the principal prize, felt under no obligation to play their second round. I was disappointed that they should think nothing of acting in this manner, especially as such action could be interpreted as being something of an affront to those players who had been balloted out of the competition. The standard of play among the leading players was very high and afterwards, in the sociable atmosphere of the casual bar, I had the pleasure of presenting the cup to the victor, Paul Gault (Westerwood), who returned a score of 138 (70, 68) to win by three strokes from John Ashton (St. Nicholas) and Gordon Boyle (Ayr Dalmilling).

Paul Gault (Westerwood) with Arrol Cup, flanked by Hon President
Bill Andrew and myself

Immediately prior to the trophy presentation, David Steele and Rhona entered the clubhouse for an evening meal and enquired whether Jeanette and I would join them. This necessitated a telephone call home to Jeanette, and David's driving to Ayr to collect her, since I would be officiating at the prize-giving. That is indeed what happened, and the four of us had a very pleasant time together in the Tom Morris Room – the Dining Room being utilised for a private function.

Sunday, 19th September: Prestwick Rosebowl

It is no exaggeration to say that, for golf historians, a visit to Prestwick Golf Club is an absolute must; an experience not to be missed. The clubhouse exudes an atmosphere of tradition and permanence, suffused with the ghosts of golfing legends, whilst the course itself defies modern concepts of architectural design and retains much of the character of a bygone age. It is difficult to imagine how anyone with an abiding interest in golf could fail to be captivated by its unique appeal, or warm to the challenge of its exquisite links. How fortunate for me that in my period of captaincy the venue for The Prestwick Clubs' Rosebowl should be 'Old' Prestwick itself! Each Prestwick club is represented by a team of eight players and the competition is played on current handicaps in a format comprising four groups of three-ball sixsomes; two players from each club playing against the other two clubs simultaneously and each game decided upon 'holes up' over eighteen holes. The overall winner of the competition being the club with the greatest net aggregate of holes won.

The teams met for coffee at 8.45am and the first group, in which the respective captains were involved, teed-off at 9.30am. I had invited Jim Kelman to be my partner, and we were paired against Brian Morrison and Niall Scott representing Prestwick GC and Billy Gibson and Bob Cord representing Prestwick St. Cuthbert GC. Jim was an old acquaintance of mine from Motherwell, our having played in the same former pupils' football team almost 40 years previously and both having been members of Colville Park Golf Club where, incidentally, Jim was Club Champion in 1984. For most of the round we acquitted ourselves reasonably well but, due to a couple of aberrations on my part at the 17th and 18th holes, our result was not as favourable as it might have been; we finished nine up on Prestwick but, more significantly, two down to St. Cuthbert. Not that my lapses were crucial in deciding the eventual destination of the Rosebowl as St. Cuthbert won with a net total of 13 up; St. Nicholas finished 3 up and Prestwick 16 down. Due to shortage of time, Captain Brian Morrison was unable to stay for the lunch and Past Captain Peter Kennedy-Moffat acted as host in his stead. As St. Nicholas captain, it behove me to say a few words upon conclusion of the prize-giving ceremony. Thereafter Peter invited some of us to share with him the comfort of the Smoke Room and, upon finding a common interest in cricket, he regaled us with reminiscences of his having played cricket in Kent and of having seen Bradman bat at Canterbury; and all the while we partook of Port and Kummel On The Rocks. What a delight to be at Prestwick Golf Club in such absorbing company!

Monday, 20th September: Taste of Turnberry

The St. Nicholas Constitution recognises only two Office Bearers, *viz.* Captain and Vice-Captain. The significance of this denomination suggests to me a working partnership; the active participation and co-operation of two people in promoting the best interests of the Club, whether in relation to its members or in its association with other clubs and governing bodies. Too often, I would suggest, a vice-captain is perceived as being a captain-in-waiting, the next man in line, when in fact his current role should be one that is proactive. His may well be a year of preparation, but he is also the person on whom the captain relies to provide the necessary support, counsel and encouragement that will make his tenure of office a time of fulfilment and satisfaction. It was a great joy for me to have Alan as Vice-Captain and, as a token of my appreciation, I invited him to join me in a Taste of Turnberry Golf Day. The package consisted of coffee and bacon roll on arrival, a round over the Ailsa course, and a meal in the Turnberry Clubhouse. We had a super time together and afterwards, in the relaxed atmosphere of the Tappie Toorie Lounge, we took time to discuss the format of the forthcoming Committee Outing.

Alan on 9th tee Ailsa Course, Turnberry

Wednesday, 22nd September: Practice hole opened

As befitted David Breckinridge's sentiments, the ceremony marking the official opening of the practice facility was a very modest affair and was not intimated in advance to the general membership. In fact the event was so informal, and arranged at such short notice, that I was unable to attend due to my having a previously-arranged business appointment. The actual proceedings were organised by Past Captain Bill Rae and Head Greenkeeper John, and they were joined at the ceremony by Secretary Tom, Links Convener Stephen King and, of course, David Breckenridge. David was invited to play the first shot, and he struck a crisp seven iron to within four feet of the pin! A quite remarkable stroke in the circumstances; and a fitting means by which to mark the opening of the new practice hole.

Thursday, 23rd September: Bill McFarlan

Since being informed by Secretary Tom that I was responsible for inviting a guest speaker to the Annual Dinner, I had been considering whom I might approach. Gordon McKinlay, professional at Troon Municipal, had attended the Troon Welbeck dinners during the period when I was a member there, and I thought that he might be ideal for the purpose. But when I visited him at his shop, he told me that 'After Dinner' speaking was not his forte, although he could recommend other professional golfers who undertook such commissions. When a few days later Secretary Tom enquired as to whether I had made any progress in the matter, he and Margaret mentioned the names of some members within our Club who might be suitable. As time was obviously getting short, Tom suggested that, on my behalf, he approach Bill McFarlan, a relatively new member, but well-known to many of us through his journalistic career and television appearances. Thankfully Bill was happy to oblige and I was much relieved by his willing acceptance.

Prestwick St. Nicholas GC – What a beautiful practice hole!

Friday, 24th September: Ayrshire Junior Golf League

Secretary Tom was contacted by Ayrshire Junior Golf League enquiring whether the St. Nicholas links could be made available for its forthcoming finals day which was due to be held two days hence. The finals had originally been scheduled to be played at Largs Golf Club but, as a result of recent prolonged rainfall, the course was closed due to flooding and there was no prospect of its being re-opened by Sunday. Having ascertained that the matches could be accommodated without undue inconvenience to Club members, I sanctioned approval of the request.

Sunday, 26th September: Committee Outing to Whitecraigs

Reflecting upon my previous four years on Committee, I was aware that, whilst inter-committee matches were always a great pleasure and gave each committee member the opportunity to experience being part of a team, there was no identifiable golfing event which could be construed as bonding everyone together. So the prospect of introducing, or perhaps re-introducing, a Committee Outing was something which had been on my mind for some time. When I suggested it at the June Management Meeting, the proposal received immediate approval and, between us, Secretary Tom and I made arrangements to have an afternoon outing to Whitecraigs Golf Club. I thought it appropriate that the outing be of a relatively short duration to a course within one hour's journey of Prestwick rather than organising something which would involve, as some had suggested, an overnight stay. In my judgement, an afternoon round of golf followed by a meal was more likely to prove convenient to the great majority of the Committee members and to be more rewarding as a consequence.

It was through Tom's good offices that we secured Whitecraigs as the venue and, having a reciprocal arrangement with them, no green fee was involved. We hired a coach so that everyone would travel together; and that was the only cost expended from Club funds. The catering and refreshment bills were apportioned among the Committee members, and our hosts did us proud in that regard. In order to give some structure to the golf, I had discussed with Alan whilst at Turnberry my plan to form the party into two teams and to play a Captain versus Vice-Captain match using

Committee Outing to Whitecraigs GC
Left to right: *David Coid, Tom Hepburn, David Gilmour, Gary Tierney, Robin Alexander, Murray Bothwell, Bobby Hodge, Murray Liddle*

Alan Poole, Stephen King and Steven Bolland

the Stableford system and, as a trophy, I purchased from Peter Carmichael a tankard bearing the St. Nicholas crest. Thanks to the inspired play of Secretary Tom (39 pts) it was the Captain's team which came out on top. It was a very merry company that arrived back at the St. Nicholas clubhouse shortly after 10.45pm and, as the last five of us were about to make our farewells, Vice-Captain Alan challenged us to play the eighteenth hole in the darkness. What with the amount of wine and spirits that had been consumed, Gary Tierney, David Coid, Robin Alexander and I took up the challenge! As Captain, my acquiescence may be considered by some to have been somewhat rash but, no matter, we were all in a jovial mood and I arranged with Jeanette, who had come to collect me, to shine our car's headlights across the fairway; and then onto the green. If I recall correctly, only one ball was lost, and Alan and I both holed-out in four, which was probably par in the circumstances. All agreed that the outing had been a great success.

Monday, 27th September: Peter Carmichael

The car park at St. Nicholas is immediately adjacent to the eighteenth fairway and is separated from it by a post and rail fence. When preparing to play from the eighteenth tee, one's awareness of the car park on the right-hand side varies according to the prevailing conditions. At the best of times the tee shot requires to be hit straight and true but, dependent upon the state of one's match or medal score, in like measure will the influence of the out-of-bounds intrude into the golfer's mental process; not to mention the direction of the wind, the volume of cars in the car park, or one's propensity to slice tee shots. Whatever challenges the final hole provides, and it provides a few, the most obvious element for most golfers is the dreaded prospect of putting a ball into the car park, causing damage to either a car or a clubhouse window, and thereafter having to play 'three off the tee'. I must confess that consideration of such items had not been an inhibiting factor following the Committee Outing! But I digress. The fact was that there had been a serious incident in the car park the previous day; and not the result of a wayward shot from the eighteenth tee!

Upon coming out of the clubhouse Irene, the bar manageress, had discovered Peter Carmichael, our starter and shop retailer, sprawled on the tarmac beside his bicycle and bleeding profusely. She sought help from Past Captain Louis Thow and immediately put out a call for an ambulance. Both Irene and Louis were shocked by the amount of blood that Peter had lost. Fortunately a paramedic team was in the vicinity and it responded very quickly to the call. Forthwith Peter was taken to the Accident & Emergency Unit at Ayr Hospital and Louis accompanied him in the ambulance. Peter had obviously fallen from his bicycle, but it was unknown at that stage whether it was due to his having suddenly taken unwell or whether he had simply crashed his bicycle. From Ayr Hospital he was transferred to Glasgow's Southern General Hospital, which deals with serious head injuries, and there it was confirmed that he had sustained fractures to his face and skull, dislocated a shoulder and badly injured an eye. Great was the concern regarding Peter's condition, but everyone was also aware that there was no hospital better equipped to attend to him than the Southern General.

Thursday, 30th September: Committee meeting

Committee matches and inter-club matches are invariably played on a handicap basis and are generally great fun for the club golfer. So, when Secretary Tom informed me that an approach had been made by MCC Golfing Society enquiring as to the possibility of engaging St. Nicholas in a challenge match, and knowing that within our Club were several cricket lovers, I was keen that we should accede to the request. The prospect recalled past times prior to the Second World War when the Club played matches against Oxford and Cambridge Golfing Society; albeit the calibre of the golfers and the status of these matches were on a different scale to what was being suggested in this instance. On these occasions the team sheets read like a Who's Who of British Golf, for they were sprinkled with the names of Home Internationalists, Walker Cup players, national champions and even winners of the Amateur Championship. The list is impressive, and the likes of Cyril Tolley, Roger Wethered, Bernard Darwin, John Wilson, John JF Pennink, Willie Tulloch and Raymond H Oppenheimer are testament to the prestigious nature of these encounters. The background to the MCC Golfing Society's request was its annual outing to the Ayrshire coast during which it visited Western Gailes, Glasgow Gailes, Prestwick and Royal Troon; very much an itinerary of outstanding merit! For whatever reason, Royal Troon was no longer to be one of the venues and St. Nicholas had been proposed as a possible substitute. I was enthusiastic about the proposal and was quite certain that, not only was St. Nicholas well equipped to host such a fixture, but the recognition implied by the approach was something which the Club should embrace and seek to promote. So I urged Committee, the great majority of whose members had no leanings towards cricket, to agree to my recommendation that we host the fixture; and this was approved.

I reported to Committee upon my recent private visit to Wallasey Golf Club and it agreed to my request that, as a token of appreciation for the hospitality shown to me, two courtesy tee-times be allocated to that club for use by its members. In the course of the meeting I was informed that one of our own members, Lawrence Hood, a local butcher and well-known character within the Club, had suffered a heart attack and had been admitted to Hairmyres Hospital, East Kilbride.

Hickory Shafted Golf Clubs

By its very nature a change from something that was once familiar and accepted often evokes nostalgia, especially as the years go by and old habits and old practices assume a place in memory unsullied by reality and the passing of time. Only a small minority, one would assume, lamented the demise of the feather ball when it was superseded by the gutta-percha; and subsequently when it in turn was ousted by the rubber-cored Haskell. The introduction of a regular and ultimately standard ball which was more reliable and truer in performance was a great advance towards ensuring that players of all abilities could get the fullest possible pleasure out of playing the game. So nostalgia for 'featheries' and 'gutties' is probably a misplaced concept except in the mind of the avid collector of golfing memorabilia. Similarly, only a golfer who lived through the years of transition from hickory shafts to tempered steel shafts can be fully conversant with the initial impact it had on the players of that era. What it most certainly did achieve was the ready acquisition of a fully-matched set of clubs involving the minimum of maintenance. Prior to their introduction the average golfer acquired, perhaps 'accumulated' would be a more accurate description, an assortment of hickory shafted clubs most suited to his liking and, for him, that represented his set of clubs. As to the variety of clubs which constituted a set, that depended solely on the individual and, until a restriction was placed on their number, there was no limit as to how many with which a golfer could equip himself; governed only by the quantity he or his caddie was able to carry! Incidentally, a restriction as to the number of clubs that could be used in competitions was first introduced by the R&A in

1939; which was post-hickory era. For his part, Harry Vardon's set regularly comprised of only nine clubs, *viz.* Driver, Brassy, Driving Cleek, Light Cleek, Driving Mashie, Iron, Mashie, Niblick and Putter. When considering that set and the limitations of its design, it only takes a moment's reflection to appreciate the skill and improvisation that Vardon and other players of his generation must have employed in manoeuvring their way round a golf course.

Driver, Spoon, Cleek, Mid Iron, Jigger, Mashie Niblick, Niblick, Putting Cleek and Putter

As a consequence of the technical advances in club design, and the manicured condition of the modern golf course, the subtleties of shot-making and the constant need to adapt to difficult lies and uneven ground, or so it appears to me, have all but vanished from the professional golfer's armoury. Three-quarter swings, gripping down the shaft, closing or opening the club face, punching down on the ball, were all part of utilising and getting the most out of what would now be considered as being inferior implements. Winston Churchill famously defined golf as a game in which one uses weapons ill-suited for the purpose. But for many, therein lay both the charm and the attraction of the game. By today's standards the implements were indeed rudimentary; but what fun and what a challenge they engendered! And how precious certain individual clubs were to their owners, for they were quite literally irreplaceable. A broken shaft heralded the loss of that club's unique properties for, unlike modern precision parts, it could never be replaced with the identical characteristics of its predecessor. Uniformity was unachievable. Each piece of hickory was similar but different; each shaft was rubbed down and fashioned to attain the degree of stiffness or flexibility the clubmaker alone judged appropriate. A club could be copied, but it could never be replicated exactly the same as the original. Not that all clubs were of the highest quality. Many were of inferior design, poorly balanced and with few attributes to commend them; but having rejected what was mediocre, or unsuited to his particular requirements, a good hickory club was something which an owner treasured and which became an object of his affection. Each club had its own special relationship with its owner and this was augmented through the care that was required to keep it in good condition for play.

Regular preparation and maintenance of equipment is something that has now disappeared from many sports and with it the personal satisfaction of doing something that is both practical and rewarding. How some of us still recall the days when football boots required to be cleaned after every match, worn studs pulled out with pliers and replacement studs hammered into the soles, and the leather uppers softened and waterproofed with an application of Dubbin; and so with hickory shafted golf clubs. These required to be dried down after rain, the shafts lightly rubbed with raw linseed oil, the grips suitably softened with a leather preservative, rust on the iron heads attacked with fine emery paper or Duraglit wadding, and any slack whipping tightened and secured. What satisfaction was obtained when the clubs were restored to their pristine condition and ready for the next foray on the links! And no club was ever laid aside without its first being waggled about and lovingly admired.

It was pleasant to feel the texture of a good leather grip, especially when relatively new and still possessing the slight tackiness that provided confidence for a firm strike; not forgetting the underlayer of felt wrapping which gave that little bit of additional softness or cushion for the fingers. If touch was the most obvious of the five senses to be aroused by the clubs, the others were also significant. Every good quality club had its own beauty and the mere sight of it was appealing, particularly the woods with their lacquered heads, indented ornate lettering bearing the maker's name, fine patterned grooves across the face, a ram's horn inset for the leading edge of the driver or a brass metal sole plate for brassies and spoons, a lead insert on the back and whipping coiled tightly round the shaft; the whole assembly proclaimed pride in its workmanship and just begged to be admired. And the evocative smell of raw linseed oil as it was applied with a rag to the shaft which, in its turn, glistened brightly to a golden brown as it absorbed the oil's restorative properties and revealed the intricate pattern of the hickory's grain. And the noise of emery paper on iron heads as these were burnished up to reveal the shining metal beneath, which otherwise would have succumbed to being a dull, rusted, pathetic imitation of its original condition.

Touch, sight, smell and sound; all were products of the maintenance ritual. As for taste? Any suggestion of the foregoing becoming something of a chore was suitably dispelled when accompanied by a Macallan's 10 Year Old Malt Whisky!

Chapter 8

October

Halfway through my term as Captain.

Monday, 4th October: W.S. MacDonald wood
Having recently acquired the five examples of W.S. MacDonald woods, what should happen but I came across yet another club! Once again it was in a local charity shop, and this time I uncovered a No 2 wood with a persimmon head having a finely grooved white plastic insert fixed with three brass Phillips screws. The head was weighted with a lead insert at the back and was varnished in a dark brown stain with 'W S MacDonald' in scrolled white lettering, The stainless-steel soleplate, of similar design to Shoorlok, was engraved 'GRADIDGE TRIPLE CROWN' and was secured by four brass Phillips screws. The True Temper shaft had standard black whipping and was fitted with a 'Pro Only' Golf Pride grip which may well have been the original, but was now hard and in need of replacement. Whilst the club was not so obviously attractive as the set of red-painted woods, it was beautifully balanced and a very welcome addition to my collection.

. . . . 4th: Visited Peter Carmichael and Lawrence Hood
Having been informed by Secretary Tom that Peter Carmichael had been discharged from Southern General Hospital, I called round to Peter's house to see how he was progressing. On arrival I discovered that I had been preceded by another visitor, Past Captain Louis Thow, and that both he and Peter were deeply engrossed in watching the televised coverage from Celtic Manor of the final day's play in the Ryder Cup. There was no hiding the fact that Peter had been seriously injured as he was wrapped in slings and bandages, and the bruising on his face was very evident. Thanks to the swift action taken upon his admission to Ayr Hospital, where blood had been drained from behind his eye, his sight had been saved and he had been advised that his future participation in golf could be jeopardised if care was not taken regarding the shoulder dislocation. As to the cracked cranium; he was fortunate that the damage had not been more severe. I then went to Lawrence Hood's house to enquire of his health and was greeted with the good news that he was out for a short walk with his wife. I returned later and was told by Lawrence the circumstances of his having taken unwell at his shop and of the treatment he had undergone at Hairmyres Hospital. Thankfully the insertion of a stent would enable him to make a full recovery.

   I was relieved to have found Peter and Lawrence in such good spirits after their ordeals, but both were a timely reminder as to what are life's important priorities when measured against the minor aggravations of clubhouse politics.

Tuesday, 5th October: e-mail to Professor Purdie
During my conversation with Professor David W. Purdie at the cocktail party in June, he had offered to propose The Immortal Memory at the St. Nicholas Burns Supper. His reputation as an 'after dinner' speaker is of the highest order and only yesterday he had been Colin Montgomery's speech adviser at the Ryder Cup match, having performed a similar role for Sam Torrance when the latter

had captained the European team in 2002. Among his many associations are membership of Sunningdale Golf Club and of The Royal Burgess Golfing Society of Edinburgh, but I was aware that he had applied recently for membership of St. Nicholas, where he had commenced his golfing life as a junior member fifty years previously. It demanded no hesitation on my part to decide that the Club should accept David's offer to speak at the Burns Supper and, having cleared matters with Committee, I contacted him by e-mail and took the opportunity to update him on his membership application, the which I had endorsed by acting as his proposer. The following morning David telephoned to say that unfortunately, due to previous commitments, the proposed date for the 2011 supper was unsuitable to him but that he would be happy to speak at the 2012 function.

Wednesday, 6th October: Meeting with Bill Andrew

There was no doubting that compliance with the proposed Equality Act was the most significant topic of my Captaincy. Dependent upon how matters developed, it had the potential to alter radically the historical character of the Club. At our meeting two months previously, it had emerged that Honorary President Bill and I were alike minded that the Club should proceed with caution and should not introduce measures hastily in anticipation of what compliance with the act might eventually entail. 'Ca' canny' is the old Scottish term for such an approach, and that was our maxim in this instance. Both of us recognised and supported implementation of The Law's requirements, but we considered that it would be prudent to await guidance from the Scottish Golf Union rather than push ahead with our own perceived interpretation of the new requirements. In particular, if it could be accommodated, we were anxious that a means be devised whereby compliance with the new act did not mean the demise of the Ladies' Club and that its unbroken history since 1893 should continue. This was the backdrop to our current meeting, which was but an update on the previous one. As a result of the changes to the Club's Constitution agreed at the AGM in March, ladies were now eligible to become Ordinary Members of the Club but, as yet, none had applied and so remained as Associate Members with no voting rights in Club affairs. Bill expressed his approval of Committee's decision to make 31st October the final date in the current year for applications to upgrade from Associate to Full Membership. Among the various equality issues which he wished to discuss were the criteria (or lack of it) for men seeking Associate Membership, the drive by a small number of ladies on membership issues, and the possible erosion of the benefits currently being enjoyed by many lady members. We talked at considerable length on these subjects and I assured him that I would relay our deliberations to the Membership Development Sub-Committee.

I checked with Bill that, in accordance with past precedent, he would say Grace at the forthcoming Annual Dinner. He said that he was prepared to do it once again, but was unhappy about his not being accorded a place at the top table. The Grace has indeed been offered 'from the floor' by previous Honorary Presidents, and without resentment, but I rather agreed with Bill's sentiments and thought it only proper that the post of Honorary President should be duly acknowledged; so I arranged for a place to be provided.

Friday, 8th October: Male Associate Membership

I was aware that Secretary Tom had already issued offers of Associate Membership to a small number of gentlemen but, in light of the concerns intimated to me by Honorary President Bill, and having conversed with Vice-Captain Alan and John Errington, I requested Tom to refrain from issuing any more offers until the situation had been reviewed.

. . . . 8th: Letter to Roy Bulmer
Having obtained Committee's agreement to making courtesy tee-times available to members of Wallasey Golf Club, I completed the draft of my letter to Roy Bulmer informing him of the offer and also thanking him for the hospitality that I had received during my recent visit to Wirral.

Saturday, 9th October: Complaint re Junior Room
Over the years the Club has always had a thriving Junior Section; predominately consisting of boys, but with a few girls among its number. The Club Constitution defines Juniors as being between the age of ten and eighteen years, and states the permitted maximum number at any one time to be 50. For many years junior members had no facilities within the clubhouse but, as part of alterations and additions to the building carried out in 1997, the Junior Section was allocated a small room on the ground floor. The room itself is of modest proportions and serves only as a changing area and a meeting place where juniors can relax before and after play. A wall board records the names of Junior Captains and Champions, and a display cabinet houses all of their trophies; but there is no locker accommodation. Margaret McLean and her staff provide the same level of cleaning services to the Junior Room as they do to the remainder of the clubhouse, but the juniors themselves are expected to keep the room reasonably tidy. It therefore came as something of a surprise to me to receive an early morning telephone call from Past Captain Don MacLaren informing me that, whilst attending a Rotary dinner in the clubhouse on the previous evening, he had occasion to look into the Junior Room and had found it to be in a very untidy state. As someone who had actively promoted the juniors being accorded better facilities when the clubhouse was renovated, he was dismayed by the apparently careless and slovenly manner in which the facilities were being treated. I went down to the clubhouse and was fortunate to find Vice-Captain Alan and House Convener Gary Tierney already there. By this time the mess had been cleared away, but Gary was able to confirm that Past Captain Don's complaint had been totally justified. Committee subsequently arranged a meeting with representatives of the Junior Section and it was made part of the Junior Captain's responsibilities to ensure that the room was kept tidy and the furnishings treated with care and respect.

Friday, 15th October: Refurbishment completed
The major alteration and extension works that were carried out in 1997 to the Mixed Lounge and Dining Room greatly improved these amenities but, as is only to be expected, the passage of time, and the constant use to which the facilities are subjected, necessitated some remedial action; albeit the rooms have always been well cleaned and maintained, but the decoration and carpeting had become 'tired', and in the intervening years standards of interior lighting and ventilation had moved to a higher level. What had been perfectly acceptable a decade ago was now less than adequate. Thanks to the professional expertise of Past Captain Bill Rae as Special Projects Convener, the main contract and interior design works were completed on programme and the

newly refurbished Mixed Lounge and Dining Room were now re-opened for the use of all members.

Sunday, 17th October: Commemorative round
The first Open Championship was played over Prestwick Links on 17th October 1860. Although entry to that particular competition was restricted to professional players, it is nevertheless regarded as being the inaugural event in the history of the championship. Having attended Prestwick Golf Club's 150th Anniversary celebrations in July, and having been aware of Tom Morris's involvement in the setting up of that first competition, I thought it would be appropriate if St. Nicholas GC commemorated the actual day of the anniversary with an event or function of its own.

'Harris Tweed and Hickories'

(Alan Poole)

Watching Gary Tierney's Approach Shot to the 17th Green

(Alan Poole)

Among various ideas, it had crossed my mind to suggest organising a golf competition over twelve holes (possibly using hickory shafted clubs), a putting competition (which would thus accommodate any elderly or infirm members), or even a celebratory dinner in recognition of our own association with Tom Morris and Charlie Hunter. The ongoing refurbishment works made all of these ideas impractical since the Mixed Lounge was crucial to each of the events and, of course, the remaining resources of the clubhouse were already being fully utilised. Nevertheless, I was keen that a token commemoration be observed of what was a singularly significant date, and I enquired of Vice-Captain Alan and House Convener Gary whether they would wish to join me in privately marking the occasion. My suggestion was that we use clubs from my own collection to enact the various eras of The Open Championship; I would play with a set of hickory shafted clubs as representing the first 70 years, Alan would use steel shafted Tom Stewart clubs of 1930's vintage to represent the next 25 years, and the pre-metal wood era would be celebrated by Gary playing with Dai Rees New Master clubs of 1950s vintage. Happily, both Alan and Gary were enthusiastic about sharing the experience with me and we arranged to meet at noon when we knew the first tee was likely to be quiet. Suitably attired, and without preliminaries, we set out on the course for our little adventure, armed with clubs that were both unfamiliar and unforgiving, but fortified by the knowledge of a hip flask from which to drink a toast at the tenth tee. We played off the medal tees and recorded our best-ball score at each hole. Alan and Gary entered into the spirit of the event with their accustomed good humour and were philosophical as to the rare mixture of superb and mediocre shots that was uncharacteristic of their normal play. A best-ball score of 78 was somewhat higher than I had expected but, with only a modicum of practice beforehand, that return might easily have been reduced by four or five strokes – or so I would like to believe!

Tuesday, 19th October: John Gray cleek heads

Tradition and history cannot be bought, but a good reputation can be lost in an instant. Not perhaps the most original of thoughts on my part but something which I believe every Captain should have uppermost in his mind when considering his responsibility as guardian of the Club during his term of office. The St. Nicholas Club is blest with having a rich heritage dating back to its establishment in 1851, when Tom Morris and a group of artisans founded what they called the Mechanics' Club and played over the links of Prestwick Golf Club. By 1858 most of its members were either businessmen or from a professional background, and the original name was considered to be no longer appropriate. At the AGM of that year it was decided that the name be changed to 'St. Nicholas Golf Club'; after the saint with whom the town of Prestwick has ancient associations. The present course was acquired in 1892, and for the next 50 years the Club was famed for producing players of national and international repute and for hosting competitions and matches involving the leading professional and amateur golfers of the day. But the Club's reputation extended beyond having Tom Morris as a founder member, or of James Robb having won the Amateur Championship in 1906. In John Gray it not only had another founder member, but it had a man who was destined to be the finest cleekmaker in the West of Scotland. Examples of his craft are much prized by collectors of golfing memorabilia, and quite unexpectedly the Club received an offer from one of his descendants, Ian Morton, to make a long-term loan of two cleek heads which had been forged by John Gray. Ian had recently visited his mother in New Zealand and, whilst there, had been given them with a view to seeing whether they would be of interest to the Club. She told him that the shafts had been removed to make them easier to pack when the family had first moved to New Zealand! Needless to say the Club was happy to accept this offer, and the heads are now suitably displayed in the clubhouse.

Thursday, 21st October: Committee match v Prestwick GC

In addition to the annual match with Turnberry Golf Club, Committee has a similar fixture with our friends in Prestwick Golf Club. Not only had it been my good fortune to be involved in the 150th Anniversary Celebrations of The Open Championship and to have participated in the Prestwick Rosebowl event, but it befell Prestwick to host this year's fixture. As is the Prestwick manner, lunch is taken in the grand Dining Room prior to the golf match, and one is liberally supplied with generous measures of Kummel before setting out on the links. This undoubtedly ensures the conviviality of the meeting but, as an opponent, one suspects that it marginally tips the balance of the match in Prestwick's favour. Peter Graham, the Club Chairman, acted as host and welcomed everyone to the afternoon's proceedings. The weather conditions were cold and dull but, thankfully, there was no suggestion of rainfall. Playing in the first game, Peter and his partner, Graham Bell, outplayed Alan and myself to the tune of 7 and 6, but our dignity was salvaged by others in our team and the match was drawn at two games each. Back in the clubhouse we enjoyed a post-match refreshment in the Smoke Room and I spoke a few words on behalf of the St. Nicholas party.

Chairman Peter, Gentlemen of Prestwick Golf Club:

On behalf of the Committee of Prestwick St. Nicholas, I wish to thank you for the hospitality shown to us today. It is always a great pleasure to experience the conviviality of your clubhouse and to enjoy playing upon your fine links.

Our thoughts are with your Captain, Brian Morrison, as he traverses the Spanish countryside; although I suspect that we are far from his own thoughts at this moment.

We of St. Nicholas are particularly pleased to find that Ian Bunch was selected for your team today. In light of his imminent retirement, this has given us the opportunity to say;

'Thank you, Ian, for all the assistance and support that you have given to us over the years. You have helped maintain the happy relationship which our clubs enjoy, and we acknowledge your promotion of tourism in this area with the introduction of Scotland's West Coast Golf Links, and the Prestwick Pass; two items that have been of considerable benefit to all three Prestwick clubs. We also commend you for your contribution to the planning and success of the celebrations marking the 150th Anniversary of The Open Championship; that was a magnificent weekend. Ian, you have been a good friend of St. Nicholas, and we wish you well in your retirement.'

As to the match itself, I shall say nothing of individual performances; suffice to note that, much to the relief of some of us, the match was drawn. I consider this to be a very happy outcome.

Next year's match will be played at St. Nicholas, and we shall look forward with anticipation to once again meeting up with our good friends from Prestwick Golf Club.

Friday, 22nd October: Annual Dinner

Among the various golf clubs in Ayrshire has evolved a set pattern as to the timing of each club's

Annual Dinner & Presentation of Trophies, and as to the representatives invited to the respective functions. This is a very practical arrangement which ensures that there is no clashing of dates and allows prospective guests to plan in advance. Of the circle of five clubs in which St. Nicholas operates for this purpose, our dinner is first on the rota and is generally held in the latter part of October. The evening commences with a private reception for our invited guests in the Tom Morris Room, followed by dinner in the Mixed Lounge.

(Prestwick St Nicholas Golf Club)

Annual Dinner and Presentation of Trophies 2010
From left: *Jamie Murray (The Irvine GC), Bill McFarlan, Bill Rae, David Miller (Kilmarnock (Barassie) GC), David McPherson (Troon Portland GC), Gordon Gilchrist, Ian Logan (Prestwick St. Cuthbert GC), Gene O'Donoghue (Prestwick GC), Alan Poole*

Before commencing the meal, I briefly introduced the top table persons to the assembled company; and upon its completion, continued with my duties as Chairman.

Honoured Guests, President Bill, Past Captains, Gentlemen:

It is my pleasant duty to introduce to you a very good friend of St. Nicholas Golf Club who has generously agreed to propose the toast to our Club.

It strikes me that there is something of a conundrum in asking someone to propose a toast to oneself. The essence of such a toast, at least as I understand it, is that it is something that is offered rather than invited; so one needs to be very sure that any invitee shares one's own enthusiasm for the subject.

In that regard, this evening we are on firm ground.

Eugene O'Donoghue, or Gene as he is affectionately known, is someone with whom we have a close affinity, and it is always a pleasure to have him in our midst.

As I said in my earlier introduction, Gene is a Past Captain of Prestwick Golf Club, but his early influences are all south of the border. I assume that Golf was always destined to be one of his passions. After all, he was born in Hoylake; home of Royal Liverpool Golf Club, several times a venue for The Open Championship and other major events, and the club which produced the first non-Scottish Open Champion.

He was educated at Stonyhurst College in the Ribble Valley, where he and his collegiate peers refer to themselves as 'OS' – Old Stonyhurst. I shall not attempt to draw any parallels between that college and Prestwick Acadamy, save to say that the college has its own 9-hole golf course tucked away within its grounds. A fellow OS of Gene's, although of an earlier generation, is one George Walker, who became President of United States Golf Association and who donated a trophy for the bi-annual match between the Amateurs of Great Britain and United States, viz. the Walker Cup.

Purely as an aside, the same George Walker is respectively the grandfather and great-grandfather of two US Presidents, George Bush and his son George W.

Gentlemen, without further ado, I would ask you to welcome Gene to propose the toast to Prestwick St. Nicholas Golf Club.

Gene, as always, spoke genially and complimentary; Vice-Captain Alan replied on behalf of the Club; Past Captain Bill proposed a toast to the guests; and Ian Logan replied on the latter's behalf. It then behove me to introduce Bill McFarlan.

And now, Gentlemen, we come to our Guest Speaker. Someone who contributed regularly to a variety of diverse publications, and who became a 'well kent' face on our television screens. Whether on news items, magazine programmes, sports reports or the like, Bill McFarlan's name and the sound of his voice were never far from the scene. He projected an aura of decency and fair mindedness, of reasoned argument and clarity of thought – and despite these qualities still managed to succeed in the mad world of journalism and broadcasting. And today he continues to be to the fore, not just in broadcasting, but as a media consultant and author.

I can assure my colleagues at the top table that there is no substance to the rumour that Bill is having tonight's event secretly recorded so that it can be used in one of his training courses.

Gentlemen, I would ask you to give a very warm welcome to our guest speaker, Mr. Bill McFarlan.

Bill delivered an interesting and entertaining account of his experiences in journalism and broadcasting, suitably interspersed with humorous anecdotes, and concluded with details of his current involvement in media consultancy. With ample references to his time presenting football and golf programmes on television, his was a major contribution in ensuring the success of the evening.

Tuesday, 26th October: Meeting re equality issues

For almost the entire period of its existence, Ladies' St. Nicholas Golf Club has enjoyed a harmonious relationship with what it quaintly refers to as the Parent Club. Over the years issues arose which required to be resolved, accommodations made and rules reviewed but, generally speaking, the two clubs co-existed to their mutual benefit. When the Ladies' Club lost the tenancy of its own course in 1936, it was afforded increased playing rights on the Gents' course, and the clubhouse was extended to incorporate a lounge, locker room and toilets for the ladies, all of which facilities were upgraded in subsequent improvement works. The Ladies' Club has no direct responsibility with regards to the management of the course and clubhouse; is largely autonomous in that it has its own committee; receives an annual allocation of funds to run its affairs; organises its own competitions; and its members pay a lesser annual subscription than their male counterparts. And so the advent of the Equality Bill raised questions as to how its implementation would affect the current arrangements and alter the historical character of the Club. It was my hope, one shared by President Bill, that the Club's legal obligations might be achieved without recourse to disbanding the Ladies' Club and that the rights of any lady members who wished to retain their current status as Associate Members would be preserved. As one of the country's oldest ladies clubs, we wished to see its continuance within the ambit of Prestwick St. Nicholas Golf Club. There were many convoluted, indeed contradictory, issues to be addressed and these were the very matters which it was the remit of the Membership Development Sub-Committee to consider. In summary, the sub-committee was seeking to achieve a solution whereby any ladies wishing to become Ordinary Members could be so upgraded, but all ladies, whether Ordinary or Associate Members, would automatically be members of the retained Ladies' St. Nicholas Golf Club. For ladies upgrading to Ordinary Membership and acquiring full voting rights, it would mean having dual membership on one subscription.

In my opinion, the Club's aspirations were respectful of the ladies and of the historical significance of their club's existence. There was no doubting that many awkward issues regarding the initial monetary and practical implications of instituting changes had yet to be resolved, but without goodwill and forbearance the process could prove to be divisive. Sadly that was beginning to become apparent in the tone and content of correspondence being received by Secretary Tom. As a result of these developments Tom, Vice-Captain Alan, Membership Convener Robin and I had a lengthy afternoon meeting to consider Management Committee's response to the questions and comments emanating from the Ladies' Club.

. . . . 26th: Visited Robin Boyd

Secretary Tom had previously informed me that on Thursday of last week Past Captain Robin Boyd had slipped on the wooden sleepers at the 2nd Hole and had sustained a broken ankle. It had become apparent in recent times that golf shoes with soft spikes were liable to skid on wet sleepers, and that appeared to be the case in this instance. I visited Robin at his home and he confirmed that this had indeed been the cause of his fall. He told me that he had been taken to Ayr Hospital immediately following the accident and that there was the possibility of his bones requiring to be pinned together. Little prospect of winter golf for Robin this year!

Thursday, 28th October: Archie Thomson driver

Since assuming the Captaincy I regularly visited Secretary Tom in his office, and I had periodic chats with President Bill. The other key person in my estimation of priorities was the Head Greenkeeper, John MacLachlan, and I made a point of calling in at his workshop on a monthly basis to have an informal chat. On this visit I told John of the little commemorative round that Alan, Gary and I had played recently and mentioned that I had used a driver bearing the name of a previous professional at Girvan Golf Club. Knowing that John is a member at Girvan was the sole reason for my using that particular club on the day, so imagine my surprise when John told me that the name of the former Girvan professional was Alec Thomson, not Archie. Had I known that in advance I would certainly have used a club more suited to my purposes as that one was shorter than any of my other drivers, its having been owned by a lady golfer. This revelation set me off on a quest to discover the actual maker of the club, and I have concluded that it was almost certainly the Machrihanish professional, Archie Thomson; father of the 1936 Amateur Champion, Hector.

. . . . 28th: Committee meeting
This meeting proved to be one of historical significance in that it sanctioned the first transfer of ladies from Associate to Ordinary Membership of the Club. The fact that Mara Lindsay and Rosalind Purdom had shown sufficient faith in the Club's intentions as to apply for full membership, despite the minutiae of the transfer arrangements being as yet unresolved, was welcomed by the Management Committee and the announcement of their successful applications was greeted with spontaneous applause. In recognition of their new status, and of the unique place which they had created for themselves in the recorded history of the Club, I subsequently wrote a personal letter to both of them and welcomed them as the first lady members of what had hitherto been a 'male only' club.

Friday, 29th October: Telephone call from Lady Captain
The complexities and anomalies which arise in relation to the concept and implementation of sexual equality are without limit, as the Membership Development Sub-Committee had so clearly discovered. Nothing alters the fact that males and females are both different and complimentary at one in the same time; that both crave a measure of independence whilst requiring to co-operate for their mutual benefit; that one should not be master of the other; that patience and trust are a necessity if relationships are not to be soured. That at least is my rather simple analysis of the situation; albeit it might be at odds with other people's perception. An early morning telephone call from Lady Captain Eileen illustrated this dichotomy quite succinctly. I was already aware that tonight was Ladies' St. Nicholas Golf Club's Annual Dinner and, as is customary, arrangements were made by Secretary Tom for a basket of flowers to be presented to the Lady Captain. Eileen's call was to inform me that the Gents Captain usually provides a welcome drink for the ladies on their arrival at the Dinner, and she was enquiring as to whether I had attended to that matter. No one had previously advised me of this protocol, but I accepted it in good faith and arranged with the bar staff that a sufficient number of bottles of wine be supplied at my personal expense. Interpret my action as you will, but this little episode encapsulated the absurdity of the situation. For the previous four months Eileen and her committee had been less than complimentary of the Club's deliberations over the terms of transfer for lady members but, critical or not, as Lady Captain she instinctively assumed that old-fashioned civilities and courtesies still applied in this new world of sexual equality.

. . . . 29th: Prestwick St. Cuthbert GC Annual Dinner
Past Captain Jim Pettigrew had long asserted that there are two distinct periods in a Captain's term of office, *viz.* the playing season, followed by the cholesterol season. And I was now about to embark upon the latter, having been afforded a precursor at our own dinner of the previous week. As is customary at the St. Cuthbert Dinner, it fell to me as St. Nicholas Captain to reply to the Toast to the Guests, and that rather concentrated my mind in the days preceding the dinner and throughout the meal itself. Until one has gained the necessary experience and confidence of addressing an audience, it can prove somewhat difficult to do proper justice to the proffered meal and to relax

during the accompanying conversation; nervous tension lingers just below the surface as one endeavours to project an air of composure and self-assurance befitting a captain.

The chauffeur driven limousine, which conveyed Sir John Craig to Colville's Steel Works in the 1950s, used to drive past Shields Glen as I stood waiting at the bus stop on my way to high school. Although the sight of its passing was a familiar occurrence, there was something magical each time it appeared round the bend and Sir John could be seen in the rear seat reading, what I presumed to be, *The Glasgow Herald*. Being driven personally to one's office conferred and confirmed, or so it seemed to me, a very special status on the person involved and was a tangible expression of the regard in which that person was held. Such dizzy heights of recognition were far beyond anything to which I aspired in life, but the provision of a taxi by St. Cuthbert Golf Club to transport me to and from the function was my equivalent experience; and I was thrilled!

Following a preliminary reception, the meal and presentation of trophies, the subsequent proceedings were chaired by Captain Billy Gibson. Jimmy Forrest, Past Captain of Prestwick Golf Club, proposed the toast to Prestwick St. Cuthbert Golf Club, Billy replied, and then Vice-Captain Graeme McGartland proposed a toast to the guests. Thereupon all eyes turned towards me as I prepared for my baptism as an 'after-dinner' speaker outwith the confines of the St. Nicholas clubhouse!

Thank you, Graeme, for such an illuminating toast:

It is always gratifying to learn that a guest's personal details have been carefully vetted before being revealed to the sensitive ears of a golf club audience. St. Cuthbert as a club has always had a reputation for being the very soul of discretion in such matters, and I for one am extremely relieved to find that it is still adhering to that principle. I can only presume that Mr George Reynolds was not consulted in this instance, otherwise the content might have been decidedly different.

Captain Billy, Gentlemen:

In replying on behalf of the guests, it strikes me that the occasion is somewhat reminiscent of the scene outside Glasgow High Court when a tall, balding, bespectacled solicitor, with a 'difficult to place' Scottish accent, issues a previously prepared statement on behalf of his clients.

Let me assure you at the outset, that there is a certain irony in my being asked to reply on behalf of the other guests. It might infer that I am the most accomplished to perform this duty, but indeed they are all more than capable of speaking up for themselves. It might infer that I am considered to be the most eloquent but, as you are about to find out, that is hardly the case. It could perhaps even be that I am considered to be the most gullible – and that may very well be closer to the truth. However, I rather suspect that the logic of inviting only one guest to reply on behalf of all, ensures that as little time as possible is taken up before the unrestricted consumption of a popular beverage can begin.

Over the past couple of years, the St. Cuthbert Club has enjoyed a fair degree of success and I see from the honours boards and the silverware, testament to the Club's and to individual members' achievements. Many of those names and competitions are familiar to me and, whilst I don't consider myself to be either a particularly jealous or a conceited person, I searched in vain among your displays to find any mention of my name, or even a modest acknowledgement of my contribution to your success. Perhaps I have been deluding myself, but prior to coming along here this evening I harboured the notion that Prestwick St.

Cuthbert recognised me as being something of a talisman. If Gordon Gilchrist is involved, we're sure to be on a winner!

Has John Kirk forgotten that, but for my participation, his name would not be engraved on our inter-club Quaich? Does Willie Murray not recall who refereed the final of the Hugh Boyd Trophy last year? I can perhaps forgive a lapse of memory in these cases. But this year!! Craig Holland and Graeme McGartland had me to thank for St. Cuthbert winning the Quaich; albeit on the night it had been misplaced somewhere along the way between Grangemuir Road and East Road. And as for the Prestwick Rosebowl, I really thought that Billy Gibson and Bobby Cord would have had the decency to acknowledge my part in their success. If my contributions have been overlooked at St. Cuthbert, I can tell you that they are still vividly remembered at St. Nicholas. However, personal disappointment aside, this dinner has been a wonderful occasion.

Captain Billy and Gentlemen of Prestwick St. Cuthbert Golf Club: The friendliness of your welcome, the sumptuous meal, the generosity of your hospitality have been a delight. As guests, we feel privileged to have been invited to this very special event. The happy association which we enjoy among our various clubs is something that we all treasure and, on behalf of Jimmy, John and Hugh, I thank you most sincerely for allowing us to be part of this evening's celebration.

Hugh Brown, a well-known snooker referee, was Guest Speaker and gave an entertaining address. Thereafter Tom Thomson delivered a poignant eulogy on Jim Glass; a much respected member of St. Cuthbert GC whose unstinting contribution to golf and its devotees was recognised throughout Ayrshire, and beyond.

Wallasey 1967

Before the opening drive was struck at The Teacher Senior Professional Golf Tournament over Ayr Belleisle Golf Course in May 1967, all of the competitors knew that the winner would be matched subsequently against Sam Snead for what was generally regarded as the World Senior Championship. The American tournament had been played in Florida some months previously and, from a large field which included a host of famous names, the redoubtable Sam Snead had won for the third time; and by a record margin of nine strokes! The venue for the play-off was the seaside links at Wallasey and the match was scheduled for the Sunday prior to the start of The Open Championship which that week was due to be played nearby at Hoylake. When John Panton rolled in his final putt to win the British event and so set up a match against Sam, I resolved to make the journey down to Cheshire to witness what promised to be an enthralling contest. But how to travel? There was no motorway north of Lancaster and, if memory serves me correctly, the journey south of Lancaster at that time was besought with road works and delays in consequence of the construction of the new M6. I made enquiries as to the availability of trains, and that is how I planned my adventure. At ten minutes to midnight on Saturday 8th July, I boarded a southbound train from Glasgow at Motherwell Railway Station and it stopped at Crewe Junction, from where I caught a 'middle of the night' connection back to Liverpool. I arrived in Lime Street Station shortly after daybreak and to all intents and purposes the streets were deserted. I had to linger about the city centre until such time as the first Sunday morning train left for New Brighton, and it transported me through the Mersey Tunnel to Wallasey Station, from where I walked to the golf course.

I do not recall there being any charge to spectate at the match, but it may have been that the accompanying programme included that cost. The elements were kind to all concerned and conditions were ideal for playing and watching a golf match. There was an air of expectancy among

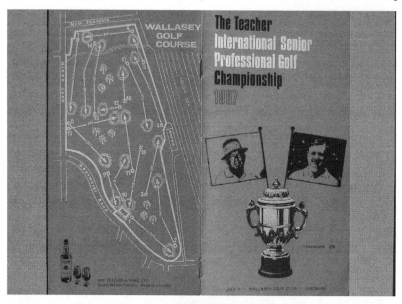

Official Programme and Scorecard

the large crowd which one estimate put at 4000 spectators, but I would have thought that at any one time half that number was probably nearer the mark. Other than a few eminent professionals who had come along to see the encounter, I do not think I came across a single person whom I knew or recognised.

John Panton's opening drive was less than impressive and his ball finished very far to the right of the first fairway, which did not auger well for the future. On the other hand, Sam's drive was ideally positioned for a straight-forward approach to the green. I suspect that I was not alone in being filled with a sense of foreboding at what was about to unfold, but the script had yet to be written! From his unpromising position out in the rough, John managed to scramble a par four, Sam three-putted, John went one up, and for the rest of the outward half John played as a man inspired. Among the many incidents which I remember of these early holes, I think my favourite one is of Dai Rees unobtrusively slipping out of the stream of spectators to give John a quick word of encouragement as he made his way along the fourth fairway. The great Sam Snead was never one to succumb easily and, from being three down at the turn, he squared the match by the 13th Hole. John recaptured the lead, won a further two holes, and then sunk a vital putt on the eighteenth green to ensure that he held a 3-hole advantage going into the second round. Lunch for me was sandwiches taken on a grass verge looking out towards the beach at Wallasey.

The spectators returned for the afternoon round and the match continued in a similar vein to that of the morning. I had always admired John's swing and found it a pleasure just to watch him play. His action could be described as anything from text book to classical; and it was one to be copied. But Sam's was something else! In my experience his was the finest I have ever witnessed; and I have seen many of the acknowledged great players in my time. Everything about his swing was perfect, and all the words that have been written as to its power, its grace, its rhythm, its balance etc. are absolutely true. However, age had inflicted the yips on his putting and he had devised a 'sidewinder' action to counteract them – a method which was subsequently banned. He was employing it at this stage in his career, but on this occasion it was proving to be somewhat unreliable; and that, together with some misjudged approach shots, was a crucial factor in determining the outcome of the match. How different from his form in the US Senior Tournament when he had three-putted only once in 72 holes! John was in a dominant position during most of that second round, but I must recount events at the last hole played; which was the short 16th (or 34th). A hole of just under 200 yards; it required a tee shot that carried all the way from tee to green over low lying ground. Sam was three down but had the honour; and no one was writing off his chances, as earlier in the match he had recovered from a three-hole deficit within the space of three holes. He struck a glorious iron shot which finished about 9 feet from the flag, presenting him with yet another birdie opportunity. John selected a No. 4 wood, and played a majestic shot which not only found the green but settled down within 6 feet of the hole. The animated applause from John's supporters which greeted this result was suffused with relief, and it was with an air of expectation that the crowd headed for the green. Sam simply had to hole his putt or the match was over – and he did! The gallery clapped appreciatively, but the mood among the spectators had changed dramatically. Would John hold his nerve and hole-out for a birdie to win the match, or would we all be heading over to the 17th tee for further drama and suspense? John proved to be more composed than some of his supporters, for he rolled in the putt for a two, thereby halving the hole and becoming World Senior Champion. His was the first British win since Norman Sutton had achieved similar success eight years previously and, by coincidence, over the links at Wallasey.

Sam Snead had the reputation of being a 'hard boiled' character, and he had been less than complimentary towards his caddie at some stages of the match, but at the prize-giving ceremony in front of the clubhouse he was magnanimous in defeat and said of John that he had never played against a more gracious opponent. There was something poignant in that Sam Snead of all people should express so succinctly what countless others felt about the innate integrity of John Panton. As for me, I had the daunting prospect of another overnight train journey back to Scotland!

Chapter 9

November

Wednesday, 3rd November: Visited Margaret McLean

Good housekeeping is the mark of any well-run club whatever its size. And in relation to clubhouse issues such as staff training, property maintenance, financial management and service provision, the expertise and dedication of the various members of the team is paramount. No matter the circumstances, one item in particular is foremost in creating a good impression on members and visitors alike. If it is satisfactory, it may go unnoticed except by a very few but, if it is unsatisfactory, it will be immediately obvious to everyone. I am, of course, referring to the cleanliness of the premises. Nothing is more disappointing on arrival at any establishment than to discover that it is slipshod in its attention to that vital element. For the past two decades Mrs. Margaret McLean has been employed by the Club as its Head Cleaner and she has acquired the whimsical reputation of treating the premises as her own domain. Indeed she projects a formidable presence within the clubhouse and is totally non-phased by whomsoever she encounters. Very sharp of intellect, she has a ready response to whatever is said to her, and the respect and affection which she attracts is recognised throughout the Club. Now in her early eighties, physical frailties are becoming more pronounced but, as long as she is capable of managing her team of helpers, the Club will be happy to retain her in its employ. News of her being unwell and having been taken to Ayr Hospital the previous Friday was met with understandable concern by her many friends and, now that she had returned home, I made a point of visiting her to convey the Club's good wishes for a full and speedy recovery. It was typical of her that her immediate thoughts were of the 'early birds' whom she supplies with tea and toast first thing every morning as they prepare to tee-off soon after daybreak.

Friday, 5th November: Kilmarnock (Barassie) GC Annual Dinner

A certain aura accompanies the prospect of being collected by a taxi ordered by one's host. It rather implies that one's presence is being specifically sought and promotes a wonderful sense of personal well-being. Such were the transport arrangements for my attendance at the Annual Dinner of Kilmarnock (Barassie) Golf Club and, prior to the taxi arriving and throughout the journey, I was in the most buoyant of moods. This kindly gesture by the host club once again emphasised to me the privilege and responsibility of being Captain of St. Nicholas Golf Club. The fact that I was not required to render an 'after dinner' speech contributed greatly to my anticipation of enjoying the proceedings, and the provision of a taxi to take me home was the portent of a convivial evening. An Islay malt at the Guests' Reception set the mood for social intercourse, and it was good to meet with captains from clubs outwith the St. Nicholas circuit, *viz.* Ken Arthur (Royal Troon) and Brian Dennison (Western Gailes). Captain David Miller hosted the dinner and was ably assisted by Secretary/Manager Donald Wilson.

The format of the Kilmarnock Dinner was geared to providing an entertaining evening. Speechifying was confined to the Captain formally introducing the top table guests and to Tommy Wilson's contribution as Guest Speaker. Vice-Captain Douglas Orr compered a golf-orientated quiz and the Presentation of Prizes was divided into two parts on either side of Tommy's speech. Under Captain David's chairmanship, a genial and relaxed atmosphere pervaded the whole event.

Saturday, 6th November: Experimental two-day winter medals

With every passing year, and the steady influx of new members, the demand for more medal play at St. Nicholas is unabated. Many older members would much prefer that the weekends afforded more opportunities to engage in casual golf, but the continuing trend towards medal play now means that throughout the summer months almost every weekend has an organised competition of some kind. And the demand for medal play is now prevalent in the winter months. From November to March each month contains one Saturday Medal and one Wednesday Medal. But shorter daylight hours inevitably mean that fewer places will be available for entrants and some members have expressed their discontent about having difficulty securing a place on the entry sheet for the Saturday Medals. In view of the number of members who had commented upon the situation Committee decided, for a trial period, to experiment with playing winter weekend medals over two days, and today marked the introduction of this venture. For the record, 16 players took part in the Sunday round.

. . . . 6th: Tastes of the World

Ever since the Club engaged Grant Hood as its Catering Manager the members have enjoyed a standard of food comparable with the very best restaurants. As a young chef, he immediately demonstrated a flair and an enthusiasm which transformed the Club's menu, and he set standards of presentation and quality which encouraged members to make the clubhouse their preferred eating place, especially at weekends. One of his specialities has been 'themed' dinners, and these have proved to be very popular. 'Tastes of the World' was his latest offering and he engaged a local pianist to entertain everyone throughout the evening. Jeanette and I arranged to go as a foursome with David Steele and Rhona, and we had a most enjoyable evening. Needless to say the menu was extremely varied and there were dishes on offer representing at least a dozen countries. I was more than satisfied with my selection of haggis, neeps and tatties (Scotland), prawn ticka masala (India), and crepe pancakes (France) – delicious!

Wednesday, 10th November: Visited Alan Hawthorn

One of the most interesting features in *The Golfer's Handbook* of former years was the section dealing with accidents on the course. It is an inherent, if undesirable, aspect of human nature to be fascinated by accounts of misfortunes sustained by others and, as most people will acknowledge, the media often exploits this darker side of the human psyche. It was a combination of the bizarre and the unexpected which made that section so readable and, whilst the subject itself is no longer given such prominence as previously, no amount of health and safety measures will ever succeed in making golf courses a risk-free environment. Many of the accidents that occur are profoundly serious and disturbing, and on occasions totally distressing. So far this year I had been aware of three accidents of varying severity on the St. Nicholas links, and now I was informed of another incident which had occurred yesterday morning. Whilst searching in gorse at the 3rd Hole for a partner's ball, Alan Hawthorn had been struck on the head by a miscued shot played by a member on the hole behind. Thankfully, when I visited Alan at his home, I discovered that his injury was not overly serious, but

I was acutely aware that only providence (and a couple of inches) had stood between him and a catastrophe.

Thursday, 11th November: First interviews

Back in May I had requested Robin Alexander to amend the existing interview procedure in order to make it more meaningful, especially with regard to the input and involvement of each applicant's proposer. My confidence in Robin's judgement was amply rewarded as he produced a format exactly to my requirements, and included some additional features of his own which improved the process even more. Tonight was the inauguration of this new First Interview process and Robin chaired the proceedings. His initial welcome and introductory remarks preceded his calling upon myself as Captain to address the meeting, which included 10 new applicants.

Gentlemen:

There are no doubt a multiplicity of reasons as to why anyone should wish to join a golf club such as St. Nicholas. Perhaps because a relation or friend is already an existing member; maybe due to having recently moved into the district and someone recommended the Club; perhaps having played the course on some previous occasion and enjoyed the experience. Whatever the reason – you are here tonight!

I am inclined to think that the course, particularly its setting, is probably the principal factor in enticing most people to apply for membership. At 6,000 yards it is not too long, but is still a good test of golf. Being on linksland, it has all the benefits that that implies. Good drainage, the prospect of year-round golf, super views over the Firth of Clyde, natural features and hazards commensurate with a seaside course, and variable weather conditions – from balmy days to gale force winds. In our case, we have a first class greenkeeping staff. The course is invariably in good condition, with greens that provide no excuses for missed putts; and well-tended fairways. In fact, a course that attracts important external competitions. Two years ago it hosted the Scotland v England Boys International match; last year it was the venue for the Scottish Club Championship Final; it was one of four courses chosen for the Young Professional Golfers Tournament organised by Rohan Rafferty and, when I tell you that the other three courses were Dunbar, Kingsbarns and the Renaissance Club at Archerfield, you will understand just how highly our course is regarded among those who know their golf. And next year we are co-hosting with Prestwick Golf Club the Scottish Area Team Championship which, by its very nature, will involve every leading amateur player in the country.

Another significant factor for applying is likely to be the Clubhouse facilities. We certainly have good accommodation but like any old building, this one dates from 1892, it has its limitations. At present there is a waiting list both for lockers and for use of the caddie car shed. Over the years the clubhouse has been altered, extended and upgraded, but its essential character has been retained. The general condition and maintenance of our property is overseen by our House Convener.

In recent times the Gents Shower Room has been modernised; the Gents Toilet, the Junior Room, the Rear Hall and Stairway have been refurbished; and only last month the Mixed Lounge and the Dining Room were substantially improved. In that regard we have been fortunate in having had the services of Past Captain Bill Rae who administered the project on the Club's behalf; and we are delighted with the result. Next year it is our intention to refurbish the Tom Morris Room in culmination of what has been a three-year plan of improvements.

Also, within the clubhouse we have first rate catering and bar facilities. We are able to cater for private functions, and many members have made use of the premises for a variety of family events. The food is of a very good standard and we have been complimented upon the quality of the wines on offer.

Another factor in deciding to apply is likely to be one's perception of the existing membership. We like to think that we are egalitarian in our outlook; but in any club consisting of more than 600 members there is a wide variety of characters, and a huge diversity of golfing abilities. However, I believe it is true to say that we can be described as being a generally friendly and welcoming club. One very important change that has taken place recently is the introduction of ladies as full members of the Club: all part of the new Equality legislation. To date two ladies have been admitted, and a third's application is due to be considered at next week's Committee meeting.

For your information, I would like to say a few words regarding the management of the Club. We have a Committee of 12, comprising the Captain and Vice-Captain, the Immediate Past Captain, plus nine Ordinary Members. The Committee is responsible for implementing the business of the Club. I use the word 'business' quite intentionally because, although we are a recreational club, we require to operate on a business-like manner in regard to financial and legal obligations, and as a means of promoting the best interests of our members. Each committee member is allocated an aspect of that business and, as convener, is responsible for dealing with its demands. I don't intend to go into any detail on the matter but, as a means of letting you understand the breadth of the Committee's remit, I shall simply list the various convenerships – all of which are largely self-explanatory, viz. finance, house, management, links, match and handicap, health and safety, juniors, ladies, membership, marketing and social. We employ a professional greenkeeper, and the day-to-day management of the Club is the responsibility of our full-time Club Secretary.

In closing, I shall say a few words relating to the Club's history. It was founded in 1851 and for its first 26 years played over the Prestwick Golf Club links. However, by 1877 the links were becoming so crowded that it was put to the St. Nicholas members that they really needed to find a course of their own. The parting was amicable, and Prestwick Golf Club contributed one half of the total expense incurred in acquiring a new course. It was located in the area now partly occupied by Prestwick Cricket Club, the tennis centre and the indoor bowling arena; and what is now the cricket clubhouse was in fact built originally as our clubhouse. The club remained there until 1892 when it got the opportunity to lease the ground which now constitutes the present course. The original lease was for a period of 20 years, but as time passed the club negotiated individual purchases from the various proprietors and eventually obtained ownership of all the ground in 1923.

There have been many celebrated members over the years, but I shall name only a few. The most distinguished is arguably Tom Morris, who was a founder member and who won The Open Championship on four occasions. There was John Gray, the Club's second captain, who was a local blacksmith and a renowned cleekmaker. Examples of his work are exhibited at the Golf Museum in St. Andrews. He produced the iron heads, and Tom Morris shaped and fitted the hickory shafts and wound on the leather grips; Tom Morris, of course, was a master clubmaker and ballmaker in his own right. As well as having had an Open Champion within our membership, we also had an Amateur Champion; Jimmy Robb won at Hoylake in 1906. Gordon Lockhart won both the Irish and the Scottish Open Amateur Championships, and John Wilson twice won the Scottish Amateur Championship. John was undefeated in his Walker Cup matches and, more recently, Paul Girvan also represented Great Britain in the Walker Cup. In addition to these named, the St. Nicholas Club has produced many internationalist players.

I think by now this is quite enough of the Captain's contribution to this evening's session. I hope that I have given you some indication as to the background and status of the Club to which you have applied for membership; and I shall now invite Robin to introduce the next item on the Agenda.

The nature of this gathering in the privacy of the Tom Morris Room ensured that I had the most attentive and respectful audience that I am ever likely to address. When people are unfamiliar with their surroundings and their fellow listeners, attention levels tend to be so much higher and the proceedings free of interruption. My address, which lasted about eight minutes, allowed me the opportunity to provide a summarised version of the Club's ethos and heritage but, in the context of the meeting, it also gave the new applicants time to assimilate to their situation and to be comfortable among their number. Robin spoke in detail of the Application and Waiting List processes before involving the other members of Committee in interviewing one half of the applicants and their proposers on an individual basis, whilst I provided the remainder with a conducted tour of the clubhouse. Thereafter the two groups were interchanged, and the whole business of the evening took less than 90 minutes.

. . . . 11th: Gordon Hepburn
It is always heartening within a club to find individuals who make a personal contribution to its success through their willingness to give freely of their time, talents or resources. St. Nicholas is blest with several among its number who do just that; and one of these is Gordon Hepburn. For several years Gordon has organised an annual Quiz Evening in which lady and gentlemen members get the opportunity to share in an informal social event that is both fun and competitive. The early darkness, brought about by the return of Greenwich Mean Time and the impending onset of winter, creates a tangible aura which makes this event so welcome at the conclusion of the main golfing season. Gordon's meticulous preparation and the inventiveness of his questions have made this a popular evening among a devoted group of adherents and the event is always eagerly awaited. What a calamity to discover that Committee had arranged to conduct an interview session in the clubhouse on the same evening! Much too late to retract invitations to the interviewees, both events went ahead but, unfortunately, the first guided tour of the clubhouse briefly disrupted the Quiz. It was a most unfortunate intrusion and, mindful of Gordon's personal commitment on the Club's behalf, I subsequently wrote a letter of apology to him.

Friday, 12th November: Troon Portland GC Annual Dinner
Ayrshire is rightly acknowledged as being one of the principal locations in Scotland for links golf. From West Kilbride in the north to Girvan in the south there is a succession of fine courses, each having its own distinctive character and all enjoying a close proximity to the Firth of Clyde. As to the merits of the individual courses, each has its battalion of ardent admirers but, no matter one's preference, the fact remains that all of them are without doubt wonderful locations in which to experience the challenges and exhilaration of seaside golf, and to enjoy the comfort and atmosphere of the clubhouses. And in that context, an invitation to Troon Portland Golf Club's Annual Dinner is an excellent bonus, since the dinner and presentation of trophies are traditionally held in the well-appointed confines of Royal Troon clubhouse, prior to the company retiring to the more intimate

surroundings of Portland's own premises situated 150 yards away. Having substituted for Bill Rae at the previous year's dinner, I was acquainted with the format of the evening and looked forward to it with great anticipation. In the Lounge Bar of Royal Troon GC, and suitably positioned around the blazing fireplace, Captain David McPherson welcomed myself and the other top table guests at a pre-dinner reception before escorting us through to the baronial-style banqueting hall for the meal and presentation of trophies. Captain David formally introduced and welcomed all of the guests, and Ernest Mutter of Royal Troon GC replied on their behalf. Last year was the first time I had entered the portals of this fine club and on that occasion Ernie had given me a personal tour of the clubhouse. I had found that visit to be of great interest and I was totally captivated by the profusion of historical artefacts and memorabilia on display. Following the formalities of the banqueting hall the company adjourned to the Portland clubhouse, and there the evening progressed in a more informal manner. Indeed it was the same jovial affair as I had enjoyed previously and Hugh Brown, as Guest Speaker, ensured that the relaxed and congenial atmosphere of the evening continued well into the night.

Monday, 15th November: Meeting with Hon. President and Vice-Captain

Two and a half months had elapsed since my previous conversation with President Bill and I thought it advantageous that Vice-Captain Alan should join us for a lunchtime meeting. As Convener of the Membership Development Sub-Committee, Alan was in a position to update us on its deliberations and simultaneously to make his own contribution to the various topics which Bill and I invariably debate. Our conversation extended over the whole gamut of current issues relating to the Club; from the implementation of the Equality Bill to the duties of the Club Secretary, from limitations on the number of Associate Members to voting rights at General Meetings, from extension of the joint match secretaries' duties to Constitutional amendments. We spoke openly and candidly to one another in what we considered to be the Club's best interest, and I was satisfied that I had made the correct decision in inviting Alan's involvement as his would be the Captain's responsibility in the very near future.

Thursday, 18th November: First interviews

As usual, Convener Robin chaired and organised this session of interviews. Just as I had done back in May in similar circumstances, I was able to deliver my address to the company without reference to notes, and I felt so much more comfortable in doing so. Practice makes perfection, or so it is said, but it certainly breeds confidence. Must make a mental note to apply that dictum to my golf! Afterwards Robin, Vice-Captain Alan and I spoke about membership issues, and Robin produced a very comprehensive paper for consideration as to the way forward.

Friday, 19th November: Letter from Wallasey

In response to my letter to Wallasey Golf Club offering courtesy tee-times, I received a delightful letter from John Connolly on behalf of The Stableford Society. He informed me that a group of Wallasey members had recently obtained permission from the club to institute a society in memory of Dr. Frank Stableford who had been an active member of Wallasey Golf Club when he devised the popular scoring system which now bears his name. Indeed, Dr. Stableford stated that his idea of the points system which we now employ actually occurred to him in the latter part of 1931 whilst he was on the 2nd fairway at Wallasey golf course. John wrote to say that my letter had been passed onto the Society and that it would be very interested in taking up my suggestion of playing a match against St. Nicholas members.

. . . . 19th: Italian weekend
In his continuing quest to attract members to utilise the clubhouse, especially outwith the main golfing season, Grant organised two consecutive evenings on an Italian theme. Jeanette and I opted to go along to the first of these with our good friends Andrew Taylor and Annette. In total there were about 30 diners, and yet again the fare on offer was varied and very much up to Grant's usual high standard. The following evening proved to be even more popular and Grant was able to report that in the region of 80 persons had chosen to make the clubhouse their preferred venue for that weekend's enjoyment.

Tuesday, 23rd November: SGU/SLGA seminar
The Club had received an invitation to be represented at a seminar being organised jointly by the Scottish Golf Union (SGU) and the Scottish Ladies' Golfing Association {SLGA}. Lady Captain Eileen and John Errington, a member of the Membership Development Sub-Committee, joined with me in attending on the Club's behalf. The seminar, which was being held at Kilmarnock (Barassie) Golf Club, was an 'all day' event focussing on the current management and financial issues with which all clubs were having to contend. The principal topics under consideration related to membership marketing, legislation, handicapping and golf tourism, and I thought it important that we learn how other clubs were dealing with these items. I was particularly interested to hear what advice might be given by SGU/SLGA representatives with regards to implementation of the Equality Act 2010. The presentation was very comprehensive but, when legislation was being discussed, Eileen rather took aback John and myself by raising some points which could leave no one in doubt as to her dissatisfaction with our Club's approach to the equality issue. However, she failed to find any other delegates similarly minded and, as a consequence of their responses, I was reassured in my opinion that we were dealing with the matter in a responsible and measured fashion.

Thursday, 25th November: Committee meeting
Prior to the monthly Management Committee meeting, I met with the Membership Development Sub-Committee to learn of the draft proposals which Robin and Alan had prepared for its consideration. Unfortunately two members of the sub-committee were more intent upon debating details rather than approving the broad framework which Robin and Alan were trying to establish and, consequently, little progress was made on the agenda. At the Management Committee meeting which followed, two more ladies had their applications for Ordinary Membership approved, *viz.* Lady Captain Eileen and Vice-Captain Elaine.

Monday, 29th November: Water seepage in Shower Room
It may prove to be a rash statement that the status attributed to a golf club is often commensurate with the quality of its lavatory facilities, but it is certainly a useful rule of thumb. Not that

attractiveness is necessarily a measure of worth, for even the most modest of clubhouses often has a value that is incalculable in regard to the life of the community in which it is located. In former days, especially in village and rural situations, clubhouses were but a place where golfers could change their clothing, keep their clubs in a locker and have access to a sink. If social contact other than the actual playing of the game was involved, the golfers would retire to the local hostelry and enjoy one another's company in its comfortable surroundings. Over the years as clubs expanded and standards altered, most clubs extended or rebuilt their clubhouse so that it became the place where members met, not just to play golf, but to socialise as well. To a greater or lesser extent dependent upon individual circumstances, clubs introduced bars and kitchen amenities whereby the whole concept of being a club was then enshrined within the clubhouse itself and it became the primary locus for club activities and social contact. Members of St. Nicholas GC have been well-provided for in that respect ever since the Club erected its existing clubhouse in 1892, and in the intervening years upgrading and alterations were made in conjunction with the ever-improving standards in the design and performance of welfare facilities. Only four years previously the Gents Shower Room had been completely renovated to provide the very best in sanitary accommodation and members were unanimous in their approbation of the new installations. Unfortunately, in recent weeks, signs of water seepage from some loose joints in the floor tiles had become apparent and Committee agreed that the cause should be investigated and the tiling rectified.

'Where there's muck, there's brass!' is an old saying; but where there's water where it shouldn't be, there's trouble! And so it proved to be. Committee had hoped that the Shower Room might only be closed for a few days whilst floor tiles were lifted and re-laid/renewed but, when the Contractor commenced his investigations, it soon became apparent that the solution to the problem of the loose floor tiles and the water seepage was more complex than initially envisaged. It was discovered that there was a basic fault in the design of the junction between the shower trays and the cubicle walls; which accounted for the ingress of water into the sub-floor. The question was no longer just one of remedying the fault; it now entailed establishing the extent of damage that had occurred to the fabric of the building as a result of prolonged water penetration. 'Closure for a few days' had now developed into 'closure for an indeterminate period'!

Unplanned Obsolescence

Whether or not an admirer of Prime Minister Harold Wilson, it is surely unthinkable that anyone could fail to acknowledge the iconic status afforded to his 1963 speech referring to the white heat of technological change. Advancement in all spheres of technical and scientific study is the very essence of human endeavour, but the effects of such changes are not always speedily incorporated into everyday life and often involve a long period of transition before they become universally available or accepted. Sudden change, whether welcomed or otherwise, generally results in an acute awareness of the altered circumstances, whereas a gradual change may be so unobtrusive that only on hindsight do many of the consequences become apparent. Not that golf equates to the dramatic context of that political speech, but the tenuous association drifted into my mind as I reminisced upon former days and recalled items that were once so familiar as to be taken for granted; and which quietly disappeared like melting snow. The unlikely item which set me off on this train of thought was, of all things, the golf mitt! And here arises yet another example of how the meaning and use of some words and phrases have changed over the years – and not just in golf! In modern terminology, especially when influenced by American usage, 'mitt' and' mitten' are often applied interchangeably when referring to a thermal-lined glove which encases the fingers separately from the thumb (similar to a boxing glove) and is designed to keep hands warm, especially in winter conditions. But the golf mitt to which I refer was for a completely different purpose; it was worn to provide a firm grip of the club as an alternative to the golf glove, and comprised to all intents and purposes of a smooth backless glove with the fingers cut off at the first joint beyond the palm of the hand, but with the thumb left intact. The mitt had leather pads on the ball of the thumb and on each of the truncated fingers to coincide with the pressure points where the club was gripped, and a press-stud secured it at the wrist. In my early days I much preferred wearing a mitt rather than a glove and, as I record these thoughts, it occurs to me that I was then using mostly hickory shafted clubs; and that might have accounted for my choice. Certainly, I felt my grip to be more secure when my finger-tips were uncovered, but I eventually changed over to the soft wafer-thin golf gloves that had appeared on the market; and the mitt disappeared from the golf stockist's shelves without my ever noticing that it had gone!

The sponge ball-cleaner used to be a common attachment on most bags of amateur golfers and, prior to setting out on a round, a few seconds were needed to seek out a water tap (or a puddle) and to moisten the sponge. If a piece of soap was available, all the better – as a quick rub over it improved the effectiveness of the wet sponge when cleaning the ball. There were various designs of ball washer, some with a flap to close off the sponge, but most popular was the one with a red rubber casing in the shape of an upturned bowl and which had a broad outer rim to prevent the wet sponge from falling out. It was about 3 inches (76 mm) in diameter and had a cord for attaching it to the golf bag. An additional feature of the casing was the provision of six holes into which, for convenience, tee pegs could be fitted. With many golf clubs now installing more elaborate course furniture, especially free-standing ball cleaning units at every teeing ground, the need for the old-style personal sponge cleaner is fast receding.

In order to prevent feet slipping whilst making a stroke, it was Harry Vardon's advice that nails with round heads, each about the size of a small pea, should be driven into the shoe – twenty-five on the sole and fourteen on the heel! The rubber golf shoes with which I started the game had at least thirteen studs on each shoe; my first pair of leather shoes, Stylo Matchmakers purchased about 1965, had seven steel screw-in spikes on the soles and four on the heels. Until fairly recently, the 'clip-clop' sound of golfers walking over concrete paving slabs in the vicinity of the clubhouse was a regular occurrence, especially at professional events (before the introduction of courtesy buggies) when this self-created fanfare was a fitting introduction as each competitor walked among spectators on his way to the first tee. Alas, the new soft spikes will never emulate the ringing tone of metal spikes in generating an atmosphere of dramatic expectation and heroic combat. Just imagine the Changing of the Guard at Buckingham Palace being performed in soft spikes! But now the trusty metal spikes are in danger of disappearing from the golfing scene. Many courses have already banned their use on the pretext that soft spikes are less damaging to the greens – and that is likely to prove a potent factor in determining their future prospects.

Manufacturers of leather goods have had a long association with golf, and still do, but this was particularly evident before the advent of synthetic fibres and other man-made alternatives. The list of golfing items that were made of leather was quite extensive and included golf bags, club head covers, grips, shoes, gloves, scorecard holders and various other accessories; not forgetting the outer casing of the old feather golf balls! With regards to club grips, leather is still available, but the

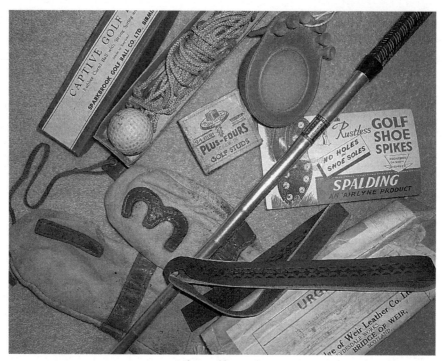

A few golfing relics

continuous improvements made in the manufacture of one-piece sleeve grips since their introduction in the 1950s hastened the demise of the old-style Kinghorn Tacky Grip and other similar strips, which were designed to be wound round the club. When fitted by a golf professional these wound grips were a work of art, their being tacked at the top to a timber plug attached to the steel shaft, and secured at the bottom with a plastic sleeve. A new grip immediately transformed the whole feel and appearance of the club, and it is no coincidence that some of the modern sleeve grips are designed to replicate the features of the very best wound leather grips.

If the demise or the decline in the availability of golf mitts, ball cleaners, metal spikes and leather grips are symptomatic of the evolutionary process, they are but of periphery significance in comparison with the changes that have taken place in the manufacture of golf clubs, both in woods and in irons. Aluminium shafts were introduced as an alternative to tempered stainless steel in the mid-1960s, but they did not attract the high level of acceptance required to sustain their manufacture and they were withdrawn after a few years. About the same time graphite shafts first became available and I associate Hedley Muscroft, then professional at Moor Allerton Golf Club, as being one of their principal proponents. New manufacturing techniques were developed which allowed the shape of iron heads to be substantially changed and the hitherto basic simple designs were soon superseded by what were described as cavity-back heads; all in the name of making the game easier for everyone! But in terms of finally eliminating hand craftsmanship from the golf professional's unique skills, the introduction of the metal-wood completed that process. Although smaller metal-woods had been in circulation for some years earlier, it was the arrival in the early 1990s of drivers with bulbous hollow heads made of Titanium that brought about the eclipse of what had been for many years the traditional shape and size of wooden headed clubs. No longer would the club professional be engaged at his workbench in producing a set of woods to order, in replacing a soleplate or renewing a plastic insert; no more would he display his skill in putting on new whipping or re-varnishing a club head – the age of standard spare parts and screw adjustments had finally arrived!

Chapter 10

December

Eight months of my term of captaincy have now been completed and for the first time my thoughts turn to the prospect of demitting office at the end of March. How odd that only now do I reflect as to what were my aims and aspirations when I accepted the nomination! In truth, I never did compile a list of items that I wished to address. Rather I had a notion as to my style of captaincy, which I hoped would meet with the members' approval, and a determination that I should be worthy of the office. As to specific items that I intended to confront, these were very much in my mind; but so few as to render making a list unnecessary. My first priority was to ensure that there was a substantial reduction in the duration of Management Committee meetings. In previous years, having commenced at 7pm, these had regularly lasted until 10.15pm, and occasionally far beyond, which to my mind put too much strain on all concerned and made committee work feel more like a chore rather than a fulfilling experience. Secondly, having attended several of the interview evenings for prospective new members, I was aware that the current format was far removed from what had been my previous conception, and I resolved to return it to more traditional ways. I was also very conscious that the continuing spread of gorse over the course was, in my opinion, adversely altering the character of some holes whereby, for elderly and less-gifted players, it was detracting from their enjoyment of the game. It was also my intention to establish a dialogue with our Honorary President, as it appeared to me that the incumbent of that position should be afforded more involvement with the current Captain than perhaps had recently been the case. Other than these items, my way ahead would be governed by issues as they arose. Regrettably, at this advanced stage, some unwelcome ones were about to arise over the next few weeks.

Friday, 3rd December: Annual Dinner Dance

There is little doubt that for many years the Annual Dinner Dance has been perceived as being the highlight of the Club's social calendar. Without fail the prospect of an enjoyable evening in formal attire, with ladies in their most attractive dresses or ball gowns, gents in dinner suits (and a few in highland wear), a sumptuous buffet, a live band to encourage constant occupation of the dance floor, and the jolly intercourse of the whole company, ensured that the event is always a sell-out; so much so that many of the revellers have to be accommodated in the adjacent Dining Room. The Dinner Dance also constitutes an opportunity for the Club to extend its hospitality to representatives of the neighbouring clubs with whom it has a close relationship and, in some measure, to foster genuine friendship among the various office bearers. The social atmosphere created at such a function is quite different to that experienced at a formal dinner or at a meal following inter-club matches. The latter often promote a sense of camaraderie and a shared passion for golf, but the dinner dance tends to be more liberating, and guests often show a personal side to their lives and character which otherwise would never be revealed. Instead of golf talk, the conversation ranges from families and holidays to employment and shared interests; spouses add anecdotes and wine stimulates the conversation. And so acquaintances become friends. As the Tom Morris Room is utilised to display and serve the buffet meal, the Guests' Reception is held upstairs in the Ladies Lounge. By tradition, all of the assembled members and their partners are seated and ready to applaud the top-table party whenever it makes its way downstairs from the reception and enters the Mixed Lounge; and the Captain responds appropriately.

Ladies and Gentlemen:
Thank you for the warmth of your welcome. For many within our Club, tonight is one of the highlights of our social calendar and this is reflected in the numbers attending – for every ticket has been sold.

This is not an occasion for speech making, but I cannot let this opportunity pass without thanking my social convener, Bobby Hodge, for his commitment and enthusiasm throughout the year in organising events such as this; and a word of thanks too to all others who have helped towards making everything a success.

A few weeks ago, my wife and I were at the Theatre Royal in Glasgow where we attended a performance of the ballet, Swan Lake. It was a full house and the only seats we could get were those with a restricted view in the upper circle. Tonight's function is also a sell-out and many of you have a restricted view – and some of you have no view at all! Nevertheless, if I may, I would wish to introduce to you those at the top table.

At the head of the table, from Kilmarnock (Barassie) Golf Club. Captain David and his wife, Sheena.
And anti-clockwise round the table; our Lady Captain Eileen and her husband, Wilson.
Our Vice-Captain Alan, and his wife Gail.
From Turnberry Golf Club, Vice-Captain Norrie and his wife, Clare.
From Prestwick St. Cuthbert Golf Club, Vice-Captain Graeme and his wife Karen.
And finally my own inspiration and personal motivator, my wife Jeanette.
In closing, it only remains for me to wish all of you a most enjoyable evening.

Saturday, 4th December: The Irvine Golf Club Annual Dinner

After having enjoyed a superb evening at our own dinner dance, Past Captain Jim Pettigrew's reference to the cholesterol season was again in my thoughts as I set out to represent the Club at The Irvine Golf Club's Annual Dinner and Presentation of Prizes. Lest anyone assumes that I am forgetful of my wife when I attend these dinners, let it be known that I booked a table for Jeanette and her sister, Susan, that they might have an evening meal at the St. Nicholas clubhouse. However, my destination was Irvine and I dropped off my wife and sister-in-law *en route* to the dinner. The course and clubhouse are located in Bogside and the club is often loosely referred to as Irvine Bogside; whereas the members are jealous of its proper name, The Irvine Golf Club. It is a club to which I travel always with a sense of expectation and pleasure. I was first introduced to it as a young apprentice surveyor about 1963, when it was the venue for the firm's annual golf outing, and my abiding memory is of being surprised at seeing Willie Kilmarnock, captain of Motherwell FC's 1952 Scottish Cup winning team, seated in the Members' Lounge. Another memory, indicative of the times, relates to Sinclair Sutherland whose bus (a Bedford Duple) transported us down to Ayrshire from Hamilton and Glasgow. Sinclair was a well-known character in Lanarkshire and the name of his business was Balmoral Coaches; a very appropriate one since Sinclair was always dressed in Highland wear when behind the steering-wheel. Attired in a kilt and Harris Tweed jacket, and not forgetting the Balmoral or Tam o'Shanter on his head, he was a one-man entertainer as he drove his passengers about the countryside. He had a microphone attached to the dashboard and used to sing Scottish songs and recount humorous stories to keep everyone amused. Later on in the evening when all the office staff were settled down in the lounge, one of the Irvine members enquired as to who was the kilted figure who had been drinking at the bar for the past hour or so. 'Oh, that's Sinclair. He's our driver!' As to the course itself, it remains a jewel whose character is all its own. In recent years the encroachment of gorse has, in my opinion, been detrimental to the holes adjacent to the railway line, but the layout is absolutely wonderful and many of the original James Braid features are still as relevant as ever.

I was welcomed by the captain, Jamie Murray, and was then pleasantly surprised to find that our own catering manager, Grant Hood, was a fellow guest in his capacity as Captain of St. Mungo Golf Club, which is affiliated to The Irvine Golf Club and whose members are associated with the licensed trade in Glasgow and the West of Scotland. As always, Stewart Brown provided an excellent meal and David Miller (Kilmarnock (Barassie) GC) in toasting our hosts spoke of the enduring challenge of the course and of the traditions of the clubhouse. The guest speaker was Bill Nolan, a communications consultant, Burns enthusiast and rugby union Board member. This was another super evening spent in good company and in a lovely relaxed atmosphere.

Tuesday, 7th December: Sub-committee meeting
I attended an afternoon meeting of the Membership Development Sub-Committee in the Ladies Lounge. Because of widespread disruption of traffic throughout the region caused by prolonged snowfall, Secretary Tom was unable to attend.

. . . . 7th: Foreword for Handbook
Throughout my years in the Club, the annual Fixture Card issued to members has always contained a Foreword by the Captain. There was no set formula as to the content of the Foreword; its being at each Captain's discretion as to what he wished to contribute. Some used it as a vehicle to convey good wishes for the forthcoming season, others to remind members as to the good etiquette required of them, whilst others reproduced some pertinent extract from golfing literature as took their fancy. I decided to try and raise awareness of the Club's regulations and to be informative of current issues, bearing in mind that less than 25% of the membership ever attends an AGM.

Whether described as a Foreword, Preface, Introduction, or any other similar designation, there is an implied assumption that the publication to which it relates is going to be read. I must admit that in my eagerness to get started upon a book I have often dispensed with consulting the Introduction, especially in those cases where it extends beyond a few pages. As to St. Nicholas G.C. Fixtures and Regulations 2011, I know that throughout the year the Fixtures section will receive close attention from the great majority of members but, as to the Regulations, that section is more likely to be accorded only the briefest of glimpses by those who no longer consider themselves to be 'new' members. However, 2011 will be a significant year in the continuing development of the Club, and I would urge everyone to devote a little of their time in familiarising themselves with the current regulations.

History is perceived as being a record of past times, but history is moulded by the present, and each of us plays a part in determining its outcome. Our 2010 Annual General Meeting assumed the mantle of historical importance when it was agreed that ladies could apply for full membership of the Club and, in that regard, the names of Mara Lindsay and Rosalind Purdom are recorded as being the first ladies accepted into St. Nicholas Golf Club as Ordinary Members. This year will see us co-host with Prestwick Golf Club the Scottish Area Team Championship and, reminiscent of former times when Oxford and Cambridge Golfing Society used to play matches against us, we are scheduled to welcome visits from members of Marylebone Cricket Club (MCC) and Wallasey Golf Club (The Stableford Golf Society).

The past year witnessed the construction of a practice hole and the refurbishment of the Mixed Lounge and Dining Room. Improvement of our amenities, both on the course and in the Clubhouse, is an ongoing commitment and I would encourage everybody to support the Management Committee in its endeavours to promote the best interests of the Club.

To those members seeking some kind of guidance, encouragement or message in this Foreword, the best advice I can offer towards their continued enjoyment of golf is 'Keep your head still, and make sure that your shoulders are square at impact'.

Having composed the Foreword, I turned my attention to the current Club Regulations with a view to establishing whether there was a requirement for any amendments to be incorporated in the new Fixture Card.

Wednesday, 8th December: Winter Foursomes dispute

The protocol relating to the playing of match play competitions within the Club is very much dependent upon the parties themselves. In the past there were procedural rules governing how ties were to be arranged, whereby the first player on the drawsheet was the challenger and was responsible for complying with various stipulations relating to the timing and issuing of a challenge to his opponent and to the number and variety of the dates being offered. Although the system was well understood, disputes sometimes arose and these were often referred to the Match Secretary for a ruling. Referrals eventually became so onerous upon the Match Secretary that Committee agreed to accede to his suggestion that, in future, the onus be put on the players themselves to make the necessary arrangements as would ensure that their tie was decided before the cut-off date. If the tie had not been resolved by that date, both parties would be eliminated from the competition. This approach proved to be very successful and has been in operation for the past five years. However, golfers being as they are, the occasional hiccup is encountered and one had occurred at the end of November.

A Winter Foursome tie which was due to be played by 28th November had been delayed to the very last day, principally due to one of the players having been abroad on holiday for several weeks. This had restricted the options as to when all four players could be available at the same time, and that was the crux of the problem. On this particular Sunday, the prevailing conditions were not conducive to affording a pleasant day's golf owing to the exceptionally cold weather that had enveloped the country; the frosts had been so severe in the preceding days that temporary greens were in operation. Crucially, the course was still open for play, but there had been an altercation between two of the participants on the previous day when the question had arisen as to whether the tie should be conceded, or decided by the toss of a coin, rather than having to endure the extreme weather conditions. This friction had re-emerged on the first tee on the morning of the match as they were about to tee-off; it had developed into an argument; un-parliamentary language was used and one of the parties conceded the tie in anger without a ball having been struck. The player who had conceded the tie submitted a report of the incident for the attention of Committee and apologised for his part in the disturbance. The Match & Handicap Convener was informed; Secretary Tom requested, and obtained, a response from the other parties; the Joint Match Secretaries offered their opinion; and I was given copies of all the correspondence. All of us agreed that the matter should not be allowed to develop into a series of claims and counterclaims and, if approved by Committee, that a letter be sent to each member of the foursome expressing disappointment at the incident. At its next meeting, John Errington (Match & Handicap Convener) provided Committee with a brief résumé of events; and approval was obtained to send the proposed letter. In the meantime, a more serious breach of conduct was reported to the Secretary – but that would require considerably more circumspection and the unequivocal involvement of the Management Committee.

Monday, 13th December: Christmas cards
As its name implies, the festive season is a time to be enjoyed but, as most households will agree, it sometimes can prove to be filled with domestic chores, anxieties, frustrations and seemingly endless preparations totally out of proportion to the eventual outcome. The writing of Christmas cards is often laborious and time consuming, and is rarely done in the relaxed and harmonious atmosphere as portrayed by novelists or as shown on the silver screen. If only our lives were better ordered and our fantasies realised, we would be so much more contented! This year the writing of the Club's official Christmas cards was my responsibility and I acquiesced to the task in a mood of serenity and goodwill towards all of the recipients. After all, it would be but for one year and each of my fellow captains was already a soul mate on our mutual twelve-month journey. So it was in the joyous spirit of the season that I penned my greetings to our friends in other clubs and to a special few within St. Nicholas.

Wednesday, 15th December: Meetings and Committee Dinner
If one was asked to say which of the Management Committee meetings was considered to be the most agreeable, the December gathering would probably take pride of place simply through its generally being arranged to coincide with the evening of Committee's Christmas Dinner. This entails its requiring an earlier start than usual as the dinner is traditionally served just before 8 o'clock. Ever since the November meeting Membership Convener Robin, in consultation with Vice-Captain Alan, had continued drafting his proposals for dealing with the equality issues (he was currently on Version 6) and had reached the stage whereby something meaningful could at last be presented to the Ladies' Club for discussion and comment with a view to establishing a consensus upon the way forward. As a first step, Alan and Robin required to consult with the other members of the Membership Development Sub-Committee; so it was arranged that Tom Andrews, Bobby Hodge, John Errington and Secretary Tom meet with them and myself at 4pm, two hours prior to the Management Committee meeting, in order that Robin could explain the logic behind his proposals and obtain their approval. Unfortunately, John Errington was unavailable for the sub-committee

meeting. Not surprisingly the two hours flew past in the twinkling of an eye but, nevertheless, agreement was reached and the Management Committee meeting beckoned.

It too was a flurry of reports, but the critical item which demanded action related to the closure of the Shower Room. The fact that only four years previously it had been totally upgraded was a major concern, and one upon which the litigiously minded members of the Club would most likely be expected to express an opinion. In the meantime, the Contractor who had just completed the upgrading works in the clubhouse had been invited to submit a quotation for the investigative work necessary to ascertain the cause of the water penetration and to bring forward proposals for reinstatement of the Shower Room facility. A quote had been submitted within a few days and, although the amount was somewhat higher than might reasonably have been anticipated, time was of the essence, and it was agreed to accept the offer rather than embark on a series of competitive quotes from other contractors which would further delay matters and might possibly only secure a saving of a few hundred pounds. Accordingly, Committee decided to appoint an emergency executive sub-committee to deal with all aspects of the proposed contract, *viz.* Gary Tierney (House), Bill Rae (Special Projects) and David Coid (Finance), so that action could be instigated without any unnecessary delay. The Committee meeting closed at 7.40pm and we all repaired to the Mixed Lounge to greet our invited guests.

Not only is the dinner a welcome diversion from the concerns of Committee business, it is an opportunity to meet socially, and for Committee to show its appreciation of the valuable contribution made to the Club by the four people invited as its guests; Joint Match Secretaries, Malcolm Foggo and Bob Ellis; Starter & Shop Retailer, Peter Carmichael; and Honorary President, Bill Andrew. This is invariably a very jovial occasion, made all the more so by the presence and active participation of our guests whose wry humour and cryptic comments always add immeasurably to the enjoyment of the evening.

Gentlemen:
On behalf of the Committee, I extend a very warm welcome to the four friends we have as our guests this evening: Honorary President Bill, Match & Handicap Secretaries Malcolm and Bob, and Starter Peter. It is a great pleasure that you are able to join us for this dinner. The invitation to you is but a token of our thanks for all the support and encouragement that you have given to us throughout the year, and it is good that we can meet up in a convivial atmosphere free from the stress and complexities of golf club administration.

Before having our meal, I shall say Grace.

'We are conscious of the privilege of being members of this golf club; aware of the recreation afforded on the course, and of the warmth and hospitality of the clubhouse. Grant as we partake of this meal that we are mindful and thankful of all the benefits we enjoy. Amen.'

Friday, 16th December: Meeting with Ladies' Club
After more than five months of detailed discussion and six drafts of the ensuing documentation, the Membership Development Sub-Committee's proposals were at last in a suitably coherent state to put before representatives of the Ladies' Club. Until it had agreed the basis and parameters of its remit, I was content to let the sub-committee proceed as it thought best, and I was satisfied that

that had been accomplished. The whole process required to be treated with circumspection and, when considering the obligations set out in the Equality Act 2010, I appreciated totally the sub-committee's need to fully ascertain the likely consequences of any proposals it might put forward. This was the day when Vice-Captain Alan and I, along with Secretary Tom, were able finally to meet with Lady Captain Eileen and her Vice-Captain, Elaine, and to inform them of the sub-committee's draft proposals which, it was hoped, would act as the blue-print from which all future discussions and negotiations could be undertaken. The meeting was very amicable indeed; the ladies indicated their broad approval of what was being proposed, intimated a number of specific items which they wished to have addressed, said that they would report back to their own committee, and would respond thereafter. And so the meeting ended in a spirit commensurate with the season.

Malcolm Foggo and Bob Ellis (Joint Match Secretaries)

Thursday, 23rd December: Cancellation of Christmas competition
The course having been covered in snow since Sunday, and with no prospect of the bitterly cold weather abating, the Christmas competition due to be played on Boxing Day was cancelled.

Monday, 27th December: Staff party
According to its Constitution, St. Nicholas is a members' club. The accepted version of Tom Morris's advice as to forming a golf club is that as many friends as possible should get together and simply advertise that a club has been instituted; and that was all that was required in 1851. In the intervening years the administration and governance of the game have meant that there is a considerable number of other factors which need to be taken into account before a club can be recognised, but the basic premise still applies; like-minded enthusiasts form a club to their own liking and decide the format of its structure and its activities. At least that is how it was, and still can be, but there are now a multitude of new clubs whose genesis is a multi-million pound development company or hotel chain whose primary aim is to generate profit by means of the leisure

industry or through the sale of new houses adjoining the golf complex. It constructs the course along with the associated amenities and advertises membership packages to the general public; but its ethos, or so it appears to me, is essentially that of a financial institution or business concern. By this means some of the finest golfing venues in the country have been created, and that is to be applauded, but it is a totally different concept from that of the old-established clubs which were founded and funded by their members out of a mutual interest and desire to play golf. A consequence of the proliferation of these commercial developments has been a corresponding erosion of potential new members for the established clubs, and many of the latter are now experiencing financial difficulties as a result of diminishing membership numbers.

The members of St. Nicholas each enjoy the rights and share the obligations which membership entails. But whilst they consider rightly that it is their club, within its confines there is another group of persons who also take pride in being associated with it and who are jealous of its reputation. That latter group is its employees and they, sometimes to an even greater degree than many of the members, daily promote and project the essential character and uniqueness of the club in such a way as identifies them with it and demonstrates their own sense of belonging to it. Members would do well to reflect that, whereas for them the club is a haven for social and recreational pursuits, for the staff it is a vital and personal means of livelihood. Happily, for many years St. Nicholas has enjoyed the loyalty and commitment of its employees and, just as important, the Club has recognised the valuable contribution made by them in furtherance of its ideals. The Staff Christmas Party is one of the occasions in which an expression of gratitude is conveyed to them.

The party is usually held in the Mixed Lounge and by prior arrangement the staff itself chooses what specific dishes it wishes to have served on the evening. Cleaners, bar staff, secretaries, greenkeepers and their respective partners are all gathered together, are waited upon by members of the Committee, have unfettered access to a free bar and, this year, have the evening's music provided by the Club's own Richard Merry. It is a very informal and light-hearted time in which everyone can be relaxed, joke, have fun, dance and be free to enjoy the hospitality of the Club and its amenities. And the organiser of this annual event? None other than our Head Cleaner, Mrs Margaret McLean, now fully recovered from her recent illness! Not only does Margaret make all the arrangements for the party, but she invariably organises a fund-raising raffle in conjunction with it and donates the proceeds to a charity of her choice. This year she raised £160 for the Children's Hospice Association Scotland (CHAS) and, as in past years, the Club contributed an equal amount; thus achieving an overall sum of £320.

David Kinnell (1879-1951)

In William Galbraith's excellent *History of St. Nicholas Golf Club*, published in 1950, mention is made of the former Club Professional, David Kinnell, but no indication is given as to his character or of his contribution to the ongoing life of the Club; albeit he is credited, along with Charlie Hunter, of laying out in 1906 a new 18-hole course for the ladies, and reference is made to his participation in some exhibition/challenge matches. In the context of the book this brevity is understandable; it is after all a history of the Club and its members, but it is nevertheless scant recognition of the contribution that he and other employees made to the Club. However, the mere fact that his name is quoted in the narrative is of itself significant simply because it aroused my interest in the man and prompted my research into his life as a golf professional. And what an enthralling search that proved to be!

My investigations were in connection with a contribution which, in 2007, I had volunteered to make towards the production of an updated history of Prestwick St. Nicholas Golf Club whereby a few paragraphs could be included concerning some of its former prominent professionals and clubmakers. The research was undertaken over a relatively short period of time and without access to the wealth of information that is now readily available on the Internet. It consisted solely of referring to old books and newspaper cuttings already in my possession and of contacting club archivists who might be able to assist me with some specific details. At the outset I knew a little of James (Jimmy) Kinnell, but as to the relationship, if any, between him and David Kinnell I had no knowledge. Might he be a brother, a cousin, a nephew, an uncle? I would need to find out!

My initial enquiries among the older members of the Club revealed that nobody had any knowledge whatsoever of him and, as I have since established, it is highly probable that at the time of my researches even the longest-serving member had not been in the Club during David Kinnell's era as its professional. For my part, I knew that Jimmy Kinnell was originally from Leven and therefore I decided to commence my investigations by writing to the Secretary of Leven Thistle Golf Club and by inserting an enquiry into its local newspaper, *East Fife Mail*. As a result of these overtures, I received replies from Jim Scott, Secretary of Leven Thistle, from Past Captains Jim Nisbet and Ian Gerard, and from John McCallum who it emerged was related to the Kinnell family through his mother. I had made my first breakthrough in uncovering the story of David Kinnell!

David Kinnell with his sons, James and Lindsay circa 1922

I was able to establish that Jimmy and David were brothers, David being the younger, but a search through Leven Thistle's archives had failed to unearth any photographs of him. Jim Scott provided me with the address of a Mrs. Cooke who lived in Cumbria and he understood that she might be able to help me with something of the family history. It was about two months later that I was contacted by Julie Cooke and she indeed was able to furnish me with details of both Jimmy and David. Julie informed me that David Kinnell was her grandfather and that some years previously she had compiled a dossier of him; hence Jim Scott being able to put me in contact with her. Julie sent me a copy of the dossier which not only included her account of her grandfather's life but also details of the Kinnell family's background, the family tree, census returns, birth and death certificates, newspaper extracts and family photographs. Among the latter were two which included David; so at last I had an image of him! Naturally, I was in contact with Julie by telephone and in the course of a conversation she told me that David's youngest daughter, Janet (Bunty), lived in Ayr. That was a huge surprise to me, but the most exciting of prospects towards learning something of David at first hand and on a personal level.

I managed to speak on the telephone to Bunty and explained the reason for my call and the background to my having obtained her address. At the outset she treated me with some reservation, as was only to be expected, but eventually she invited me along to her house to meet with her and her husband, Archie. And that proved to be a heart-warming occasion. She was genuinely surprised that anyone should be enquiring about her father and that his career should be of interest outwith the family but, with the encouragement of Archie, she had looked out what little memorabilia she possessed. In truth there was not very much, but she did have a very good photograph of her father - much superior to those that I had hitherto received. Just as important was the fact that she was able to talk about her father and to speak of family life as she remembered it as a young girl. Following a second meeting with Bunty I had sufficient information for my purposes and was able to allocate a couple of paragraphs to him within the chapter on Clubmakers and Professionals. Having started from almost scratch, his entry in my little dissertation was the one which gave me the greatest satisfaction.

David Kinnell was born on 10th May 1879. He was the second son of James and Janet Kinnell of Scoonie Burn, Leven; his elder brother, James (Jimmy), having been born in 1876. The family lived in close proximity to Leven Links, one of the great golfing centres in Fife. Alexander Patrick, the well-known ball and clubmaker, was Jimmy and David's uncle and both of them served their apprenticeship in his workshop opposite the Leven Thistle clubhouse. In addition to having his club-making business, Alex Patrick was for six years the professional at Royal Wimbledon Golf Club where he was succeeded by his own brother, David. As for Jimmy Kinnell, he had a notable playing career whilst attached to Prestwick St. Nicholas, Royal Norwich and Purley Downs golf clubs and played in eleven Open Championships. In the period between 1899 and 1905 he competed in five Opens and finished fourth, sixth, seventh (twice) and fifteenth; ample evidence of playing at the highest level during a period dominated by The Great Triumvirate. Through his attachment to various clubs and his regular involvement in tournament golf, Jimmy's name has been better remembered than that of David; but my findings would suggest that David also merits an honourable mention when reflecting upon that period of golfing history.

In 1897, at the age of eighteen, playing a Medal Round in a prize competition over Leven Links he returned a score of 74 which equalled the record for the course. He was appointed golf professional to Leven Thistle G.C. and the following year (1898), playing in The Open Championship for the first time, he finished in sixth place; what a marvellous performance considering that the field was packed with all of the leading players of the day! Later that same year he reduced the record for Leven Links by two strokes to 72. It was another five years before he played again in The Open Championship and in the interim he had been appointed golf professional at St. Nicholas Golf Club, Prestwick in succession to his brother, Jimmy, who had moved to Royal Norwich G.C. This absence from competing in the major championship would suggest that he was actively engaged in undertaking his duties as a club professional, the which would involve making and repairing clubs, administering a shop, giving tuition and possibly acting as starter. At this time St. Nicholas had several Scottish Internationalists among its number and was considered to be one of the most progressive clubs in Scotland. Its name appeared prominently against entrants for many of the important amateur tournaments in the country and one might reasonably speculate that David's influence contributed to some of the successes achieved. As for the 1903 Open, which was played at Prestwick, David tied in eighteenth place, one stroke behind his brother. Three years later he played at Muirfield and once again put together four consistent rounds to finish in eleventh place. In 1907 he competed in the inaugural Scottish Professional Championship, which was played over the Panmure Club's course at Barry, and he and Willie Fernie (Troon) finished joint runners-up one stroke behind John Hunter (Prestwick). His fourth, and what proved to be his last, Open was in 1908 and once again the venue was Prestwick. In what was a particularly strong field he demonstrated just what a fine golfer he was; this being amply confirmed when he tied with Harry Vardon in 5th place.

The first of the matches to which William Galbraith alluded in his history of the Club took place in 1902 shortly after Alex (Sandy) Herd had won The Open Championship at Hoylake using one of the new Haskell rubber-cored balls. At the instigation of the Club Captain, Mr. J.K. Hunter, Sandy Herd was invited to play a 36-hole challenge match against the recently appointed St. Nicholas professional. David had no previous experience of using the Haskell and therefore opted to play a gutta-percha ball. At the end of the morning round Sandy was three up, and in the afternoon went on to win the match 3 and 2. In the evening a foursome was played in which Sandy, partnered by Mr. William Hunter, defeated David and Mr. James Robb by 3 and 2; the latter pair again playing a 'gutty' ball. Within a very short time of this challenge match the rubber-cored Haskell ball became the preferred choice among all golfers, and the 'gutty' was condemned to a similar fate as the 'featherie'!

The other references made by William Galbraith are to exhibition matches which took place after The Great War. The first of these was in July 1919 when, at the invitation of Captain James Ferguson, Harry Vardon, Andrew Kirkcaldy, James Braid and J.H. Taylor played a series of four-ball matches on the last weekend of the month. On the Friday afternoon, in what was a very close match, David Kinnell, partnered by Club Secretary Robert McFadzean, defeated J.H. Taylor and Andrew Kirkcaldy by one hole. The following year, on Saturday 28th August, George Duncan and Abe Mitchell played over the St. Nicholas links and in an afternoon four-ball match against David and the newly appointed Club Secretary, Gordon Lockhart, these two celebrated golfers were beaten 3 and 2 by the home pair. Incidentally, Gordon Lockhart had a very distinguished amateur career, winning the Irish Open Amateur Championship in 1912 after having been a semi-finalist in The Amateur Championship the previous year. As well as being a Scottish Internationalist, he was a prolific winner of amateur tournaments and four months after this match resigned as Club Secretary to take up a post as golf professional at Gleneagles.

In 1908, at the age of 29, David married Margaret Heirs in Monkton and lived the rest of his life at 40 Ayr Road, Prestwick; a mid-terrace red sandstone bungalow (since painted white) within a short walking distance of the golf course and immediately across the road from the ladies' course. David and Margaret had four children, Margaret, Lindsay, James and Janet: none of whom followed their father into the world of professional golf. However, the Kinnell family had a very strong golfing pedigree. Jimmy and David's two younger brothers, John and Alexander (Alec), were also golf professionals and their younger sister, Jane, was an accomplished player. John was appointed the first professional at Chipstead Golf Club in Surrey and served there from 1906 until 1909, whilst Alec moved to Africa, as did two nephews who secured appointments with clubs in the vicinity of Nairobi.

Although David was not a regular entrant in The Open Championship, he did play in many professional prize competitions and he was reputed to be a very good instructor. Along with his elder brother Jimmy, he established and operated a club-making business in Prestwick under the name of D & J Kinnell.

In addition to his normal duties as club professional of St. Nicholas, David's services were also sought in regard to golf course design. In 1903, the year following his coming to Prestwick, he was approached by Girvan Burgh Golf Club and commissioned to lay out a nine-hole course on the sea front immediately north of the harbour. The result was the creation of a splendid sporting course in the most idyllic of settings beside the Firth of Clyde. In 1906, when Ladies' St. Nicholas Golf Club succeeded in leasing additional ground adjacent to its existing course, he collaborated with Charlie Hunter (Prestwick GC) in laying out a full-length 18-hole course for the ladies. His abilities as a designer were obviously recognised elsewhere and his 9-hole course for Carsphairn Golf Club in Dumfriesshire, laid out in 1914, is but a further example of the good reputation he acquired in that aspect of his profession.

For health reasons, a few months short of his 57th birthday, David retired as the Club's professional, having held the post for almost 34 years, and he was awarded a pension in token of his long service and commitment throughout that period. In his retirement David found congenial employment as caretaker of Prestwick putting green which at that time was a favourite amenity among locals, comprising four circuits, and renowned for the intensity of the competitions which it hosted. David died at home on 10th January 1951 and is buried in Prestwick Cemetery.

Chapter 11

January

Saturday, 1st January: Captain's Reception

New Year's Day is celebrated within the clubhouse by the provision of the Captain's Reception, which commences at noon. It is something of a misnomer in that those who attend probably assume that the Captain is responsible for footing the bill, especially for the drinks offered upon arrival, whereas his roll is principally one of meeting and greeting, and of saying some appropriate words to the assembled company just prior to the buffet being served. Of necessity, he requires to be present in good time for the arrival of the members and their guests, so Jeanette and I were in our place by 11.45am. I had hoped to introduce some minor variations to the normal proceedings and to that end, at my own expense, to offer a dram of whisky in addition to the usual selection of wine and soft drinks, and to provide some background music, the likes of which was unlikely to have been heard previously within the confines of the Mixed Lounge. I had also given some thought to the content of my address to the company so that it would not appear bland and predictable, and would be appreciated on that account. So much for my planning – the outcome proved to be somewhat different!

It had crossed my mind to set up the microphone stand the previous afternoon in preparation for my address, but in the end decided that I would have sufficient time to attend to that immediately prior to the reception getting underway. On reflection, that was a big mistake! By the time Jeanette and I arrived in the clubhouse, the bar staff had already set up tables at the Mixed Lounge doorway and had laid out the drinks and glasses thereon, and one of the tables was so positioned as to ensure that the entrance door remained propped in an open position. Having exchanged New Year greetings with the bar staff, I handed over my CDs and, not surprisingly, was met with total bewilderment as to the artists featured on them. For the record, they comprised Al Bowlly, Perry Como, Elvis Pressley (from his Sun recordings), Robert Wilson, Anne Lorne Gillies, and Will Starr. I enquired as to where I would find the microphone stand but was met with the same blank expressions as had greeted my handing over the CDs. What about the lectern? But once again no one appeared to be even aware of its existence. I looked for these items in the Mixed Lounge, Dining Room and Tom Morris Room without success, and then went upstairs to the Committee Room. Again without success! Jeanette suggested that I put a couple of wine boxes on top of a table and to lay my notes thereon, but I was uncomfortable as to how that would look in the context of the event.

The first party arrived about 12.15pm and thankfully thereafter there was no surge of arrivals, but rather a steady procession of couples and families, which allowed Jeanette and me to give a personal welcome to everyone, and was for me an ideal introduction into the finer art of meeting and greeting; not something of which I had much previous experience. White wine and fruit juice proved to be the most requested drinks, but there was a sufficient number of gentlemen who opted for a glass of whisky as to reassure me that its presence was welcomed. By 1.15pm about eighty people were present and our caterer, Grant Hood, brought through the buffet from the kitchen.

Because of my preoccupation in speaking to members as they arrived, the matter of preparing myself mentally for what I was about to say to the assembled company had been overlooked and I was somewhat unnerved when our barmaid, Caroline, suddenly handed the microphone to me. A few years earlier I had my only previous experience of using a hand-held microphone and it had been a total embarrassment to me. On that occasion the hand holding my notes started to shake so violently that I had been unable to read anything of what I had prepared, and I vowed that I would never put myself in such a predicament again. However, I automatically accepted the microphone from Caroline and thereafter found myself venturing into another self-inflicted nightmare. Of course, I should simply have laid the microphone aside, concentrated upon speaking sufficiently loudly and trusted that my voice would carry throughout the lounge. But in my unsettled condition, I stepped forward and found myself leaping in to my prepared speech. I had hoped that it might be received as being a little different from the usual words of welcome but, whilst that was probably still the case, the whole effect was ruined by my delivery. Being unfamiliar with the technique of holding the microphone and at the same time engaging people on opposite sides of the room, I quickly became aware that as I turned my head the microphone was not picking up my voice. My brain was experiencing its own private turmoil, perspiration exuded from every pore, eighty pairs of eyes were looking at me, and I just wanted to be somewhere else. I should have ditched the microphone as soon as I became uncomfortable but somehow, in the midst of my travails, that notion did not occur to me. I soldiered on, had the presence of mind to omit any reference to the background music which I had selected (for that was now discarded from my plans), and to my own and, I am sure, to everyone else's relief, I completed my little dissertation.

Ladies and Gentlemen, Friends, Family and Guests:
It is my pleasure to host the Captain's Reception for 2011.

I recall during the nineteen-nineties how I used to speculate as to how we would all refer to the individual years in the new century. Somehow 'nineteen-four', 'nineteen-ten', 'nineteen-sixteen' all tripped off the tongue quite naturally; but would we refer to 'twenty-o-four', 'twenty-ten', 'twenty-sixteen' or to 'two thousand and four', 'two thousand and ten', 'two thousand and sixteen'? Well, the first decade of the twenty-first century has now expired and no clear pattern has yet emerged. Perhaps the main reason is the proliferation of mobile 'phones. Modern 'texters', I suspect, are probably inclined to think in terms of '20 something', whilst the older, less dexterous, generation is more likely to think of 'two thousand and something'. However, that is just an aside.

Today we bid farewell to 2010! At moments like this, I so wish that I was an accomplished singer and could invite all of you to join in the chorus of a suitably seasonal song. But lacking such talent, I am resigned to reverting to a more comfortable mode which is more akin to Reverend I.M. Jolly or Father Ted.

2010 will have been memorable for many of you. Perhaps there has been the announcement of a couple's engagement, a wedding in the family, the birth of a baby, the arrival of a granddaughter, an important anniversary, the trip or holiday of a lifetime; perhaps even the winning of a trophy at the golf club! But we are all aware that there is another side to life. Mingled among the happy times there may have been illness, even bereavement; insecurity of employment, regret or disappointment – that fluffed chip or wayward drive at a crucial point in the match; 'But for that I might have won', or much worse 'But for that the team would not have lost'. However, that is now all consigned to the past.

Occasionally Scots are described as being dour, but I have known very few to whom that applies. I suspect such a description emanates from sources outwith Scotland from folk who misinterpret a natural reserve, reticence or modesty and equate these qualities with dourness. What other country is so associated with revelry and goodwill at this season of the year; where happiness is wished upon all and sundry; where the outlook is one of optimism and good cheer? Happiness is not a memory of the distant past; it is something to be experienced in the present:

> *'If Happiness is what you seek*
> *Here's advice from which you'll profit,*
> *The ready outcome of your search*
> *Is to 'ken it whilst you've got it!'*

And as we bid farewell to 2010, whether at home, among family or in the comfort of St. Nicholas Golf Club, I wish A Guid New Year to Ain and A'.

May 2011 be indeed A Happy New Year!

This was without doubt the lowest point in my period of Captaincy. For the majority of the people at the reception, this would be the only occasion upon which they would come across me in my Captain's role and I had so wished to make a good impression. But I failed miserably with a poorly delivered address; all emanating from my inability to find the lectern and microphone stand. Yet again the genius of Robert Burns captured the moment aptly and concisely:

> 'The best-laid schemes o' mice an' men
> Gang aft agley,
> An' lea'e us nought but grief an' pain'.

As for the microphone stand and the lectern? At the end of the Reception, upon the bar staff re-positioning the furniture, both items were discovered behind the entrance door that had earlier been propped open by one of the tables!

Thursday, 6th January: Letters of complaint

After having looked in at the Greenkeepers' compound to extend to the men my compliments of the season, I met with Secretary Tom to discuss, among other items, two letters of complaint which had been received almost four weeks previously. They related to the conduct of a prominent member towards one of the bar staff in the course of the latter carrying out his duties in the Mixed Lounge. An undesirable subject at the best of times, but made the more awkward by the high profile of the member concerned and by the open aspect of the area in which the alleged incident had taken place. I had discussed the contents of the letters at some length with Vice-Captain Alan and Secretary Tom, and we were agreed that the issue was not one that could be ignored, irrespective as to how it might develop. We decided that Committee be advised of the complaints at the December meeting and, without divulging any specific details, to seek its approval to defer the matter pending further enquiries. Having so decided, Tom then wrote to the accused member stipulating the nature of the complaints against him and requesting his response. Approval to postpone any detailed discussion was obtained at the December meeting, and the member's written response was received thereafter during Christmas week. I considered it important that the matter be settled expeditiously and impartially, and today I requested Tom to arrange a Special Meeting of the Management Committee to deal with it.

Wednesday, 12th January: Equality issues

The meeting with Lady Captain Eileen and Vice-Captain Elaine on 16th December had been very friendly and had instigated a better understanding of the Membership Development Sub-Committee's progress towards resolving the equality issues. As agreed, Eileen and Elaine relayed the sub-committee's proposals to the Ladies Committee for its consideration and reaction. The subsequent response as submitted by Lady Captain Eileen was very positive and, thankfully, heralded the prospect of closer co-operation and progress towards agreeing an acceptable solution. Vice-Captain Alan distributed a note of his comments relating to the items raised by the ladies and, having studied the contents this afternoon, I concurred with his conclusions.

Thursday, 13th January: Special Committee meeting

An inherent requirement within golf is the observance of good etiquette; so much so that the first section of *The Rules of Golf* relates to that very subject in regards to the playing of the game. As to the acceptable standards of dress and conduct of members within the clubhouse, that aspect of etiquette is generally enshrined within each club's rules and regulations. Nevertheless, the basic precept, whether stipulated or otherwise, is that everybody within the club and its environs is entitled to be treated with respect. Members have a right to expect that they will be afforded suitable courtesy in their dealings with staff and fellow members, especially within the clubhouse, and the staff is entitled to have such conduct reciprocated. This was the philosophy governing my appraisal of the issues which Committee was required to consider at a Special Meeting dealing with the recent complaints as to a member's conduct. The scenario was reminiscent of my experiences of forty years previously when, as President of The Glasgow & District Former Pupils' Football League, I had regularly to consider what action Committee should take following the receipt of referees' reports concerning misdemeanours on the football field.

All notifications and information relevant to the Special Meeting were issued to the parties but, as events turned out, neither complainants nor accused made a personal appearance before the Committee. In my opinion that was fortuitous, as it enabled Committee to proceed on the basis of the available evidence (which was corroborated) without being harangued by claim and counter-claim. Committee decided that there was substance to the complaints but, in circumstances peculiar to the case, I deemed it inappropriate that the matter be publicised or that the member be subjected to any form of penalty or suspension. Accordingly, the accused member was reprimanded and warned against any repetition of his ungentlemanly conduct. Upon receiving his letter of reprimand a few days later, he contacted me by telephone and apologised for having been responsible for such an incident occurring during my term as Captain. And there the matter was concluded.

Friday, 14th January: Meeting with Ladies

Now that the Membership Development Sub-Committee had been given the opportunity to consider the Ladies' Club's response, a late afternoon (4pm) meeting was arranged to take matters forward. As my car was receiving its annual service, Vice-Captain Alan collected me from my home and we drove to the clubhouse, where Secretary Tom joined us for our meeting with Lady Captain Eileen and Valerie Stephen. All of the matters which had been raised by the ladies in their response were discussed fully and only one item was left in contention, and that related to the transfer status of one senior lady member who, as it so happened, was Valerie. I assured Eileen and Valerie that the views of the Ladies' Club would be communicated to the Management Committee, and the meeting closed on that positive note. Alan and I retired to the Mixed Lounge to review what had been discussed and, in light of the general consensus that had been achieved, Alan agreed with me that the outstanding contentious item be resolved in compliance with the wishes of the Ladies' Club.

Wednesday, 26th January: Meeting with Bill Andrew

Back in December my thoughts had turned to the prospect of demitting office and I had reflected upon what aspirations I had nourished at the outset of my captaincy. But the time for reflection had now passed and I was being confronted daily with considerations regarding the forthcoming Annual General Meeting and the future direction which the Club would take in consequence of any decisions taken thereat. President Bill, as ever, had been cogitating on the same theme and he suggested that we meet to discuss a number of issues that he thought worthy of debate; so we arranged to meet in the Tom Morris Room for a private discussion. As to the direction which our conversation might take, I allowed Bill to raise the topics and we discussed each of them at some length and in considerable detail. Bill has a great appreciation of the Club's heritage, and no one is more passionate than he of upholding its traditions and preserving its character. In particular, he is a fervent advocate of retaining Ladies' Prestwick St. Nicholas Golf Club and of promoting its historical association with the Parent Club.

(Prestwick St Nicholas Golf Club)

Ladies' St. Nicholas Clubhouse

As always, we entered into our conversation on the understanding that all details and comments would be strictly confidential; and that is how it must remain. No confidences are being broken when I say that the range of topics which we discussed was wide, substantial and ultimately crucial towards determining the composition and character of the Club. Our deliberations related to the future utilisation of the Tom Morris Room, membership issues, the appointment of trustees, and the position of Honorary President. At the conclusion of our meeting Bill handed over to me, for viewing by Committee, a photograph album which he had compiled of the Celebration Lunch.

Thursday, 27th January: Committee meeting
Robin Alexander presented his paper containing the recommendations of the Membership Development Sub-Committee following its consultation with the Ladies' Club, and it received the approval of the Management Committee. The meeting itself was something of a personal disappointment in that two items which I particularly wished to see implemented did not receive support from my fellow Committee members. As I had made clear in my acceptance speech ten months previously, it was my desire to conduct the business of the Management Committee on a democratic basis and I knew that a rebuff of this nature was always a possibility. I had employed this mode of captaincy in the knowledge that issues might arise which would entail my having to convince Committee members of the logic of my opinions, but I had rather hoped that I might obtain their accedence upon such an eventuality. By its very nature democracy entails implementing the wishes of the majority; but it does not guarantee that the majority opinion is necessarily the correct one. However, my democratic credentials would not have prevented me from considering my position of Captain as being untenable were a decision of Committee contrary to the fundamental tenets of the Club.

Golf's Communicators

How wonderful it is that the pace and ambience of golf lends itself to fostering the talents of those with a gift for expressing themselves by the written word or through the medium of broadcasting. From its earliest days cricket was similarly endowed and provided a vehicle for musings and flights of fancy which raised appreciation of the game beyond the mere recording of events and statistics into a world of rapture and reflection. The first classic writings on cricket arguably pre-date those on golf by several decades, and successive contributors advanced the literary skills and perspectives by which the game, its participants, its matches, its methods and its enchantments were described and eulogised. Neville Cardus took literary contributions on cricket to a new height in the period between the two World Wars, and commentators such as John Arlott, Brian Johnston and Richie Benaud, each in his own manner, communicated to the listener or viewer the endless fascination of the game.

But what cricket created by way of inspired writers and commentators, so likewise did golf. In 1887 was published *The Art of Golf* written by that great friend of Robert Louis Stevenson, Sir Walter Simpson, Bart.; and other classic writings followed shortly thereafter. Just as Neville Cardus had taken cricket literature to another level, so Bernard Darwin produced reports and writings which received a similar approbation among golf's *aficionados*. The list of distinguished contributors, both in this country and abroad, is now considerable and much could be written on the subject. Indeed, so many are worthy of acknowledgement that their contribution to the enhancement of golf's attractions would constitute a study in itself. There are four upon whom I would wish to comment; and whose observations I was able to enjoy at the time of their first delivery.

It would be quite erroneous were it surmised that I was a regular and avid reader of *Golf and Golfers*, a weekly article that appeared during the winter months in *The Glasgow Herald*, but it was a feature which, when I first came across it, I read with considerable enjoyment. This was in my formative years when, as yet, I had no real appreciation as to the quality of the prose that I was reading; because I had no basis upon which to make comparison. All I knew was that the articles were appealing and opened up new avenues in my understanding of the diversity of topics which an interest in golf could generate. These short articles were filled with reminiscences of incidents on the links, of visits to courses both famous and obscure, of the exploits of golfing legends, and of the romance of the game. They were informative, perceptive, sometimes light-hearted, often serious, but always entertaining; and they were attributed to 'Our Golf Correspondent'. It was many years later I learned that the author of these articles was Sam McKinlay, Editor of the *Evening Times* and a former Walker Cup player. By that time my awareness of journalistic skills had matured and, on re-reading many of these articles, I immediately recognised the merit of their composition and of the language employed. Sam's contributions were the equal of anything that the best golf writers have ever produced and his name deserves to be mentioned whenever good golf-writing is discussed.

As regards the reporting of golf tournaments, my favourite correspondent was undoubtedly Norman Mair of *The Scotsman*. Like Sam, he communicated a certain mystique and passion for the game and its participants, and always impressed me with the eloquence and incisiveness of his narratives. Although generally better known for having been a Scottish internationalist in both rugby union and cricket, he had succeeded Frank Moran as the newspaper's golf correspondent. He had a gift for description which at times ascribed to the execution of a golf shot something of beauty bordering on an art form, and he displayed an affinity with the players which never descended to undue adverse criticism. His reports personalised the players in a manner which showed them as vibrant individuals rather than as a succession of abstract, but familiar, names. Brief anecdotes and little asides interspersed his reports and, most significantly, he appeared to write as an observer rather than as one relating second-hand accounts. In the course of a few short paragraphs he conveyed the essential elements of a full day's golf. Each report was informative not only of the leading players and their scores, but of the related factors that contributed to the whole golfing experience. He was a reporter of the very highest quality.

In my recollection, prior to the introduction of televised events, golf reports on radio tended to be of very short duration; usually a brief summary in the midst of, or more often at the end of, a sports programme. Even with the introduction of television, broadcasting of golf tournaments still tended to be of very limited scope and cameras were often only able to cover a few of the holes. I recall the venerable Bill Cox providing excellent comments on the style and technique of the various players as they were captured on camera during these early transmissions, but it was the advent of extended coverage which created the basis for commentary to be more expansive and for every aspect of play to be televised 'live' as events unfolded. The improved technology provided a means whereby commentators had time and opportunity to express themselves in a conversational manner, and no one more exemplified that capacity than Henry Longhurst. As a journalist and writer he had already many admirers who followed his every word on the printed page; whilst others knew of him through his contributions on radio. But televised golf exposed him to a new audience, many of whom had previously known nothing of him and who were captivated by his commentaries. Being an accomplished communicator on paper provides no guarantee of similar success on the air waves, but Henry proved to be equally adept in both media. His mellifluous voice, sagacious observations, memorable turns of phrase and pregnant pauses so endeared him to the viewers that he became something of a national institution. His commentaries epitomised the values and traditions of the game, conveyed the atmosphere of the moment and conferred a quiet dignity to the proceedings. In his time he was The Voice of Golf.

Henry's broadcasts were so wonderfully idiosyncratic that the prospect of his retirement suggested the possibility of our never seeing or hearing his like again. His departure threatened to leave a void so difficult to fill that any successor was likely to be compared unfavourably against the quality of his commentaries. But thankfully, when that day inevitably arrived, there was someone who not only shared the same golfing values as Henry, but who was able to express these sentiments in a most personable manner and who, in addition, had played tournament golf at the very highest level. That man was Peter Alliss. Others in the BBC television team made significant contributions towards the success of golf coverage, but Peter emerged as the person who could truly be described as Henry Longhurst's successor. Whereas Henry had introduced new viewers to the delights of golf and to the numerous attractive locations in which it is played, Peter's background as a Club and Tournament Professional probably accounted for his instinctively encouraging non-golfers to take up the sport, and existing players to improve their game. Not only did he comment on the action as seen by the viewer, but he was able to convey the mental processes and anxieties that individual players were likely to be experiencing at any given moment and in any particular situation; and by so doing he added a new dimension to the viewers' enjoyment and understanding of the stresses and complexities of 'big time' golf. Without disrespect to his colleagues, one could not fail to be uplifted by that most welcome of introductions 'And now I shall hand over to Peter Alliss to continue the commentary'. In a trice the whole atmosphere of the proceedings was transformed, the senses awakened, expectations raised and the attention span enhanced. His every utterance was a potential gem not to be missed. Through a multitude of broadcasting and publishing ventures, roadshows and 'after dinner' speeches -and not forgetting his own dazzling play when on the tournament scene – few there are who have matched Peter Alliss's benevolent influence in promoting the game of golf.

Chapter 12

February

Friday, 4th February: Turnberry GC Dinner Dance
The prospect of enjoying the hospitality of Turnberry Golf Club at its Annual Dinner Dance is yet another of the pleasures afforded to the St. Nicholas Captain and his partner. In recent years this function has coincided with the St. Nicholas Burns Supper and, on such occasions, successive Captains have attended the former event. Without enquiring into the matter, I assumed that protocol demanded of me that I represent the Club at the Turnberry dinner which, incidentally, is held in the Spa building. Needless to say Jeanette was delighted at the notion of accompanying me that evening and, in order to ensure our full appreciation of the social aspect of the event, we took advantage of a special deal offered by the hotel for an overnight stay to those attending the Dinner Dance. The journey from our home to Turnberry takes only twenty-five minutes by car and we chose to set off early in the afternoon so that we could savour the peaceful atmosphere of the hotel and relax in our bedroom prior to preparing for the evening's entertainment. It was a dry, crisp day and, as is our wont, we took the coastal road via Dunure and Maidens; a journey that is a succession of impressive views and of enduring pleasure. The road rises steadily from Ayr until it gains an outlook over the prominent headland known as Heads of Ayr. On the landward side the farms and homesteads have the reassuring backdrop of the Carrick Hills, and looking westward over the broad expanse of the Firth of Clyde the snow covered peaks of the Arran Hills dazzle in the sunlight. The road is undeniably one of outstanding beauty as it offers unrestricted views of the old smuggling village of Dunure, the isolated protuberance of Ailsa Craig, the Kintyre peninsula and, on a clear day, the distant hills of Antrim. The Electric Brae, Culzean Castle and the iconic Turnberry lighthouse are some of the many other features of interest on this most beautiful of scenic routes.

The evening commenced with a Reception in the comfortable confines of Brown's Room within the main hotel building where wine, soft drinks and *canapés* were served to the assembled guests. We were welcomed by the Turnberry Captain, Peter Wiseman, whom we knew well from previous events, and he introduced us to our fellow guests. It was good to meet up with John McMillan, an architect whom I had often come across in the course of my surveying work and with whom I had worked on several construction projects in South Ayrshire. From Brown's Room, Graeme Rennie, Turnberry Golf Club's Social Convener, conveyed us through the adjoining subterranean corridor to the Spa building and thence to the upper floor function suite. Jeanette and I were seated at the top table beside Peter and his partner, Barbara, whilst Ken Arthur from Royal Troon GC, whom I had met previously at the Barassie dinner, was seated on their other side along with his wife, Marion. Also at the top table were Vice-Captain Norrie Stevenson, Ladies Captain Esther and Secretary Tom Paterson, each accompanied by their respective partners. As was only to be expected at such a prestigious venue, an excellent meal preceded the evening's dancing; the music for which was provided by Stack, a popular band from Hamilton. During the interludes when the gentlemen were talking among themselves and golf-club business was the topic of conversation, equality issues was the predominant theme; so St. Nicholas was not alone in its wrestling with the subject! What for me was especially pleasing, was being approached by people who had a connection with St. Nicholas and who made a point of introducing themselves. That was a kind gesture on their part and much appreciated by me. In particular, I recall speaking to Marjorie Mitchell, a member of Ladies' St. Nicholas; Margaret McPike, whose husband had recently joined the Club; and Past Captain Alan McKinlay. After having had such a superb evening of dining and dancing, it was bliss to know that the comfort of a Turnberry Hotel bedroom was but only a few minutes away!

Saturday, 5th February: Hangover Trophy

Turnberry Links– a golfing paradise as viewed from the hotel

What a pleasure it is to wake up in the morning in the knowledge that you are in Turnberry Hotel and are about to partake of one of its delicious breakfasts! Luxuriating in the bedroom facilities and then strolling along the carpeted corridors and down the main staircase is the perfect prelude to entering the welcoming grandeur of the main Dining Room with its sumptuous display of fresh fruits, cereals, yogurts and juices all vying for your attention; its array of white-clothed tables each suitably adorned with gleaming cutlery and complemented by a delicate posy – every table simply begging your patronage; its high ceiling and distinctively decorated walls; its columns, dentils, mouldings and chandeliers oozing a muted opulence; and its expansive bay windows flooding the room with bright daylight and conversely presenting a panoramic view that is a delight to the eye. And the ultimate thrill of being conducted to a table positioned beside the window! Life doesn't get much better than this! But that is only the beginning, as the menu is then presented from which to choose your main course – and that can only mean the full Scottish breakfast; grilled bacon, eggs prepared to your choice, pork sausages, black pudding, haggis, potato scone, mushroom and tomato, all accompanied by tea or fresh coffee, toast, butter and marmalade. Wonderful – but don't tell your dietician!

The morning was cold but dry and I was scheduled to be on the first tee of the Arran course shortly after 10 o'clock to play in the Hangover Trophy competition with Ladies Captain Esther and her husband, Raymond. The sharpness of the air and the absence of any wind were the ideal conditions for all concerned and a most enjoyable round ensued over the nine-hole course. After watching us tee-off, Jeanette chose wisely in seeking the comfort of the hotel to await completion of our round. There were no winners in our group, but Vice-Captain Norrie came out on top with twenty Stableford points – the same score as won the Ladies' event. The informal prize-giving ceremony was a jolly affair held in the Tappie Toorie Restaurant and was the perfect finale to what had been a memorable visit to one of golf's finest resorts.

Tuesday, 8th February: Funeral of Jock Reid

In any club or organisation having in excess of 600 members, many of whom have already reached the age of retirement, it is highly likely in the course of any 12 months period that death will account for some along the way. Upon such an occurrence a Captain would consider it his duty to represent the Club at the funeral; both as a mark of respect towards a fellow member, and as an expression of support to the bereaved relatives. This was an aspect of the Captain's duties of which I was conscious at the very outset but, after ten months into my tenure of office, I was beginning to harbour hopes that mine might prove to be a year in which the grim reaper spared totally the St. Nicholas' membership. Sadly, it was not to be. On the second day of the month I was informed that one of our older members, John Reid, had died overnight. He had been in the clubhouse just a few days previously; so news of his death was all the more unexpected. John was an Ayrshire man, originally from Annbank; like so many others of his generation he had left school at 14 years of age to commence work as a coal miner; upon marrying, he and his wife set up their first home in Patna; afterwards he worked as a janitor, and was employed latterly in customer services. John was one of our members directly inconvenienced by the introduction of the Government's smoking ban in 2006; for he was an inveterate pipe-smoker, and was thereafter to be seen standing at the side entrance steps puffing contentedly on his pipe whilst acknowledging the comings and goings of fellow members in the vicinity of the clubhouse. On a very cold but dry morning I, along with many of his golfing buddies, attended John's funeral service at Masonhill Crematorium.

. . . . 8th: Meeting with Bill Andrew

President Bill had requested a meeting with me to learn of Committee's reaction to the photograph album which he had made available for viewing at the January meeting. So, following our attendance at John Reid's funeral, we repaired to the clubhouse and talked together in the Committee Room. I informed him that I had presented the album for inspection at the recent meeting, but had not sought directly any comments from among the Committee members. Nevertheless, I was able to assure him that everything that had been said regarding it had been complimentary. Bill emphasised that the introductory passage which he had included was but an incomplete draft and that he wanted me, in my capacity of Club Captain, to provide a Foreword. I must say that I considered Bill's Introduction to be highly satisfactory and suggested that I might provide him with a few notes of my own should he wish to incorporate them into what he had already produced. Bill was less than enthusiastic about my suggestion, and it was obvious that he was already resolved upon how he wished the album to be presented. It emerged that Bill had already settled the invoice for its production and that he regarded the whole transaction as being his donation to the Club.

In the privacy of the Committee Room it soon became apparent that Bill wished to continue with many of the themes discussed at our meeting of two weeks previously. These were all reiterated and expanded upon at some considerable length, and our discussion extended beyond these to include members' adverse comments regarding the recent Burns Supper, standards of dress code, duties of the Starter, and staffing levels of the greenkeepers. I was very aware that my imminent relinquishment of the Captaincy was the motivation behind Bill's introducing such a wide range of topics and I shared many of his concerns, but we both acknowledged that it would be the prerogative of the incoming Captain and his Committee to decide what action, if any, should be taken. As always our meeting was focussed and incisive, and thoroughly stimulating. From 11.45am until 5pm we were totally consumed in the business and aspirations of St. Nicholas Golf Club and its members.

Thursday, 10th February: Finance sub-committee
The level of annual subscriptions and Committee's accountability for expenditure (incurred and projected) are two of the most sensitive issues to engage members in the weeks preceding the Annual General Meeting. That is the time when notice of the meeting is accompanied by the Financial Statement and the proposed budget for the ensuing year. The former is detailed and audited, and provides all members with information as to how finances have been managed during the previous twelve months; the latter is a projection based upon previous experience and achievable ambitions commensurate with the status of the Club. Every February the Finance Sub-Committee convenes to consider the Club's priorities for the forthcoming year and to set a budget for the consideration and, hopefully, the approval of the members. As a general rule the composition of the sub-committee for this exercise comprises the Captain, Vice-Captain, Finance Convener, Links Convener and House Convener, with the Secretary in attendance. Each person contributes to the discussion according to his individual role, but it is principally to the Finance Convener and to the Secretary that recourse is made for specific information. By profession Secretary Tom Hepburn is a chartered accountant and the Club benefits enormously from the commitment and business acumen which he brings to all of its financial arrangements and transactions. In advance of the meeting Convener David Coid and Secretary Tom had collated all of the relevant facts and figures, and they presented these to the members of the sub-committee as draft budget proposals. Each of the entries was explained and analysed, consequences of possible amendments ascertained, and the corresponding amount of members' annual subscriptions established. Once again discussions were expansive and very much focussed upon producing a budget that would be sustainable and acceptable to the members. When all aspects of the Club's financial obligations were fully debated and agreed, the annual subscription element resulted in a proposed increase of 3%; which the sub-committee thought reasonable in the prevailing economic conditions.

Thursday, 17th February: Prof. David Purdie's talk
At the end of October, just a few weeks after I had arranged with Professor David Purdie that he would propose the Immortal Memory at the Club's Burns Supper in 2012, he contacted Secretary Tom and offered to deliver a supper talk upon the origins and evolution of golf. Needless to say

Committee was happy to accept David's offer and our Social Convener, Bobby Hodge, was delegated to communicate with him and to make arrangements for the talk. This was an excellent opportunity to inject an informative and entertaining event into the Social Calendar; and made all the more appealing following upon the success of the talk given by Dr. David Malcolm in 2008 on the subject of Prestwick St. Nicholas's place in golfing history. Professor Purdie had expressed to Bobby a desire to play a match over the course prior to the evening talk, and Bobby invited Vice-Captain Alan and me to make up a four-ball. David was already in the Mixed Lounge when we arrived and I introduced him to Bobby and Alan. We partook of bacon rolls to give us sustenance for our round and then went forth for our game in which Bobby partnered David against Alan and myself. The pairings were well suited and to no one's discomfort the match finished all square on the eighteenth green. Thankfully the weather conditions had been reasonably favourable, for there were no shower facilities available because of the ongoing remedial work in the Changing Room.

Bobby Hodge, Prof. David W Purdie, and Alan Poole on 18th Tee

Just as I had experienced difficulty in locating the microphone stand at the New Year Reception, so Bobby struggled to find the projection screen that was required for the illustrated talk and, having found it, discovered that it was too small for David's purposes. A search needed to be undertaken to find suitable power leads, and this was followed by a decision to project directly onto a plain wall surface, which meant a rearrangement of the seating in areas where viewing would otherwise have been restricted. All of this took up so much time that we had to dispense with treating David to dinner at a local restaurant, and it ended with Bobby making up ham rolls in our own kitchen and serving them to us in the Casual Bar. What we lacked in efficiency was compensated by good fun and lively exchanges, and Bobby's status as Social Convener was exemplified by the high quality of his filled rolls! Everybody took the disruption in good humour, but it served as a further reminder that nothing should be taken for granted whenever the use of equipment is involved.

There was no charge or booking requirement for attendance at the talk; it was simply advertised about the clubhouse and we awaited the arrival of members on the night. And they turned up in such good numbers that the lounge was completely filled – and I made a point of speaking without the use of a microphone!

Honorary President Bill, Past Captains, Ladies and Gentlemen:
Prestwick enjoys a rich golfing heritage, and all of us in St. Nicholas who value tradition, and who have an awareness of history, are conscious of the legacy that we have inherited. It is no credit to ourselves that our club possesses a uniqueness which fate has bestowed upon it, but as guardians of that legacy we surely have a responsibility to preserve what is distinctive to us, and to ensure its continuance amidst all the pressures to conform to what is 'in vogue', or to what other clubs may have seen fit to introduce for themselves. History and tradition cannot be purchased and, whilst we must move with the times and embrace what is beneficial, we should hold on to what is unique to us. As for the town of Prestwick, it is steeped in golfing history; and tonight we welcome one of her champions in the cause of preserving and promoting her rightful place in the development of golf as we know it today.

David Purdie is a Doctor of Medicine and a Fellow of the Royal College of Physicians of Edinburgh. Brought up in Prestwick, and a junior member of St. Nicholas, he was educated at Prestwick High School and Ayr Academy prior to studying medicine at University of Glasgow. In 2006 he retired from his medical academic and research career, and is currently engaged in actively pursuing his passion for everything pertaining to the life and works of Robert Burns – he is editing a new edition of the Burns Encyclopaedia. A past captain of the Scottish Universities Golfing Society, he is a member of Royal Burgess Golfing Society of Edinburgh, and was speech adviser to two recent Ryder Cup captains, Sam Torrance and Colin Montgomerie.

David is well known to many of us within the club, having spoken at our 150th Anniversary Dinner in Brig o' Doon Hotel. He has an avid interest in all matters relating to golf and his most recent publication, 'The Greatest Game', formed the backdrop to the poster advertising this event.

This evening's talk is entitled 'Prestwick – and the Coming of The Open', and it is with great pleasure that I now invite David to address the company.

David enlightened and entertained his audience with a captivating address in which he expounded upon King Robert the Bruce's gifting of lands to Prestwick, the origins of golf, Dutch and Chinese claims in that regard, early golf at Leith and Bruntsfield Links; and he illustrated his talk with old photographs, paintings and aerial views of Prestwick. It was a masterly presentation and enthusiastically received by everyone present. Copies of David's recent book, *The Greatest Game*, were made available for purchase and he announced that for each book sold £5 would be allocated to the Club's Junior Fund. As David had given freely of his services, he was invited to name a charity of his choice to which the Club might make a donation in lieu and, appropriately, he nominated Burns Memorial Fund – after all, he was back in Ayrshire!

Friday, 18th February: Scottish Golf Awards 2011
As later in the year St. Nicholas was due to co-host, along with Prestwick Golf Club, the Scottish Area Team Championship, an invitation was extended to me as Captain to attend the Annual

SGU/SLGA Awards ceremony at Crowne Plaza Hotel in Glasgow. Because this team event would be taking place after I had demitted office, I thought it appropriate that my Vice-Captain should also come along, as it would be an ideal opportunity for him to make his acquaintance with the SGU officials responsible for organising the championship and, as always, having him in my company would add to the enjoyment of the evening. Accordingly, a ticket was purchased for Alan and we travelled up to Glasgow in my car. This mode of transport was not such an odd arrangement as a first reaction might suggest; after all, being among invited guests we could look forward to being treated with appropriate hospitality. In actual fact my wife, Jeanette, had a previous engagement in Glasgow that same evening and, having travelled there by rail, was more than happy to make her way afterwards to Crowne Plaza and to act as our chauffeuse for the journey back to Ayr.

Irene Taylor (Bar Manager) and Prof. David Purdie

The event was a 'black tie' function to celebrate the achievements of Scotland's golfers over the previous 12 months and to raise funds for the development of junior golf in Scotland. A special feature of this year's event was the display of the Ryder Cup which the European team had won at Celtic Manor under the captaincy of Colin Montgomerie. A personal feature of attending such functions was my repeatedly encountering David Miller and Alasdair Malcolm, and this was yet another occasion in which we came across one another at a pre-dinner reception. Alan and I were at the table reserved for guests of SGU and I had the pleasure of being seated between Jimmy Gibson, Manager of Nairn Dunbar Golf Club, and George MacGregor, twice Captain and five times a playing member of Great Britain and Ireland's Walker Cup team. Following the dinner, the presentation of awards, and a humorous turn by comedian Eric Davidson, the evening culminated with Paul Lawrie receiving a Lifetime Achievement Award for his contribution to Scottish Golf. A similar award was also conferred, but in his absence, on Colin Montgomerie. Conversation around the table, and our host's hospitality, extended far beyond the time of the official proceedings; so much so that it was after 2.15am before we met up with Jeanette in the hotel foyer for our conveyance home.

Monday, 21st February: Amalgamation seminar

Throughout my Captaincy I met with Secretary Tom on a regular basis, usually twice per week, when we discussed and attended to the business of the Club. These were always harmonious affairs in which Tom updated me upon current issues, sought my approval for actions he proposed to take in furtherance of Committee decisions or in relation to items of correspondence, advised me of administrative matters which required my input, and generally gave me the benefit of his own knowledge and experience. For my part, I made him aware of the issues which I wished to see progressed, and together we conversed at length on all aspects of club management and members' interests. This morning was typical of these meetings. On Thursday Tom had forwarded to me an e-mail from The Ayrshire Golf Association concerning the proposed amalgamation of Scottish Golf Union (SGU) and Scottish Ladies' Golfing Association (SLGA), details of which were to be discussed at this evening's seminar at Kilmarnock (Barassie) Golf Club, and I returned home to study the proposals in preparation for the consultation exercise.

Vice-Captain Alan accompanied me to the seminar and we were met on arrival by Secretary/Manager Donald Wilson. In the course of the evening we exchanged pleasantries with Norrie Stevenson (Turnberry), David Miller (Kilmarnock (Barassie)) and Graeme and Karen McGartland (Prestwick St. Cuthbert). The presentation on behalf of the Amalgamation Working Group was given by Hamish Grey, Chief Executive Officer of SGU, and it appeared to receive general approval among the Club delegates. By an odd quirk of fate the seminar was chaired by a member of Ladies' St. Nicholas Golf Club. At the end of the meeting, as an act of common courtesy to a fellow member, I approached and complimented her on her handling of the proceedings, only to be met with a rather aggressive response regarding the proposed arrangements for St. Nicholas ladies transferring to Ordinary Membership. If her attitude was symptomatic of those representing Ladies' Prestwick St. Nicholas in consideration of the Equality Act 2010, I suspect that the Membership Development Sub-Committee would have struggled to reach any kind of consensus had ladies been co-opted at the outset of its deliberations. Vice-Captain Alan thought her behaviour quite inappropriate in the context of the seminar and complimented me on the restraint which I showed in extricating myself from an awkward encounter. The travails experienced by Peter Sellers in *The Battle of the Sexes* came instantly to mind! Following the seminar, we returned to Alan's house where we discussed the proposed constitutional changes which we intended submitting to the St. Nicholas members for their approval at the forthcoming Annual General Meeting.

Tuesday, 22nd February: Bill Andrew re another dinner

No doubt as a result of the success of the Celebration Lunch held in June, Honorary President Bill telephoned me early this morning with the suggestion that a similar lunch be arranged sometime during the coming months to mark John Winter's attaining 75 years of membership, Malcolm Foggo's 60 years of continuous membership and Professor David Purdie's re-joining the Club. As this was something which would post-date my term of captaincy, I advised Bill that I felt it would be inappropriate for me to bring this matter before Committee, but that he had my approval to speak directly with Vice-Captain Alan on the subject.

Thursday, 24th February: Meeting with Bill Andrew

Only two weeks after our previous meeting, again at the behest of Honorary President Bill, we met for a lunchtime meeting in the Tom Morris Room. Bill had obviously being pondering over the issues which we had discussed recently and had made further enquiries of his own. He expressed his concerns and opinions on these and other topics, and it was quite obvious to me that he was uneasy as to some aspects of the Club's immediate future. Our conversation lasted for two and a half hours, and in that time we took matters as far as we possibly could.

. . . . 24th: Committee meeting

Past Captain Bill Rae reported that reinstatement of the Gents Shower Room was now complete and that it, and the Trolley Store immediately underneath, would be available for use as from Saturday first. Both of these facilities had been out of operation since water penetration had been discovered at the end of November. Among other business, Committee was informed by Secretary Tom of a member's dispute with the Club Caterer over an unpaid bill. Tom had initially attempted to deal with the matter in a 'low-key' manner, but the member responded by submitting a formal letter of complaint. On the basis of all the information received, Committee decided that the member be advised of Committee's displeasure as to how the matter had escalated and instructed him to settle his meal account within seven days.

Friday, 25th February: Ayrshire Golf Association Dinner

Having hosted Ayrshire Ladies County Championship back in April, it was with considerable pleasure that St. Nicholas agreed to its clubhouse being the venue for the Annual Dinner & Presentation of Prizes of The Ayrshire Golf Association (AGA). As is customary, the captain of the host club is invited to attend the event, and it was with eager anticipation that I looked forward to renewing acquaintance with many of the other officials and team members with whom I had come in contact during my time as Captain. The Association held its pre-dinner reception in the Tom Morris Room where I had the opportunity to speak briefly to its President, David Miller, the recently retired captain of Kilmarnock (Barassie) GC, and to Ken Arthur, due to retire in June as captain of Royal Troon GC. I had a longer conversation with Billy Gibson, who had just retired as captain of Prestwick St. Cuthbert GC, and with John Duncan of Troon Portland, who is an Executive Member of AGA. As happened at other functions which I had attended, conversation was dominated by the Equality Act 2010 and the manner in which individual clubs were addressing the issues. Once again it was evident that all clubs were coming up against the same questions and that St. Nicholas's approach was consistent with others in similar circumstances.

As captain of the host club I was seated at the end of the top table and had Alan Tait, Professional/Manager at Dalmahoy Country Club, at my left elbow. Alan is a former Scottish Boys Champion and Amateur Internationalist, and holds the course record at Carnoustie with a score of 64. It was good to be paired with him as our conversation tended to revolve around aspects of professional golf of which I had no previous experience; and all of which I found very illuminating.

President David introduced the top-table party to the company and invited me to deliver my welcome address on behalf of the Club.

President David, Fellow Guests, Ladies and Gentlemen:
On those occasions when our Club is called upon to host a national or district competition, there is a distinct air of anticipation amongst our greenkeeping staff in the weeks leading up to the event. Just as the players prepare and look forward to the challenge, so the greenkeepers apply themselves assiduously to ensure that their course is in the best possible condition. And I do mean THEIR course. Whatever plaudits may be received by the Club officials, welcome as these indeed are, theirs is but a reflected glory. A dedicated and enthusiastic greenkeeping staff is at the very heart of every successful club; greenkeepers who take a pride in their work and whose sole objective is to satisfy the membership. And when an invitation arrives to host an external event, they are appreciative of the compliment that is being paid to them, and acknowledge it as recognition of their daily commitment to the Club.

And the same sense of recognition and appreciation applies to the Clubhouse Staff when we are invited to make our premises available for a dinner such as this evening's. To our cleaners, bar staff and catering staff this is an opportunity to show to others the same level of service as they provide day and daily to the members; for, whenever they are on duty, individually this is THEIR Clubhouse.

So, from Prestwick St. Nicholas Golf Club, I extend a warm welcome to all of you. We are delighted that you have graced our Clubhouse with your presence, and I sincerely hope that everyone will have a most enjoyable evening.

Grant and his kitchen staff provided a meal that was absolutely first class, and our own Bill McFarlan proposed the toast to The Ayrshire Golf Association. Alan Tait was the guest speaker and he gave a humorous and generally self-deprecating talk about his experiences in professional golf; which caught the celebratory mood of the dinner and was much appreciated by his audience. The entire evening was a delight, and I had the pleasure of speaking to many friends and fellow office bearers with whom I was already well-acquainted, and also to others whom I met for the first time at this dinner. For me there was the awareness of a unique period in my life drawing to a close as I reflected upon this function being the last at which I would be representing St. Nicholas Golf Club as its Captain and, of course, being in the presence of others who were in a similar situation.

Servants of the Club

I rather approve of this somewhat archaic means of collectively describing employees of a golf club. In this age of political correctness, there are no doubt some who would instinctively find cause to object to such a reference, suggesting that is somehow derogatory or demeaning, but I can assure anyone so minded that the motivation behind my use of the term is quite the contrary; for it is intended as an acknowledgement of the commitment which so many employees willingly make towards providing a club with the best service possible – and of their pride in achieving it. Indeed, the term 'club servants' is used extensively in establishing their degree of responsibility or otherwise as stated in the rules, constitution and insurance policies of golf clubs at large, and defines the relationship between employees and members.

For many members, personal contact with the club's servants will be confined to dealing with the bar and catering staff and, if there is one, the club steward. The greenkeeping staff will perhaps be given a wave in passing and the Secretary only approached in regard to a specific request or query. That was certainly my experience until such time as I was elected onto Committee, whereupon the world of the club servants was opened up to me and I became aware of the organisation and dedication which underpin the functioning of a golf club. If my awareness was heightened upon becoming a member of Committee, my indebtedness to the Club's servants was boundless when it came to performing my duties as Club Captain. My innate capacity to go through life accepting what I see about me and yet failing to appreciate the significance of what lies behind it all, I find utterly embarrassing. Just occasionally, in a moment of enlightenment, something which previously hadn't registered with me suddenly becomes blatantly obvious. One such an example is the relationship that exists among the Servants of the Club. Without ever having given thought to the subject, I had simply accepted each of them in their individual roles and recognised them as small

Tom Hepburn (Secretary) and his assistant, Margaret Low

groups within the clubhouse or out on the course; kitchen staff, bar staff, cleaners, greenkeepers, secretarial staff and starter – each performing an important role in the ongoing life of the Club; but I had never appreciated their being a composite unit, nor had I realised just how much interaction took place amongst them. Shame on me perhaps, but I suspect many other members have never been sufficiently close to, or involved in, the practicalities of running a golf club as to have even considered the matter. It was something of a revelation to me when I first encountered the bonhomie that existed among the Club's servants and of the camaraderie they felt for one another. They shared a common bond and were as committed as any member in upholding the reputation and standards of the Club.

Throughout my Captaincy I remained in gainful employment, but was in continual contact with the Secretary by telephone or e-mail and I visited his office on a regular basis. Occasionally during one of these visits the Bar Manageress, the Starter or the Head Greenkeeper would call in to attend to some item of business and I was conscious of the Secretary's role as Club Manager, but I thought nothing further of it. Similarly, I made a point of looking in at the greenkeepers' compound every few weeks and being updated on what had been happening with regards to maintenance of the golf course and upon what was scheduled for the immediate future. It was only when the Staff Christmas Party was being arranged that I fully appreciated that all of the Club's servants saw themselves as a single entity; their being the staff of Prestwick St. Nicholas Golf Club. And, of course, this became abundantly clear on the evening of the party, and what fun that proved to be!

I had been aware for some years that Mrs Margaret McLean, the Head Cleaner, was held in great affection by the 'Early Birds'- a group of regulars who invariably set out onto the course at first light – as she opened the clubhouse for them and provided tea on their arrival. Whenever I looked in at the clubhouse of a morning around 10 o'clock, Margaret was often seated in the Mixed Lounge, relaxing after having completed her cleaning duties, and exchanging banter and chat with anyone who cared to engage her in conversation. She knew more about what was going on within the Club than did most of the members; and with what was going on behind the scenes! As for her fellow helpers, they had always departed the clubhouse before ever I arrived and it was at the party that I met some of them for the first time; very much a reminder of the unseen but vital services that are being performed systematically outwith the gaze of the general membership.

This revelation prompted me to consider the pattern of events that takes place on a daily basis, all for the smooth running of the Club and for the benefit of its members. From the arrival of the cleaners and the greenkeepers at the break of dawn until the bar staff locks up the clubhouse in the evening, the rhythm of each day is a succession of arrivals and departures, of specialist tasks and combined efforts, of manual work and secretarial duties, of members' services and visitors' needs; the bar staff serving refreshments to members and their guests; the starter meeting and greeting visitors; the Secretary's Office dealing with correspondence, telephone enquiries and multifarious administrative duties; the catering staff providing and serving meals; and the greenkeepers tending the course and maintaining machinery – a daily routine of talents and responsibilities which all combine to ensure a satisfactory service to the Club and its individual members.

Whether or not a Club Manager has been appointed to co-ordinate these diverse operations, the Servants of the Club are at the very heart of its activity and are deserving of the gratitude due to them; not just on the part of the Captain, but from every member.

Chapter 13

March

Only one month of my Captaincy now remains and the proposed amendments to the Constitution have become the primary matter of concern to me. Members require to have 14 days notice of the AGM, together with all the associated papers; and time is now of the essence to ensure that everything is in place to meet that deadline. My attention is taken up mostly with reviewing the wording of the proposed amendments to ensure that everything is coherent and logical, and that it covers as many eventualities as can reasonably be foreseen at this stage. The amendments are not nearly so radical as they might appear at a first reading but, because they are interconnected, it will not be practical to vote in isolation upon certain individual clauses. Should a particular item prove to be contentious, and were the proposal rejected, the repercussions elsewhere could render the whole package inoperable. I have already decided that I shall seek the AGM's approval to deviate from the normal sequence of the Agenda and to vote upon the proposed constitutional amendments prior to considering the level of subscriptions for next season. In truth, we are treading a path which borders upon items which are more akin to Rules and Regulations rather than Constitutional issues, but it is the only obvious means of introducing the changes at this juncture.

As usual, the month begins by my counter-signing payment cheques in settlement of invoices. Tom has drafted a letter to the member who was withholding payment to our caterer and he requests my vetting of it. There is also an e-mail from Prof. Purdie in response to my thanking him for his recent talk.

Monday, 7th March: Celebration of Malcolm Foggo's birthday
Within most golf clubs there are members whose life-long commitment to the club has afforded them a status of general respect. As is also probably the case, among a small number of members the degree of respect will be less effusive; but that is the nature of the diverse opinions found in all organisations. I vividly recall a Match Secretary who gave sterling service to a club for many years and its committee, in recognition of his exceptional contribution to the club's success, proposing at the AGM that he be made a Life Member; and the motion being defeated! Match Secretaries, in particular, are likely to be the subject of petty jealousies and aggrieved egos simply due to the arbitrary decisions which they are often required to make; and in some cases such grievances can last a lifetime.

There are currently several members who have contributed enormously to the well-being of St. Nicholas Golf Club, and one of those who epitomises its ethos over past decades is our current Match Secretary, Malcolm Foggo.

This morning, when I called in at the Secretary's office, I interrupted a little informal celebration that was just getting underway. Present were Secretary Tom, his assistant, Margaret, and Joint Match Secretaries Bob Ellis and Malcolm. I was already aware that they enjoyed taking periodic mid-morning breaks together, but it turned out that today was rather special in that it was Malcolm's birthday and they had purchased a lemon cake to do justice to the occasion. Naturally I did not want to intrude on what was a very personal gathering, but they invited me to participate. I explained to them that Jeanette and I were *en route* to Livingston and that she was waiting for me down in the Mixed Lounge. Notwithstanding, they would not hear of our leaving and they asked that Jeanette come up and join the celebration. It was a happy, light-hearted twenty minutes. I found it so uplifting just to have been included, and a lovely insight to the amicable working relationship that exists among those whose daily duties are in the clubhouse.

Wednesday, 9th March: Early afternoon meeting with Tom, Alan and Robin

Over the past few weeks Secretary Tom had been drafting the proposed changes to the Club's Constitution consequential to the Membership Development Sub-Committee's recommendations. This was yet another example of his commitment to the Club, in that he was not specifically delegated to perform the task but had undertaken it on his own initiative. I too had been applying a considerable amount of time and thought to the subject, and we arranged an afternoon meeting with Vice-Captain Alan and Membership Convener Robin to discuss fully the pertinent details which needed agreement before formal proposals could be presented at the AGM. Robin produced a list of summarised points governing all of the changes and we discussed these in depth in conjunction with Tom's draft of the Constitution. After two and a half hours of concentrated attention and debate on many specific issues, we made significant progress towards agreement of the final draft.

Monday, 14th March: Difference of opinion re Ladies subscriptions

Shortly after 9 o'clock in the morning I received a telephone call from Robin Alexander making me aware that he had just sent an e-mail in response to one issued by Secretary Tom on Friday. Tom had made observations relating to the Ladies' subscription levels as had been discussed at last Wednesday's meeting, and Robin was expressing his concurrence with Tom's logic. In addition, Robin suggested that we reconsider the terminology which had been proposed for certain membership categories as he felt it might not meet with general acceptance. I went along to the clubhouse and spoke to Tom on the subject. It was clear that Robin, Tom and I were of the same opinion on both matters. In the afternoon Alan submitted an e-mail indicating his agreement; although he was concerned as to how, in the short timescale available for motions to be tabled at the AGM, these changes could be communicated for approval to other members of the Membership Development Sub-Committee, to the Management Committee and to the Lady Captain. It was obviously impractical to call committee meetings, so Tom offered to circulate the amendments to everyone concerned and, hopefully, obtain their approval. How the world of communication has changed in this era of electronic messaging! It was late evening before I had the opportunity to speak directly to Vice-Captain Alan but, when I did so, was surprised to learn that he was unhappy about the proposed amendments. He said that he had earlier indicated his approval rather than speak out against what he perceived to be the majority opinion. I was uncomfortable with this response but, nevertheless, as he was Convener of the Membership Development Sub-Committee, I requested that he confer with Tom as how best to contact the other members of the sub-committee and make known the proposals. He and Tom consulted the following day and, between them, they agreed the means by which the matter should be progressed.

Thursday, 17th March: Planning application for hotel

The journey along the Ayrshire coast, both by road and by rail, provides a succession of spectacular views out to the Firth of Clyde. At each turning or mounting of a rise, wide vistas compete to capture the attention of the traveller and, when the weather is favourable and the visibility clear, there is no limit as to the pleasure which the beautiful scenes evoke. Being in motion at the time has its own attraction, but sometimes the view is fleeting and the time insufficient to appreciate the full magnificence of the spectacle; and one regrets the inability to linger, if only for a few moments, to admire Nature's handiwork. But the St. Nicholas clubhouse affords just such a prospect, and in the comfort of its interior members can survey the glories of its outlook as they recline with their drinks or consume the delights of the meal table. The perfect location in which to build a five-storey hotel complex that would offer visitors a coastal panorama *par excellence*! Except that the new structure would adversely impinge on the amenities and current benefits enjoyed by almost everyone in the immediate vicinity. It was with news of just such a planning application that Honorary President Bill telephoned me this morning. When I visited Secretary Tom and made mention of Bill's call, it became apparent that the Club had not yet received notification of the planning application for the hotel development. Nevertheless, my immediate concern was to ensure compliance with the constitutional requirements pertaining to the calling of the AGM and, in that regard, Tom furnished me with his draft minute of the 2010 AGM for my perusal. I spent much of the afternoon studying the draft and made only minor amendments to the wording of two passages.

Sunday, 20th March: Guests from Troon St. Meddan's GC

At Troon Portland GC's Annual Dinner & Presentation of Trophies I was seated at the top table beside Gary Miller, Captain of Troon St. Meddan's GC. Throughout the dinner our conversation was very relaxed and uninhibited, and when it emerged that Gary had never played on the St. Nicholas links I said that I would contact him in the near future with the intention of making up a four-ball. I wished to ensure that this visit took place whilst I was still Captain, and that accounted for our game taking place so early in the year. Gary was accompanied by the newly-installed captain of St. Meddan's, Brian Lawson, and Vice-Captain Alan partnered me for the round. In keeping with the informal nature of the occasion, our game finished all square. – something that proved to be a regular feature of my Captaincy!

Monday, 21st March: Foreword to photograph album

Since my meeting with Honorary President Bill at the beginning of February, although I was consumed with matters leading up to the Annual General Meeting, it was constantly in my mind to comply with his wish that I contribute a Foreword for his photograph album of the Celebration Lunch. I was especially keen that I should attend to this task within my actual time as Captain, so I set about composing a suitable passage.

Celebration Lunch : Foreword by the Captain
If ever anyone was inclined to question the statement that 'a single photograph is worth a thousand words', this little album is surely proof as to its veracity. Words can convey only so much to the reader but, in

terms of visualising a scene or recalling a face, photographs are as fine gold amidst the minutiae of detailed descriptions and lengthy prose. We live in an age when images can be captured, when events can be recorded visually, when the sight of a photograph can immediately conjure up a vivid recollection of an experience in all its aspects; the joyous reunion with old friends, the satisfaction of an appetising meal, the sincerity of tributes paid, and the reminiscences of former days. Memories of these can be recalled with pleasure as each image is viewed, and hitherto forgotten elements of the occasion can be brought to mind once again. And to those who were not present, the photographs provide a tangible indication as to what occurred and as to who participated.

The inception of the Celebration Lunch arose from a happy combination of circumstances and personalities. In its Honorary President, Bill Andrew, the Club had a man sensible of its heritage and passionate in recognising and promoting its well-being; whilst within its number was a group of gentlemen who had been members for upwards of fifty years. Aware of the historical background, and conscious of the continuity that suffuses the Club's existence, Bill mooted the proposal that it would be appropriate to celebrate the contribution that these older members had made, and continue to make, in the ongoing life of the Club. What better way to celebrate than to have a special luncheon on the first day of June and to invite as honoured guests of the Club the seven gentlemen who had been in continuous membership for more than sixty years!

But enough of description from myself! Many persons contributed to the success of the event and their contributions, and the conviviality of the day, are portrayed splendidly within this album.

It is a fitting record of what was a most happy occasion.

Tuesday, 22nd March: AGM speeches
Only nine more days until the Annual General Meeting and I turned my attention to the various occasions when the Agenda would necessitate my formally addressing the members. I was of the opinion that the composition of my Captain's Report would be the item which I would find most taxing and, therefore, I opted to put it aside until such time as I had dealt with all other aspects of the Agenda. By so doing, I hoped that I would then be able to give it my undivided attention. Today marked the commencement of this preparatory work for the AGM; and the awareness of being very much on my own in accomplishing it I found quite daunting.

Wednesday, 23rd March: Portrait removed
On entering the clubhouse I noticed that my portrait had been removed from the wall of the Vestibule. I made no comment, but surmised that preparations for my demise were already afoot!

Thursday, 24th March: Committee meeting
There was much that required my attention in these last few days and valuable time was being compromised by my having to fulfil a speaking engagement outwith my Club commitments. I had agreed to speak for twenty minutes or so at the Men's Association of a local church on a subject unrelated to golf, and I was having to apply myself assiduously in preparing for that talk. For the first time I could truly say that I was conscious of experiencing a degree of stress in the performance of my role as Captain. The spectre of the AGM was hanging about me and I was finding this to be the most challenging period of the past twelve months. Not that I felt unequal

to the task, for I was confident that I would be able to conduct the proceedings in a satisfactory manner, but it would require a great deal of intensive preparation on my part to achieve the desired outcome.

Now that formal notice of the AGM, together with all of the relevant papers, had been issued to the general membership, rumblings of discontent emanated from a few individuals who felt that they were being disadvantaged by the proposed changes to the Constitution; one in particular, who purported to have a more profound knowledge of Committee business than did the Management Committee itself. None of these responses had any material effect on my judgement as to how Committee had acquitted itself, but they were unwelcome nevertheless. The last Committee meeting proved to be of a very routine nature and finished at 9.15pm. An analysis of the ten Management Committee meetings under my chairmanship revealed that five had not lasted beyond 9.35pm, and only one beyond 10.15pm; a considerable reduction on past years' timescales and the fulfilment of one of my original aims upon assuming the Captaincy.

Friday, 25th March: Objection to Planning Application

Ever vigilant, Honorary President Bill contacted me to discern whether the Club had viewed the drawings which accompanied the planning application for the proposed hotel development adjacent to our property. I assured him that Past Captain Bill Rae was always diligent when dealing with matters of this kind and that I was confident he would have already done whatever was necessary. Immediately thereafter I contacted Secretary Tom, who informed me that a letter of objection had indeed been posted out this very morning and that everything had been attended to. Knowing Bill Rae, the possibility of its being otherwise had never crossed my mind, and I requested Tom to furnish the Honorary President with a copy of the correspondence.

Saturday, 26th March: Captain's Report

Having prepared all of the subsidiary speeches for the AGM, I now turned my attention to the Captain's Report. At the February meeting of the Management Committee I had requested that each convener submit to me a very short report identifying the principal matters that had arisen within his remit during the year. It was not my intention to incorporate these reports verbatim into my own; rather, it was simply a means of my saving time whereby I was made aware at the outset of the key issues, and being secure in the knowledge that nothing of significance had been overlooked. It was my desire to produce a report which would be interesting in itself and would hold the attention of the meeting.

Tuesday, 29th March: Full discussion with Tom, Alan and Robin re AGM

Whilst I was very conscious of my responsibilities in conducting the business of the Annual General Meeting, I was also aware that I would be totally reliant upon colleagues assisting me in the process. The presentations which needed to be made at the AGM were outwith the province of a single person and would require teamwork to deliver them. Last week I had made arrangements to meet this morning at 9 o'clock with Vice-Captain Alan, Membership Convener Robin and Secretary Tom for that very purpose. I was aware of just how much pressure I felt under to deliver my portion of the task, but the others were very much in the same situation and I was indebted to them for their assistance. Tom had already agreed to speak to the Financial Report in the absence of the Finance Convener, who would not be attending the AGM owing to a family commitment, and Robin agreed to elucidate upon any points which might be raised concerning the proposed changes to the Constitution. These were two major items on the Agenda and they required persons with insight and command of the facts who could respond authoritatively to impromptu questioning; and both Tom and Robin came into that category. We discussed in detail the various reports, possible awkward questions, the means by which motions should be presented, the consequences of rejections in so far as they affected financial budgets, and other ancillary matters; all of which eventualities any responsible committee would take cognisance when arranging an AGM. Robin and Alan said that they had taken soundings among members relating to the proposed constitutional changes, and had encountered very little negative reaction. That was reassuring!

Wednesday, 30th March: Tom's 70th birthday

At the outset of my Captaincy, the year had begun with an uplifting day spent in the company of our team as it contested the final of the Ayrshire Winter League; and today it was about to end with a delightful cameo among the Club's staff gathered in the Tom Morris Room to congratulate Secretary Tom upon reaching his 70th birthday. The fact that the staff had organised this little informal event was testament to its regard for him and to the happy working relationships which he had fostered in his daily management of its activities. I felt honoured to have been invited to participate and to be afforded the opportunity to contribute my share towards the presentation gifts; for I would not have wished it to be otherwise. The birthday cake, the bottle of whisky, the 'three figure' voucher for Dobbie's Garden Centre and the signed greetings card were a wonderful expression of a staff's affection, and I could not but reflect that once again I had been included in a team's celebration; albeit this time it was the St. Nicholas staff! And then it was back home to finalise my Captain's Report.

Thursday, 31st March: Annual General Meeting

After all of my intense preparation for tonight's AGM, the day was spent compiling a list of bullet points and key phrases to which I could refer when linking the various items on the Agenda. It was also spent in considering the more personal remarks commensurate with demitting office and acknowledging the support which I had received throughout the year. For me, the last car journey as Captain between home and the clubhouse was one of mixed emotions; almost to the point of defying description. I was filled with adrenaline to cope with the challenge of the AGM ahead of me, but simultaneously feeling a sense of loss at another phase of my life ending, of the year having passed in the twinkling of an eye, of a responsibility about to be lifted, of gratitude at having had the opportunity to experience something outwith my wildest ambitions. Not for the first time, 'surreal' probably best describes the state of my confused sentiments!

I had a brief chat with my colleagues in the Committee Room to ascertain that no last minute issue had arisen which needed consideration. We then made our way down to the Mixed Lounge to get the AGM underway, and for me to discover the adequacy or otherwise of my preparations; commencing with my opening remarks.

Honorary President Bill, Past Captains, Ladies and Gentlemen:
I am happy to report that we have present this evening a sufficient number of voting members to form a quorum and, accordingly, I am pleased to welcome all of you to the 2011 Annual General Meeting of Prestwick St. Nicholas Golf Club. As always, there is much business of consequence to be conducted in the course of the meeting, and I acknowledge each of your attendance as being an indication of your active interest in the continuing well-being of the Club. This is the first occasion upon which ladies have been eligible to attend as Ordinary Members and, in that regard, all of us are witnesses to the creation of a little piece of history. As for Ladies' Prestwick St. Nicholas Golf Club, it will be convening its own Annual General Meeting in the Clubhouse tomorrow evening. Permit me to say at the outset, should in the course of this meeting custom and habit result in references being made to 'Gentlemen' when addressing the company in its entirety, I trust that ladies present will not perceive this to be in any way derogatory, but will recognise it as being an unintentional omission which, hopefully, time and usage will rectify.

In accordance with past practice, I call upon our Secretary, Mr. Tom Hepburn, to read the notice calling this meeting.

Tom duly performed this function, and also intimated the Apologies for Absence that had been received for this evening's meeting. The next item reverted to myself.

Ladies and Gentlemen:
I am sorry to intimate the death since last year's AGM of one of our gentleman members, John Reid, who died on 2nd February at the age of 79.

Jock, as he was generally known, joined the Club in 1978. He was well known about the Clubhouse to a wide circle of friends and acquaintances. To those who were unfamiliar with him – he was the man who smoked his pipe at the back steps. When I first joined the Club, in one of the very first competitions in which I played, I was paired up with Jock. And upon completion of our round, knowing that I was a comparatively new member, he said that if ever I was looking for a game or wanted to get in with a regular group, I would be welcome to join his. It would like to think that Jock was typical of how the Club makes new members feel welcome.

Also during the past twelve months, several members within our Club have suffered personal bereavement through the loss of loved ones; we remember each of them at this time and offer our condolences.

As a mark of respect to those who are deceased, I would invite all of you to stand with me and observe a few moments silence.

This tribute was followed by approval of the Minutes of the previous AGM. And then the moment arrived for me to deliver my report on behalf of the Committee.

Ladies and Gentlemen:
In recent days I have found it particularly gratifying that so many members have told me that they can hardly believe how quickly my tenure of the Captaincy has expired. That has been music to my ears, and I thank those who took time to express that opinion to me. The past twelve months have indeed flown by, but such a statement belies the amount of time, research, endeavour and debate in which all members of

the Management Committee have been involved in addressing and implementing the essential business of our Club. For many of them, especially those who were involved in Sub-Committees outwith their own convenerships, this has entailed many hours of additional work and commitment in the service of members, and I wish to record my appreciation of the dedication and support that they have shown throughout the year.

And it has been a very busy year!

In terms of which items within the clubhouse have caught the attention of the general membership, I suspect that the upgrading and refurbishment work to the Mixed Lounge and the Dining Room will have been the most obvious. This was a major undertaking, particularly in the Mixed Lounge, and entailed the installation of a new, more efficient cooling and heating system, improved lighting installation, new carpeting, ceiling tiles, redecoration and soft furnishings. This work was all part of the previously approved 3-year programme of clubhouse improvements. It necessitated closure of these areas for about one month, and I am happy to report that the work was carried out on time and to Committee's satisfaction. We are indebted to Past Captain Bill Rae for managing this project on the Club's behalf. Although not part of the main works, our sound system continues to be temperamental and this is being investigated.

If the upgrading work was perhaps the most visually obvious, nevertheless throughout the year there has been continuous work undertaken to ensure the satisfactory maintenance and improvement of the clubhouse. A new television set was installed in the Junior Room, leaking window frames were sealed, the coat stand in the rear hall was renewed, plus various works to cupboards, shelving and coat rails at the request of the Ladies' Club. These and other matters were overseen by our House Convener, Gary Tierney. However, an unforeseen problem resulted from the intended re-fixing of some loose floor tiles in the Gents Shower Room, which was due to be carried out in the first week of December. On exposing the tiled areas it was discovered that part of the sub-floor was affected by wet rot and that remedial work would be required. Fortunately the problem was identified before any serious structural damage had occurred to the floor joists and work was put in hand to rectify the situation. This resulted in the Shower Room being out of use until late February, and also there was some disruption to use of the Trolley Store beneath. Once again, Past Captain Bill Rae managed the project on the Club's behalf, and I am pleased to report that the cost was met in full by our insurers.

Two House items were raised at last year's AGM for Committee's consideration:

Firstly: It was suggested that the facilities for the storage of caddy cars were inadequate. The matter was referred to a sub-committee whose remit was to review the current arrangements and, if considered appropriate, to bring forward alternative proposals. After considerable discussion, and consultation with users of the store, it was decided that the current system of allocation of caddy car hooks be maintained.

Secondly: It was suggested that sources of renewable energy be investigated with a view to reducing the Club's energy costs. This matter was also referred to a sub-committee whose remit was to carry out a feasibility study to establish the types of renewable energy systems that are available, to find out whether any of them would be practical for the Club, and to compile a cost benefit analysis. This proved to be a complex undertaking which has entailed approaches to, and meetings with, various consultants and renewable energy companies. So many factors have arisen in the course of these researches, including planning controls, availability of grants, government payment schemes, etc., that I can only report that this is an ongoing matter. However, it is only right that we acknowledge the considerable amount of time and effort that Gary Tierney has devoted in pursuit of this important subject.

As regards the golf links, members and visitors alike have commented upon the high standard to which the greenkeeping staff keeps the course maintained, and this is reflected yet again by our receiving a request from the Scottish Golf Union that we co-host with Prestwick Golf Club the 2011 Scottish Area Team Championship. Recognition of this kind is a wonderful testament to John MacLachlan and his greenkeeping staff and we, as members, are indebted to them for the professionalism that they bring to their daily tasks on our behalf. Selection of our course for a national event of this importance, which will feature the very best of our country's amateur players, can only be beneficial in enhancing the current reputation and status of our Club.

Throughout the past twelve months the greenkeepers have continued to implement the current 3-year programme; the most obvious addition being the introduction of two new bunkers on the right-hand edge of the 13th fairway. Construction of the new practice hole adjacent to the 5th fairway was completed last September and, if the extent to which it was utilised prior to its being closed for the winter months is any indication, it should prove to be a considerable asset to members. In particular, it is envisaged that it will be of great benefit as a suitable venue at which to conduct coaching sessions for our Junior members. It has been decided that this area, excepting the green, shall be deemed to be an integral part of the course.

We thank Stephen King, as Links Convener, for overseeing the management of the course maintenance programme, and for retaining the harmonious relationship that already existed between Committee and the Head Greenkeeper.

On the playing side, one of the first measures introduced by the new committee, in an attempt to alleviate delays being experienced in starting times on Medal days, was to increase to 9 minutes the interval between matches after 10.00am and to extend the competition time accordingly in order that there would be no reduction in the number of places available.

Over the winter months, November to February, a trial was undertaken whereby alternative times were made available on Sundays to run in conjunction with the Saturday Medal competitions. This arose out of concern that, due to the reduction in daylight hours, a disproportionate number of members may be denied the opportunity of participating in the Medal. However, upon analysing the figures at completion of the trial period, it was concluded that an insufficient number took part on the Sundays to justify continuing with these alternative times.

Finals Day took place on Sunday, 27th June. Unfortunately, the Ladies and Boys ties were not played on that date, but Committee has decided that Finals Day shall be retained next season despite the fact that the Ladies' Club has declined to participate.

At this juncture I wish to congratulate all of the players upon the sporting manner in which the final ties were contested; and also to compliment the many members whose presence on the links greatly added to the sense of occasion.

I think it only appropriate that the names of the winners be recorded at this meeting

*Club Championship – **Alan Poole***

*Coila Cup – **Brian McRobert***

*Jubilee Bowl – **Gordon Adams***

*Ladies Championship – **Catherine Malcolm***

*Junior Championship – **Scott Low***

I would also wish to record the success of the St. Nicholas team, ably captained by Stephen King, which won the Ayrshire Winter League.

We extend our thanks to John Errington for the significant contribution he has made this past year as Match & Handicap Convener; to our Joint Match Secretaries, Malcolm Foggo and Bob Ellis for their continued and unfailing devotion to organising the competitions and in ensuring the smooth running of everything connected with the playing aspect of the Club; and to Peter Carmichael in his capacity as golf stockist, receptionist and starter.

Measures introduced in recent years to encourage junior membership have proved to be very successful and I am pleased to report that the Junior Section is not only full, but that it now has a waiting list; 28 new members having joined in 2010. Junior teams have played regularly in inter-club matches and, although with limited success, the prospects for improvement in the near future are already becoming apparent. During the five months, November to March, juniors have attended coaching sessions on a weekly basis at Roodlea Golf Centre, and throughout this coming summer further coaching has already been arranged for Monday and Thursday evenings at Prestwick GC and on our own course. Within our Club we now have eight gentleman members with Level One coaching status and we acknowledge their commitment in assisting and encouraging the junior players. The Junior Boys Open in July attracted a field of 124, and the continuing success of this event is due in no small measure to the excellent administrative skills and enthusiasm of our Junior Convener, Walter Bryson, and to the members and staff who assist on the day.

Numerically, membership of the Club is in a healthy condition and, unlike many other Clubs, we still have a Waiting List, currently 94. Over the past year there have been five interview sessions; two in May for 23 prospective members having their second interview, one in June for a further 13 also having their second interview, and two in November for 29 applicants attending their first interview. Our convener, Robin Alexander, amended the previous format for first interview sessions by ensuring that proposers and seconders now take more direct responsibility for the applicant they are introducing.

Four ladies have transferred to Ordinary membership following last year's AGM decision to allow ladies to become Ordinary Members of the Club. That decision, however, presented the likelihood of further changes being required to the Club's membership, and to membership conditions, in consequence of the Equality Act which was due to be effective as from October 2010. Accordingly, in June, I appointed a Membership Development Sub-Committee under the convenership of my Vice-Captain, Alan Poole, to thoroughly investigate these matters with a view to our conforming to the requirements of the Act and to ensuring the continued well-being of the Ladies' Club.

This is a subject which all mixed clubs will require to resolve, but we are particularly aware of the historical significance of Ladies' Prestwick St. Nicholas Golf Club as it applies to ourselves, and we would wish to preserve that tradition. No doubt over the next few years the consequences of the Equality Act will be established but until then our approach, I believe, should be to proceed with caution. In time the issues will be clarified, and that will dictate whatever subsequent action is required. For over six months the sub-committee has investigated, considered, debated and consulted upon the whole matter as it presently stands and, following approval of the Management Committee, the result of these deliberations is contained in the series of proposed Constitutional Changes which have been tabled before you this evening.

Our Ladies Convener, Tom Andrews, was in regular contact with the Ladies' Club and communicated issues and concerns as they arose. By far the most prominent matters related to the Equality Act and to the implementation of last year's decision concerning transfer to Ordinary Membership. Having already noted the gentlemen's success in the winter league, I would wish to congratulate the Ladies' Club upon gaining promotion to Division 1 of the Greenlees League by virtue of its winning the Division 2 Championship.

Once again throughout the year, members were provided with ample opportunity to attend and enjoy social events within the Clubhouse. Social Convener, Bobby Hodge, arranged functions to suit all tastes; dinner dances, themed events, magician, pianist, and a most informative and interesting talk by Professor David Purdie.

And this would be an appropriate time to acknowledge the excellent service we are given by Grant and his catering staff, and by Irene and all of the bar staff. The quality of the food provided and the array of drinks on offer, together with the attentiveness of the staff, are much appreciated and commented upon by members and visitors. And a special word of thanks to Margaret and her cleaning staff for all the work they do on our behalf; the biggest compliment to them being that, for many, the work goes unnoticed.

Thankfully our Health & Safety Convener, David Coid, has not been overtaxed with work. However, last May a serious incident occurred at the 2nd Hole when a guest player, who was seated adjacent to the teeing ground, was struck on the head by a golf ball and required emergency surgery to remove a blood clot. In consultation with our health and safety consultants, the seats at both the second and third tees have been removed to obviate any further risk.

In the current economic climate, when so many golf clubs are experiencing a dramatic decrease in revenue, when membership numbers are falling and visitor income is being substantially reduced, effective marketing and advertising techniques are at a premium in securing whatever financial rewards are attainable. In that regard, St. Nicholas Golf Club has been served mightily by its Marketing Convener, Murray Bothwell. The quality and professionalism of his input is surely apparent to every member who has consulted our website, and the inventiveness of his productions, coupled with translation pages to French, Swedish and German, and the introduction of a video of the course, have pushed our website further up the rankings in the search engines; to those who are unfamiliar with computer jargon – that is wonderful!

There remains one other item of importance of which members should be informed. It is not appropriate at this juncture that I should go into this matter in any detail, but it should be known that it has recently come to the Club's attention that a developer is seeking planning permission to erect a five-storey hotel on the site currently occupied by the fitness club adjoining our car park. Suffice to say that we have submitted to South Ayrshire Council a letter of objection to this development.

And that, Ladies and Gentlemen, concludes the Committee Report.

Secretary Tom spoke eloquently and in detail to the Finance Report; Robin did likewise to the motions for Alterations to the Constitution; and I proposed the motion for the following year's Annual Subscriptions. Each of these items elicited questions and comments, but all received an overwhelming approval from the members. The meeting had now reached the stage where the next item on the Agenda was the Election of Office Bearers and, consequently, would mark the end of my period as Captain.

Ladies and Gentlemen:
Before proceeding to the next item on the Agenda, which inevitably heralds my demission from office, I would wish to say a few words relating to my year as Captain.

'Highlights' is a deceptive term; for it perhaps implies that anything that is not included must have been mundane. But that is far from being the case. My year has been filled with treasured memories; events that were uplifting and challenging; functions that were a joy to attend; little acts of personal kindness and words of support that encouraged and sustained me.

And let me say at the outset, how much I have appreciated the courtesy with which I have been treated by members and staff at all times. Mixing in company, recalling names, recognising faces and engaging in small talk has never been something in which I am comfortable, and I thank you for your forbearance on that account.

As to 'Highlights' – the ones that spring immediately to mind:

..The Celebration Lunch for our long-serving members. What a happy afternoon that proved to be! As Chairman, I was probably too involved to make a balanced judgement, but I thought it was a superb event and one which did the Club proud.

..The final of the Ayrshire Winter League at Troon Welbeck. What a thrill that was as I scampered about the Darley course following the various matches. That day I was Colin Montgomery, but without the use of a buggy. And the result was perfect.

..Ladies Day; and Alan and my pairing with Eileen and Elaine. As office bearers, it could be said that we set a poor example as to course etiquette, but a ready supply of wine, spirits, sandwiches and chocolate snacks can produce such a reaction.

..I was particularly fortunate that my period in Captaincy coincided with the 150th Anniversary of The Open Championship; fortunate indeed that we enjoy such a close and friendly association with Prestwick Golf Club as to be invited, on your behalf, to the lavish celebrations commemorating the event. Believe me, although it was very much in the line of duty, I found it to be no great hardship, and I was delighted to oblige. The cocktail party, the round of golf, the Anniversary Dinner will forever be fresh in my mind and a source of contentment to me.

I have already acknowledged the assistance and support that I received from all of my colleagues on the Management Committee. The business acumen and variety of talents which they brought to all our deliberations made my job as Chairman so much easier, and devoid of stress.

There are, however, some individuals to whom I would wish to refer.

Firstly, our Honorary President, Bill Andrew. The stately bearing and imposing presence that Bill exudes is matched only by his commitment to the continuing welfare of the Club. His attention to detail, his perceptive observations, his knowledge of the Club's past and its valued traditions are attributes which were of great benefit to me as a result of our periodic discussions, and provided me with the means of more fully assessing the wider role of Captain. My thanks to you, Bill.

Secondly, our Secretary Tom. Throughout the year he has been assiduous in attending to the business of the Club, in keeping me informed and advised of what my duties entailed and, on his own initiative, immediately taking upon himself tasks which he could so easily have ignored unless specifically requested to undertake. As far as he and his very able assistant, Margaret, are concerned, nothing was ever too much trouble, and everything was dealt with expeditiously and efficiently. The Secretary's Office, for me, was the cornerstone of my Captaincy. Thank you, Tom.

And finally, my Vice-Captain, Alan. It has been a delight having him as my right-hand man. When I invited Alan to be Vice-Captain, I envisaged an exhilarating experience. And so it has proved to be. There has been nothing downbeat, negative or mundane throughout the year. Everything has been vibrant and positive. He brought a vitality to all our dealings whether on the course or in the Clubhouse, entertaining guests or playing matches, attending seminars or meeting counterparts. He has been a great foil to myself, and I thank him for ensuring that, for me, my year as Captain has been full of happy memories.

Let me say now that I have worn this Captain's badge with pride, and that it has been a joy to represent and serve this fine Club and its members.

What will I miss most when I stand down? That's easily answered: The reserved space in the Car Park. If true to form, and if I continue to play in medals at my usual time, I shall most likely be parked in the Public Car Park across the road – a very good reason for opposing the Planning Application!!

My final duty was to propose that Bill be re-elected as Honorary President, and that Alan should succeed me as Captain. Both proposals were approved by acclamation and thereupon I attained the status of Past Captain.

Captain Alan presented me with my Past Captain's tie and badge, together with a tie and Certificate of Life Membership of the Scottish Golf Union. In addition, I was elected an Honorary Vice-President of St. Nicholas Golf Club and, in accordance with the Constitution, became a Trustee of the Club for the following three years. Alan then chaired the meeting to its conclusion.

As the Immediate Past Captain is required to serve one further year on Committee, this meeting does not mark the end of my involvement in the management of the Club; but it does mark the completion of my period as an Office Bearer and the culmination of a year that, for me, was without parallel in its diversity.

Stone Bridge Trademark

Whilst it is easy to dismiss them as coincidences, isn't it remarkable how often, when in unfamiliar surroundings, one's first personal contact develops thereafter into a lasting attachment? I'm thinking in terms of, say, first day at college, first time at a meeting, first attendance at a function; indeed anything that might be construed as being a new venture. By some strange form of osmosis, hitherto total strangers are drawn to one another; perhaps after having stood side-by-side in a queue or having sat together because no other chair was available, they find each other's company congenial, and a lasting relationship is forged out of sheer happenstance. I'm also thinking of adherences to brand names; items to which at an early age one was attracted, either by personal fascination or as a result of an elder's influence, and which have remained so for a lifetime. Bicycles, motor cars, sports goods and the like come readily to mind. My personal attachment to John Letters golf clubs, those bearing the stone bridge trademark, comes into the category of happenstance.

My early golfing years were spent using an assortment of clubs which I had acquired at random from my school chums – mostly hickories, but including a couple that were steel-shafted. The great day came when, as a birthday present, my parents said that I could purchase some golf clubs of a better quality. As neither of them played golf, it was left to myself to choose which clubs I wanted; and so we visited the David Adams sports shop in Royal Exchange Square, Glasgow. As chance would have it, no doubt influenced by the salesman's advice and an attractive price, I selected five second-hand matched iron clubs – Fred Daly Masters Model fitted with corklike all-weather grips; and I adored them! Over the next few months, out of my apprentice's salary, I added to them with purchases of my own and, although I was unable to find individual clubs to match my Fred Daly model, I made sure that each additional club bore the 'John Letters' trademark. Several years later, as a gift for acting as best man at the wedding of my good friend, Ian Barnstaple, I chose a John Letters Power Master driver; a club which I utilise to this day!

The Original Masters Model

And that is how matters stood until 1969, when I came across, in the window of Sportsman's Emporium in Hamilton, seven matched Stroke Master irons (No 4 to double-duty wedge) bearing John Panton's name; all for 14 guineas. As I already had in my possession a No 2 and No 3 iron of that series, I bought the clubs and sold my existing irons to one of my office colleagues. By this time I was aware of the good reputation that Letters clubs possessed, and also of the staff players who used them. Twenty years later I decided to get the irons re-shafted and made enquiries of Ian Ross at the Colville Park golf shop. Ian was the shop retailer, and not a golf professional, but he was able to quote me a price for the job and said he would send the clubs to Normandy Golf Range at Renfrew where John Mulgrew would undertake the work. I was a bit apprehensive as to how my request to have such old clubs re-shafted might be viewed by a professional, considering that his livelihood is dependent upon marketing and selling new goods. About a week later, Ian informed me that the clubs had been re-shafted and were ready to be uplifted. Imagine my surprise when he told me that John would have much preferred to have kept them for himself. Considering all of the 'advances' that had been made in club design in the intervening thirty years, here was a golf professional who still held them in high regard!

A similar situation arose about 2005 when I came across four Fred Daly irons at an outdoor market in Glasgow and among them was a Sand Master. Believe it or not, I had not previously known that John Letters had produced such a club; the double-duty wedge had been the limit of my knowledge. The shafts were badly rusted, but I bought the clubs for the sake of acquiring the Sand Master, and I rather sheepishly took them along to David Gemmell's shop at Ayr Belleisle Golf

Course to see if I could have them re-shafted. In truth, I had previously taken them to Prestwick Golf Range, but the assistant in the workshop had been unable to separate the heads from the original shafts. On returning to collect the re-shafted clubs, the Belleisle assistant, upon handing them to me, quoted Davie as having said 'These were the best clubs ever made'. Quite a coincidence, that on those two separate occasions, and unsolicited by myself, complimentary remarks from both professionals had been relayed to me – and my having been somewhat concerned lest they be dismissive of the job!

John Letters – all bearing the Stone Bridge trademark

Until the mid-1950s the stone bridge was displayed prominently on the soleplate of the woods, and on the back of each iron head; thereafter it was positioned rather unobtrusively, and of miniscule size, at the top of the hosel. I have concluded, rightly or wrongly, that the change was probably a token acknowledgement of the clubs' pedigree on the part of Dunlop Sports Co. Ltd. following its acquisition of the original John Letters company in 1955. An earlier modification, not related to the registered mark, was the name given to the Fred Daly clubs. The first batch, which appeared about 1948, was described as being Masters Model, but within a very short time 'Masters' plural was reduced to 'Master' singular – I wonder why?

There is a little anecdote relating to Stroke Master clubs, the likes of which would be unthinkable today:

On the eve of the 1954 Open Championship at Royal Birkdale, Peter Thomson was 'out of form' with the American clubs which he had intended using in the championship, and he sought the assistance of John Letters Jnr. Could John help him? That same evening both men went down surreptitiously to the exhibition tent and, as Peter described it, 'broke into' the Letters' display stand. He was shown the range of clubs available and was offered the use of any that took his fancy. He selected a set of Stroke Masters bearing the Panton autograph and played with them throughout the championship. At the conclusion of the event, which he won with a score of 283, Peter handed back the borrowed clubs; and no mention was ever made, nor advertisement issued, to indicate that John Letters clubs had been used to win The Open Championship.

Marketing managers, eat your heart out!

Epilogue

What a difference a day makes! Although I had now relinquished the Captaincy, I remained one of the signatories on the Club's bank accounts and, on the morning following the Annual General Meeting, Secretary Tom requested that I call in at his office with a view to my endorsing some 'end of the month' cheques. The atmosphere pervading the clubhouse and its surroundings was very much one of 'the morning after the night before'; the car park was almost deserted and no golfers were to be seen on the course. I was immediately conscious of no longer qualifying for a reserved parking bay and the sense of having returned to the rank and file of the membership was only too apparent. But if confirmation was needed that my time in office had expired, it was awaiting me the moment I put foot into the entrance vestibule; for there on the wall was the photograph of the new captain. A seamless transition in a world of change! And so it proved to be.

The amended Constitution which had been approved so decisively at the AGM never gravitated to the printer's block. Many, but not all, within the Ladies' Club expressed reservations as to the Club's means of dealing with the equality issues and, less than two weeks after their election, made these views known to the new Office Bearers. This resulted in Committee acceding to the ladies' proposal that the special measures introduced to preserve the heritage of the Ladies' Club should be rescinded, and that there should be but one composite club, *viz.* Prestwick St. Nicholas Golf Club. Accordingly, within three months of the AGM, a Special General Meeting was convened at which Committee recommended a series of amendments to the Constitution which, in effect, would herald the disbandment of Ladies' Prestwick St. Nicholas Golf Club after 118 years of existence, and elicit its transmogrification to the status of a Ladies Section. The amendments were approved; and with them one of golf's oldest ladies clubs, which in 1904 had hosted the second Scottish Ladies Championship and whose then immediate Past Captain, Miss M.V. Hamilton Campbell, along with its Match Secretary, Miss M. Allison, had planned, proposed and instituted the Scottish Ladies' Golfing Association, was consigned to oblivion in the name of sexual equality! Whilst so many old-established clubs are proud of their heritage and jealous of their traditions, St. Nicholas, or so it would appear to persons of my persuasion, jettisoned a uniquely historical asset that others would not have surrendered even under threat of reprisal. One can only speculate as to how these pioneering ladies, and their successors in the Ladies' Club, would have reacted to its demise in such circumstances! *(A copy of the ill-fated Constitution of 31st March 2011 is appended).*

Following very quickly upon, but not related to, the constitutional changes, Secretary Tom decided to retire a few months earlier than he had originally intended; and several weeks thereafter Peter Carmichael, the Starter and Shop Retailer, was informed that Committee had appointed a Golf Professional to take over all of his duties. Due to his business acumen and economic prudence, Tom left the Club in a very sound financial position at a time when many other clubs were experiencing hardship in the midst of the nation's difficult monetary conditions but, none the less, Committee decided that most of the accounting procedures which he had undertaken would not be performed by his successor, but would be outsourced to an independent practitioner.

As to what impact these changes will have upon the perceived ethos of St. Nicholas Golf Club only time will tell. But time and tide wait for no man, and a fine balance will always need to be struck between retaining that which is considered to be traditional and that which must change as the world evolves. One thing, however, is quite certain – gorse seedlings will eventually usurp heather; and I doubt that I shall ever be reconciled to that inevitability.

Appendix

PRESTWICK ST. NICHOLAS GOLF CLUB CONSTITUTION
(as amended 31st March 2011)

1. NAME OF CLUB

The Club shall be called Prestwick St. Nicholas Golf Club.

The purpose of the Club shall be to foster the game of golf, to provide a Golf Course, Club House, catering, social and recreational facilities for the enjoyment of the game by Members, their guests and visitors.

The Club is a non-profit making organisation dedicated to the supply of the foregoing objects. Any profits or annual surpluses of the Club shall not at any time be distributed to Members but shall be devoted to the maintenance or improvement of the Club facilities. On a dissolution of the Club in terms of Article 17 any surplus funds will be distributed only to Members at the time entitled thereto, or if so decided, at the dissolution meeting to another non-profit making Club/Clubs or organisation(s).

2. PROPERTY

The Club House, heritable property, effects and moneys of the Club shall belong to the Ordinary, Life, Senior, Veteran, Honorary and Associate Members of the Club, equally during Membership. The right and interest of each Member shall be personal and limited to himself/herself and shall not be assignable or passed to the Member's executors or successors. The Club House and other heritable property of the Club shall be vested in the trustees who shall be the Captain and the three preceding surviving Captains resident in Great Britain. A majority of the trustees shall, always, be a quorum.

The said trustees or quorum, shall have no power to borrow money, either on the security of the heritable property belonging to the Club or otherwise, nor sell or dispose of any part thereof except when approval is given by at least two-thirds of the Voting Members present and voting at an Annual General Meeting or Special General Meeting called for the purpose.

3. MEMBERSHIP CATEGORIES

The Membership categories of the Club shall be as follows:

Voting Members	Non Voting Members
Ordinary Members	Honorary Life Members
Life Members	Honorary Members
Senior Ordinary Members	Associate Members
Veteran Ordinary Members	Senior Associate Members
	Veteran Associate Members
	Country Members
	Non-Playing Members
	Junior Members
	Intermediate Members
	Corporate Members
	Temporary Members

The total number of Ordinary/Associate Members shall be limited to 650.

4. MEMBERSHIP DEFINITIONS

(a) Ordinary Member:

An Ordinary Member shall be a Lady or Gentleman aged eighteen years and over who has satisfied the conditions of entry as described under Article 6 of the Constitution.

The number of Gentlemen Ordinary Members shall be limited to 475 unless the number of Lady Ordinary/Associate Members falls below 125, in which case their number may be increased to a maximum of 490.

The Committee may, on application to the Committee, admit any Associate Member of the Club as an Ordinary Member of the Club. Associate Members will be given priority of application over those on the Waiting List to the extent that their original membership application pre-dates those on the Waiting List.

(b) Life Member:

Any Member of the Club, not in arrears with his/her subscription, may, at the discretion of the Committee, be admitted as a Life Member. The sum payable will be twenty times the annual subscription in respect of those aged 18-59 and ten times the annual subscription in respect of those aged 60 or over. The number of Life Members shall be limited to 15.

(c) Associate Member:

An Associate Member shall be a Lady or Gentleman aged eighteen years and over who has satisfied the conditions of entry as described under Article 6 of the Constitution. They shall have the privilege of playing on the Course and of using such parts of the Club House as are approved by the Committee for their use, subject to such conditions and restrictions as the Committee may from time to time lay down. The number of Gentlemen Associate Members shall be limited to a maximum of 50. The number of Lady Associate Members shall be limited to a maximum of 125 in accordance with Article 5.

The Committee may, on application to the Committee, admit any Ordinary Member of the Club as an Associate Member of the Club.

The subscription payable by Associate Members shall be equivalent to two- thirds of that payable by Ordinary Members.

(d) Senior Member:

The Committee shall have the power to transfer to Senior Membership, on application, Members who have been Ordinary/Associate Members of the Club for 30 years and have attained the age of 65, on payment of a subscription of one half of the annual subscription. With effect from 1 June 2012, eligibility for Senior Ordinary membership is restricted to those who have been Ordinary Members for a minimum of 10 years immediately prior to application. On application, no Annual Subscription shall be payable by a Senior Member who has been an Ordinary/Associate/Senior Member of the Club for 40 years and has attained the age of 80.

(e) Honorary Life Member:

Any Member or non-Member, in recognition of special service or distinction to the Club or to Golf, may be proposed for Honorary Life Membership by a Member's written proposal to the Secretary not later than 31st December in any year. The admission of such a Member shall require the approval of at least two-thirds of the Voting Members present and voting at an Annual General Meeting. Honorary Life Members, on admission, submit themselves to the

Constitution and Regulations of the Club and on these conditions alone are entitled to the privileges of the Club House and Course.

(f) Honorary Member:

Transfer to this category of membership ceased after 11 November 2004. No Annual Subscription shall be payable by an Honorary Member.

(g) Veteran Member:

The Committee shall have the power to transfer to Veteran Membership, on application, Members who are Honorary Members of the Club or who have been Ordinary/Associate Members of the Club for 40 years and have attained the age of 65, on payment of a subscription of one quarter of the Annual Subscription. With effect from 1 June 2012, eligibility for Veteran Ordinary membership is restricted to those who have been Ordinary Members for a minimum of 10 years immediately prior to application. On application, no Annual Subscription shall be payable by a Veteran Member who has attained the age of 80.

(h) Country Member:

The Committee may, on application and subject to the payment of a modified Annual Subscription, admit any Member of the Club as a Country Member of the Club, provided such a Member:

(i) has made payment of any outstanding subscriptions;

(ii) does not reside within a radius of 60 miles from the Club House;

(iii) does not have a place of business within a radius of 30 miles of the Club House.

Any Country Member may, on application to the Committee, be re-instated as an Ordinary/Associate Member without payment of any other entrance fee but subject to the payment of the annual subscription then ruling or such proportions thereof in the year of re-instatement as the Committee may deem appropriate. Such applications shall have priority over applications on the waiting list. Country Members shall be entitled to the same rights and privileges as Ordinary/Associate Members, except they shall have no voice in the management of the Club.

(i) Non-Playing Member:

The Committee shall have the power to transfer to Non-Playing Membership, on application, any Ordinary/Associate Member who wishes to relinquish playing rights but retain an association with the Club. He/she shall be entitled to the use of the Club Premises but not entitled to play on the Course. He/she shall pay a subscription as agreed from time to time at a General Meeting.

(j) Junior Member (Maximum 80):

(i) Juniors must have attained their 10th birthday in that year or hold a valid handicap certificate and be under 18 years of age at the time of entry.

(ii) They shall have the privilege of playing on the Course and of using such parts of the Club House as approved by the Committee for their use, subject to such conditions and restrictions as the Committee may from time to time lay down.

(iii) Junior Membership shall cease on a boy's or girl's 18th birthday.

(iv) Immediately on attaining his/her 18th birthday, a Junior Member may, on application, be admitted to Intermediate Membership or to Ordinary/Associate Membership. Such applications shall have priority over applications on the waiting list. No entry fee will be payable by applicants for Ordinary/Associate Membership.

k) Corporate Member:

The Committee shall have the power to admit up to a maximum of twelve Corporate Members on an annual basis, subject to the restrictions as laid down by the Committee and at an annual subscription per Corporate Member of not less than twice the Ordinary Member's annual subscription.

(l) Intermediate Member:

The Committee shall have the power to admit to Intermediate Membership, on application, those Junior Members who have attained their 18th birthday. Such Members shall have no voice in the management of the Club and their annual subscription shall be equivalent to one third of that of an Ordinary Member. Intermediate Members may apply for admission to Ordinary or Associate Membership up to the age of 25, at which age Intermediate membership will cease. Such applications shall have priority over applications on the waiting list. No entry fee shall be payable by applicants.

(m) Members' Guests and Temporary Members:

(i) Members' Guests

Members may introduce for a day up to three playing guests with whom they must play and who will be entitled to all the privileges of the Club House and Course under conditions laid down by the Committee. Their names and full addresses and the period for which they have been admitted shall be entered in a Club register to be kept for that purpose.

(ii) Temporary Members

The Committee may at its discretion admit visitors as temporary Members for the day or for such other period as may be fixed by the Committee. Such visitors will be entitled to all the privileges of the Club House and Course subject to the Club's regulations and such other conditions as the Committee may impose from time to time.

(n) Numbers of Members:

At the discretion of the Committee, the number of Ordinary and Associate Members may be increased on a temporary basis only to accommodate transfers from Country, Junior and Intermediate categories.

5. LADIES' ST NICHOLAS GOLF CLUB

All lady Members of the Club shall, ipso facto, be members of the Ladies' St Nicholas Golf Club which will have power to operate independently, subject to its adherence to the terms of this Constitution and of the Club Regulations. Membership of the Ladies Club will include a maximum of 125 Ordinary/Associate Members.

6. ADMISSION OF MEMBERS

(a) A candidate for Membership shall be nominated, in the form prescribed by the Committee by two Members to both of whom the Candidate is personally known. The application will be accompanied by letters giving personal particulars of the candidate from proposer and seconder. The name and address of a candidate so nominated shall be displayed, as soon as is practical after receipt, in a conspicuous place in the Club House, for a period of at least 14 days. A notice inviting Members to comment in confidence to the Committee as to the suitability of the candidate shall be displayed alongside the application.

(b) After the above period the candidate shall be interviewed by a panel of Committee Members of which four shall be a quorum and shall include the Captain or Vice-Captain. The proposer or seconder shall attend at this interview. If approved, the candidate's name shall be presented to the Committee for entry on to the waiting list. Thereafter the candidate shall be advised that his name will be displayed in the "Candidates for Membership" book and that a minimum of 6 supporting signatures, including the proposer and seconder, will be required before he will be considered for election to Membership.

(c) The election of all candidates on to the waiting list shall be by ballot of the Committee. Six Members of the Committee shall form a quorum for this purpose and three dissenting votes shall exclude the candidate. The Committee shall not proceed to the election of any candidate until at least 14 days have elapsed from the date of the candidate's name being posted on the notice board.

(d) At least four fifths of all candidates admitted to the waiting list shall reside in Prestwick, Ayr or Monkton.

(e) Candidates shall be advised by the Secretary that their names have or have not been placed on the waiting list.

(f) Immediately before admission to membership, candidates will be interviewed again by a panel of at least 2 Committee Members, notice of this final interview being given to the candidate and displayed in a conspicuous place in the Clubhouse for 14 days prior thereto.

(g) The Secretary shall give intimation of admission to each person elected as a Member of the Club, but such a person shall not be entitled to the privileges of the Club until his/her entry fee, pro-rata subscription and any levy due have been paid.

(h) A period of three years must have elapsed before a new Member may propose or second a Candidate for Membership.

(i) A member may not propose or second more than four candidates in one year.

(j) Applications for Ordinary/ Associate membership from former Members, sons/daughters of Members whose father/mother has been a Member for at least 10 years and sons/daughters of deceased Members whose father/mother had been a Member for at least 10 years shall have priority over applications on the waiting list.

(k) It is a condition of membership of the Club that Members agree to the use of the computer for the retention of individual records relating to their membership of the Golf Club.

7. MANAGEMENT OF CLUB AFFAIRS

(a) The Office Bearers of the Club shall be a Captain and a Vice Captain, and these with nine other Members shall form the Committee. The retiring Captain shall be an additional member of the Committee during the year following his/her term of office. The Captain or Vice Captain or, in their absence, a Chairman to be elected by the Meeting, shall preside at all meetings of the Club or Committee, and shall have the casting as well as the deliberative vote.

(b) The Committee, of which six shall be a quorum, shall have power to appoint Sub Committees with powers, and may co-opt one Member of the Club in excess of the constitutional number. The Committee may also co-opt Members to fill vacancies occurring in the Committee during the year. Any such Member shall complete the unexpired term of service arising from the vacancy, if approved at the next Annual General Meeting. He/she shall thereafter not be eligible for re-election as an Ordinary Member of Committee except where the unexpired term of service referred to was less than eighteen months.

(c) The business and affairs of the Club shall be under the management of the Committee. All decisions and regulations made by the Committee shall be final and binding on all Members of the Club unless set aside by the Committee or by the Annual General Meeting or by a Special General Meeting. The Committee shall post on the Notice Board all such regulations.

8. ELECTION OF OFFICE BEARERS AND COMMITTEE

(a) Eligibility

The Office Bearers shall retire annually, but shall be eligible for re-election as Office Bearers. Members of the Committee shall be elected to serve a period of three years. Three shall retire annually and shall not be eligible for re-election, except to serve as an Office Bearer, until one year thereafter.

(b) Nomination for Election to Committee

Nomination of Candidates for election to fill the necessary vacancies on the Committee shall be in writing and signed by two Voting Members. Such written nominations shall be delivered to the Secretary not later than 28 days previous to the Annual General Meeting. The names of those nominated shall be posted on the Notice Board in the Club House and circulated to Members with the Annual Report.

(c) Election of the Committee

The election by the general body of Members shall take place at the Annual General Meeting. Each voting member in attendance will be issued with a voting paper which shall show the number of vacancies and the name of the Candidates properly nominated for election to the Committee. Each Member voting may vote for as many Candidates as he/she wishes up to the number of vacancies to be filled and shall have one vote only in respect of each such Candidate. Any voting paper which has not been completed in accordance with this procedure shall be invalid. Should an insufficient number of nominations be received to fill the vacancies at the Annual General Meeting, the Committee shall have the power to co-opt Members to complete its number. The Committee shall meet at least once monthly.

9. GENERAL MEETINGS

(a) A General Meeting of the Club shall be held annually on a date not later than April 30th for the purpose of

(i) receiving from the Committee a report on the general concerns of the Club and Financial Statements for the year to 31st December previous, examined by a reporting accountant;

(ii) electing Office Bearers and Committee for the current year;

(iii) electing Reporting Accountant(s) for the current year;

(iv)the transaction of any other business which may be competently brought before the Meeting. The Annual Report and Statement of Accounts shall be posted to the Members of the Club along with the day and the hour of, and business to be brought before such a General Meeting, AT LEAST SEVEN DAYS before the date of such Meeting. Fifty Voting Members shall form a quorum at the Annual General Meeting.

(b) A Special General Meeting of the Club may be convened by the Committee at any time, or shall be convened on a requisition being lodged with the Secretary, signed by a minimum of twenty Voting Members and stating the business to be discussed. Such a Meeting must be held within 28 days of the Secretary receiving such a requisition. Notice of such a Special General Meeting must be posted to each Member of the Club at least seven days before the date of the Meeting, and such notice must state the date and hour of, and the business to be brought before such a Meeting. Fifty Voting Members shall form a quorum at any Special General Meeting of the Club.

(c) In voting, a show of hands shall be adhered to except as under Articles 8c and 12 of the Constitution, or at the request of a minimum of five Members present and eligible to vote, a paper vote will be held.

(d) Any part of any Notice of Motion can be considered and voted on as a separate issue.

(e) An Honorary President and Honorary Vice President may be elected at any Annual General Meeting of the Club. The position of Honorary President will be for a period not exceeding three years and will be offered in turn to the longest serving past Captain who has not occupied that role previously.

10. ENTRANCE FEE, SUBSCRIPTION AND LEVY PAYMENTS

(a) The respective annual subscriptions and any levy payment shall be recommended annually by the Committee and shall be fixed by approval of at least two thirds of the Voting Members of the Club present and voting at either the Annual General Meeting or at a Special General Meeting of the Members. The entrance fee for Ordinary and Associate Members shall be one and a half times the annual subscription. From 1 June 2012, the entrance fee payable by Associate Members transferring to Ordinary membership shall be the difference between the respective entrance fees at the date of transfer. Prior to 1 June 2012, the above entrance fee payable by Associate Members transferring to Ordinary membership will be discounted by 25% in respect of those who have been Members for a minimum of four years, by 50% in respect of those who have been Members for a minimum of nine years, by 75% for in respect of those who have been Members for a minimum of fourteen years, and by 100% in respect of those who have been Members for a minimum of nineteen years.

Subscriptions and levy payments are due on June 1st and invoices will be posted to Members prior to May 1st. Members joining after that date shall pay a proportion of the annual subscription and levy corresponding to the unexpired period of the subscription year.

(b) Arrears of Payment

In the absence of an acceptable reason for non-payment, the Secretary shall have the power to intimate by recorded delivery, to any Member who fails to make payment within 1 month of the due date that if the arrears are not paid within 14 days of the said recorded delivery letter, his/her Membership of the Club shall be terminated on the decision of the Committee whose decision shall then be intimated to him/her in writing by recorded delivery letter. Thereafter he/she may only be re-admitted as a Member of the Club at the discretion of the Committee. The foregoing provisions of this paragraph shall also apply to any member who has elected to pay his/her subscription, levy or any other payment due to the Club by monthly instalments under a credit arrangement if any instalment falls more than 1 month in arrears.

(c) Levy of Members

The Club at any General Meeting of which due notice has been given, shall have the power, by a majority of Voting Members present and voting, to levy the whole Membership, other than Junior Members, for payment of such sum as the Meeting shall decide.

(d) Refund of Subscription

No refund of subscription will be made on the resignation, death, change of Membership Category, expulsion or suspension of a Member.

11. RESIGNATIONS

Any Member desirous of resigning his/her Membership must notify his/her intention of doing so, in writing, to the Secretary before June 1st. In default of such intimation, the Member shall be liable for his/her Subscription for the year commencing on that date. Members resigning and not in arrears may be re-admitted on payment of the Annual Subscription and of half the Entry Fee applicable at the time of re-admission.

12. EXPULSION AND SUSPENSION OF MEMBERS

(a) Expulsion of Members

Should the conduct of any member, either in or out of the Club, be, in the opinion of the Committee, injurious to the character, interest or good order of the Club, the Committee shall be empowered to recommend in writing such Member to resign. If he/she does not resign within fourteen days from the date of receipt of such letter of recommendation, it shall be the duty of the Committee to call a Special General Meeting. A notice shall be forwarded to every Member of the Club at least seven days previous to such Meeting, intimating the time and place of the Meeting and the business to be discussed. In the event of its being approved at that Meeting, by ballot of at least two-thirds of the Voting Members present and voting, such Member shall cease to belong to the Club.

(b) Suspension of Members

The Committee shall have the power to suspend any Member for conduct of the type described in Article 12 (a). Such suspension shall be capable of review by Voting Members at a Special Meeting called for the purpose.

13. COMPLAINTS AND PROTESTS

(a) Complaints and protests, from whatever ground arising, must be made in writing to the Secretary who shall submit the same either to the first Monthly Meeting of the Committee after the lodgement of such complaint or protest, or to a Special Meeting of the Committee called for the purpose.

(b) The decision of the Committee regarding all complaints and protests shall be final and binding on all concerned.

14. SALE OF ALCOHOLIC LIQUOR

The Hours during which alcoholic liquor may be sold or supplied in the Club House shall be in accordance with the Licensing (Scotland) Acts and posted in the Club House.

No alcoholic liquor shall be sold in the Club House except to Members and Temporary Members.

Guests of Members shall not be supplied with alcoholic liquor in the Club premises unless on the invitation and in the company of a member and that member shall upon the admission of such guest to the Club premises or immediately upon his/her being supplied with such liquor enter his own name and the name and address of the guest in a book which shall be kept for the purpose and which shall show the date of each visit.

No alcoholic liquor shall be sold or supplied in the Club House for consumption outside the premises of the Club.

No alcoholic liquor shall be sold or supplied to any person, whether member or otherwise who is under 18 years of age.

No Member of the Committee and no Manager or person employed in the Club shall have any personal interest in the sale of alcoholic liquor therein or in the profits arising from such sale.

15. EQUITY POLICY

The Club is committed to ensuring that equity is incorporated across all aspects of its development. In doing so, it acknowledges and adopts the following definition of sports equity:

(i) Sports equity is about fairness in sport, equality of access, recognising inequalities and taking steps to address them. It is about changing the culture and structure of sport to ensure it becomes equally accessible to everyone in society.

(ii) The club respects the rights, dignity and worth of every person and will treat everyone equally within the context of their sport, regardless of age, ability, gender, race, ethnicity, religious belief, sexuality or social/economic status.

(iii) The Club is committed to everyone having the right to enjoy their sport in an environment free from threat of intimidation, harassment and abuse.

(iv) All Club Members have a responsibility to oppose discriminatory behaviour and promote equality of opportunity.

(v) The Club will deal with any incidence of discriminatory behaviour seriously, according to Club disciplinary procedures.

16. ALTERATION OF CONSTITUTION

No motion for the alteration of any Article of the Constitution of the Club, or the enactment of a new article, shall be entertained by the Club, unless the terms thereof shall have been intimated to the Secretary, in writing, at least one month prior to the date of the Annual General Meeting of the Club or of a Special General Meeting called for the purpose. Such intimation shall be posted on the Notice Board fourteen days before the Meeting. Any such motion or any modification thereof as may be approved by such Meeting, as well as motions for the alteration of any of the regulations made by the Committee, must be approved by at least two-thirds of the Voting Members present and voting.

17. DISSOLUTION OF CLUB

The Club shall not be dissolved except with the consent of at least two-thirds of the Voting Members present and voting at a General Meeting called for that purpose.

Index

Hunter, George, 6, 7, 45
Hunter, J.K., 138
Hunter, John, 138
Hunter, William, 138
Hutchinson, Horace G., 55

Innes, Pat, 21
Irvine GC, The, 43, 129, 130

Jacklin, Tony, 60
Johnston, Brian, 145
Jones, R.T. (Bobby), 34, 82

Kelman, Jim, 94
Kennedy-Moffat, Peter, 94
Kerr, Rev. John, 55
Kilmarnock (Barassie) GC, 32, 77, 117, 123, 155
Kilmarnock, Willie, 129
King, S.L. (Sam), 20
King, Stephen, 12, 23, 92, 95, 168
Kinnell, David, 89, 90, 135-139
Kinnell, James, 89, 90, 136-138
Kirk, John, 113
Kirkcaldy, Andrew, 138
Kirkhill GC, 79, 83

Ladies' St. Nicholas GC, 28, 66, 67, 80, 81, 103, 109-111, 132, 133, 139, 143, 144, 176
Lappin, John, 113
Largs GC, 96
Larke, A.J., 28
Lawrie, Paul, 154
Lawson, Brian, 162
Lee, Derek, 85
Leven Thistle GC, 136, 137
Lindsay, Mara, 111, 131
Locke, A.J. (Bobby), 20
Lockhart, Gordon, 93, 120, 138
Logan, Ian, 109
Logan, Dr Jim, 35
Longhurst, Henry, 146, 147

Low, Margaret, 6, 96, 160, 171
Low, Scott, 168
Lumsden, Alex, 27
Lyle, Jolande, 60, 61
Lyle, Sandy, 58, 60

MacDonald, Willie, 75, 89, 102
MacGregor, George, 154
MacLachlan, John, 30, 62, 76, 77, 80, 92, 93, 95, 110, 168
MacLaren, Don, 104
Mair, Norman, 146
Malcolm, Alasdair, 57, 154
Malcolm, Catherine, 168
Malcolm, Dr David, 152
Maxwell, Arthur, 88
Maxwell Tom, 88
McBlain, Stephen, 80
McCall, Iain, 91
McCallum, John, 136
McCaw, Harry, 60
McCulloch, Jean, 14
McCulloch, Robbie, 78
McFadzean, Robert, 138
McFarlan, Bill, 96, 109, 157
McGartland, Graeme, 34, 49, 112, 113, 129, 155
McInally, Hamilton (Hammy), 93
McKail, Hugh, 7, 30, 79
McKinlay, Alan, 149
McKinlay, Gordon, 95
McKinlay, Sam, 146
McLagan, D., 44
McLean, Margaret, 104, 117, 135, 159
McLean, Norman, 58
McMahon, David, 11, 44, 45, 52
McMillan, John, 148
McPhee, Paul, 77
McPherson, David, 122
McPike, Margaret, 149
McRobert, Brian, 51
MCC Golfing Society, 98, 131